DETAILING FOR ACOUSTICS

Third edition

Peter Lord and Duncan Templeton

E & FN SPON
An Imprint of Chapman & Hall

London · Glasgow · Weinheim · New York · Tokyo · Melbourne · Madras

Published by E & FN Spon, an imprint of Chapman & Hall, 2–6 Boundary Row,
London SE1 8HN, UK

Chapman & Hall 2–6 Boundary Row, London SE1 8HN, UK

Blackie Academic & Professional, Wester Cleddens Road, Bishopbriggs, Glasgow
G64 2NZ, UK

Chapman & Hall GmbH, Pappellallee 3, 69469 Weinheim, Germany

Chapman & Hall USA, 115 Fifth Avenue, New York, NY 10003, USA

Chapman & Hall Japan, ITP-Japan, Kyowa Building, 3F, 2-2-1 Hirakawacho, Chiyoda-ku, Tokyo 102, Japan

Chapman & Hall Australia, 102 Dodds Street, South Melbourne, Victoria 3205, Australia

Chapman & Hall India, R. Seshadri, 32 Second Main Road, CIT East, Madras 600 035, India

First published in 1983 by The Architectural Press, 9 Queen Anne's Gate, London, SW1H 9BY
Second edition 1986
Third edition 1996

© 1983, 1986, 1996 Peter Lord and Duncan Templeton

Typeset in Univers 45 by Ian Foulis & Associates, Saltash, Cornwall
Printed in Great Britain at The University Press, Cambridge.

ISBN 0 419 20210 2

A catalogue record for this book is available from the British Library

Library of Congress Catalog Card Number: 95-71099

∞ Printed on acid-free text paper, manufactured in accordance with ANSI/NISO Z39.48-1992 (Permanence of Paper).

CONTENTS

Background to 3rd Edition

A third edition? We are surprised at the interest shown in the first and second editions of this book, particularly in the light of the narrowness of the subject covered, the acoustical performance of building components. A request from several sources directly to us for a copy of the book led to the discovery that it was out of print and so a new edition was considered. The third edition of this collection of details gives us an opportunity to add, update and correct material. About a third of the material in the book is new.

There was little point in simply reproducing the content of the earlier versions of the book. There was clearly an incentive to seize the opportunity of updating technical information where possible, after all, innovation is as much a feature of the construction industry as any other and should be acknowledged. Furthermore, thanks to constructive criticism from Richard Cowell of Arup Acoustics it was accepted that the way the subject material had been subdivided and collated could be improved.

The legends to the illustrations in the earlier editions were written by hand and reproduced in that form which occasionally made them difficult to read. The former have been replaced with typescript making it much easier for the reader.

As before, the authors are heavily indebted to the building component manufacturers, many of whom have allowed us to reproduce technical information and data about their products. This assistance is duly acknowledged on the appropriate pages.

There has always been a shortage of practical material relating to both building and architectural acoustics, compared for instance with the mathematics and physics of sound. This book is composed largely of guidance details intended for reference by architects, students, structural and services engineers and interior designers. The book does rely on some basic knowledge of acoustics although the appendices do make some attempt to provide technical detail which would otherwise have to be found from a variety of sources. Exhaustive coverage cannot be claimed nor do the contents obviate the need for specialist assistance. Component assembly and choice of materials are 'moving targets' and pages could be added ad infinitum to this selection of standard and built examples.

Sources

Wherever possible laboratory results have been obtained for the standard assemblies of materials: often the basic 'favourites' can be traced to a number of sources, with minor variations on a theme. Inevitably, for lightweight partitions or ceilings in particular, manufacturers' information has been an important source of data. Such data should be treated with some caution as results may be given in the best light. The material presented has been checked as far as possible. Exact trade name specifications and references are given only where critical, as some products are subject to frequent change and development.

Format

The material comprises details of standard elements of building construction and diagrams for assessing basics. Standard elements consider both sound insulation and sound absorption aspects. In the case of the former, a single value is normally given; for sound reduction, values are in the range 100–3150 Hz (with values generally listed for octaves with centre band frequencies 125, 250, 500, 1000, 2000 and 4000 Hz, or one-third octaves). In addition to graphs, tabulated performance values are now given. Details of specialist components are there to illustrate specific usage and are not for copying on another project: we want to encourage dialogue with acoustic consultants, not replace it. Generally for this edition, details are reproduced at 1:5 scale unless indicated otherwise.

Content

The stated sound insulation of component assemblies is not intended as a means of assigning each with a definite value. A particular assembly does not have a 'magic number' because its performance will depend on the context in which it is used. Taking a partition type as an example, the sound insulation performance depends not only on its sectional constituents but on its size, degree of constraint on all sides, flanking effects and receiving room absorption. The values stated are only an average and two elements with the same average may have widely differing sound transmission at a particular frequency. For this reason, some important examples have their performance illustrated throughout the frequency range.

The single-figure values are to be used to provide a choice of comparable elements of construction consistent in acoustical terms: a 'kit of parts' of elements can be put together where no part of the whole is significantly weaker than the rest in performance. Doors and windows are problematic in that they are inherently lighter than the wall or partition into which they are inserted and gap-prone, but all is not lost when doors and windows are not up to the performance of the surrounding walls, floors and ceilings, and composite performance of assemblies can be assessed.

A philosophy that the whole is only as good as the weakest link is analogous to components in a high quality sound reproducing system. Care in detailing junctions is particularly important where discontinuous construction details are used to achieve good sound isolation. Cost-cutting exercises through the design stage should not allow part of the 'kit' to be downgraded to meet a budget.

In the case of sound absorption values, the figures should be used in conjunction with the tabulated values to sum the total effect of absorption in a particular space. In a larger area space, for example an open-plan office, the characteristics of the ceiling and floor will be of particular concern.

Information can only reflect the current 'state of the art'. A watchful eye should always be looking for new and exciting developments which may assist in the problems which will inevitably arise in lighter buildings and with high external noise levels.

Design process

For basic knowledge of acoustics, a primer text should be consulted. The details given here are intended to help at the practical implementation end of the design process rather than the crucial concept stage.

Steps in acoustic design during a building project are summarized to show the total picture of input. Acoustic consultants should be approached where a close check of characteristics is required. In the UK a list of consultants is readily available from either the Institute of Acoustics or the Association of Noise Consultants. Consultancy costs can vary from a couple of thousand pounds for a site noise levels survey and report, to 0.5% of total construction costs for beginning to end involvement on a major project including an auditorium or studios, or even 1% or more for a project with significant specialized design needs.

1. Briefing
The client may state required standards in the finished building or, more likely, the functions stated will dictate the fabric performance. The areas of acoustic interest should be well defined, and target criteria should be set at this stage. Background noise levels may be taken to assist brief-making studies or to determine the best position of a building on the site. Quantification of adjacent noise sources may influence the design of the external envelope, in order to minimize noise intrusion. Any noise survey should proceed along systematic lines, considering the information to be collected, recording the weather conditions, giving details of instrumentation employed and calibration, measurement units involved, positions on site where the data were collected and date and times of sampling. It may be useful to refer to established procedures, for example British Standards. All measuring should be undertaken by a competent person.

2. Site selection
If a choice of sites is available noise sources may be included with other environmental criteria in a scoring matrix to determine the most suitable. European legislation requires environmental assessments for any major project of more than local importance, or projects in sensitive areas. Close collaboration with planners and landscape architects as well as architects may be entailed.

3. Outline design
The form of the building may allow 'buffer' screening of sensitive spaces, and the arrangement of rooms may allow those requiring quiet conditions to be situated remote from noisy rooms, with fenestration sealed, limited in area, and not facing any significant external noise source.

4. Detailed design

Laboratory testing of building components or systems may be involved. These can be along NAMAS (National Measurement Accreditation Service) guidelines which recommends laboratory organization to have:

- a clear management structure with defined lines of responsibility for test work;
- suitably qualified staff;
- equipment and facilities suitable for the work in hand and maintained in good order;
- instrumentation calibrated to national standards;
- written procedures held and updated;
- adequate record keeping; labelling of test samples, results preparation, description of materials, level of uncertainty of test results to be evaluated;
- confidentiality/security of premises;
- monitoring of conditions, e.g. relative humidity and temperature.

5. Commissioning

Depending on contractual obligations, the role may be either one of witnessing proving tests, or measurements. In the case of electroacoustic installation and speech reinforcement systems, introductory instruction of operating staff will be needed.

2 SOUND INSULATION

Airborne Sound Insulation

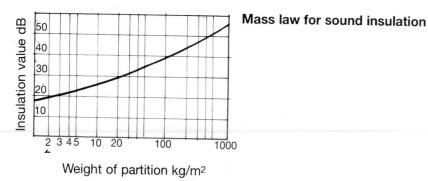

Mass law for sound insulation

Insulation value dB

Weight of partition kg/m²

For single walls the weight per unit area is an indication of insulation value only. Results below mass expectation may occur because of: resonance and coincidence effect; flanking; edge fixing. Composite construction of a series of layers improves the the sound insulation above mass law expectation as does: resilient mounting of panels; discontinuity of construction; double or triple layers with wide air space. A heavy dividing element is particularly effective for low frequency sound.

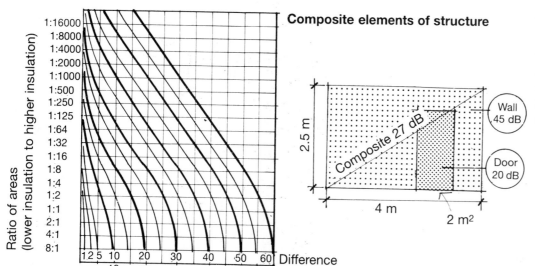

Ratio of areas (lower insulation to higher insulation)

Loss of insulation dB
(deduct from higher insulation)

Composite elements of structure

2.5 m

Composite 27 dB

4 m

2 m²

Wall 45 dB

Door 20 dB

The composite sound reduction index (S.R.I.) of partition between two rooms, or outside walls with windows in a room, can be obtained from the figure on the left. An example of the effect is also shown on the left. A hole in a 10 m² 45 dB rated wall of 100 mm X 100 mm downrates the composite rating to 30 dB.

Sound insulation

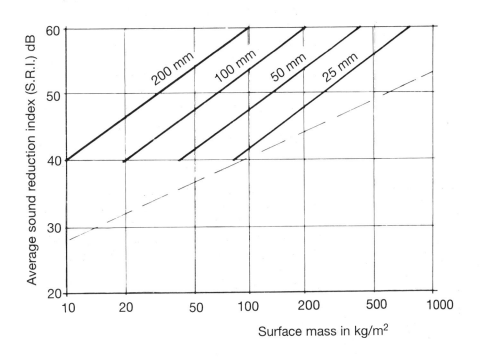

The 'mass law' for single walls has a corresponding empirical relationship between S.R.I. and weight per unit area for double leaf partitions. As with single walls, these curves are an indication only because the S.R.I. will vary with frequency.

Maximize spacing to leaves (d) relative to total mass (m) to keep resonant frequency (f_r) below 50 Hz:

$$f_r = \frac{120}{\sqrt{md}} \text{ Hz}$$

Empirical relationship for a double skin partition

— — — Single skin partition

dimensions are for different cavity widths between leaves.
$R = 34 + 20 \log (md)$
where R is average sound reduction index (dB) m is total mass (kg/m^2) and d is separation between skins (m).

Sound insulation

Mass law for most frequencies and over a wide range of incident angles on a solid division element:

$$R_{field} = 7.6 + 20 \log M \text{ dB} \quad \text{where } M \text{ is in kg/m}^2. -\blacksquare-$$

Further prediction formulae are as follows:
1. National Physical Laboratory, for sound reduction index over 100–3150 Hz:

$$R = 14.5 \log M + 10 \text{ dB}. -+-$$

2. AAC mass law, found by Airo/Celcon Ltd/ Thermalite Ltd. To compare closely to aerated concrete blocks of varying thicknesses, in field tests:

$$R = 22.9 \log M - 4.2 \text{ dB} -\times-$$

and

$$R_w = 27.7 \log M - 11.6 \text{ dB}.$$

Building Regulations Part E offers guidance on the calculation of wall leaf mass; other surface mass values can be obtained from BS 648:

Coordinating height of masonry course (mm)	Formulae to be used
75	$M = T(0.79D + 380) + NP$
100	$M = T(0.86D + 255) + NP$
150	$M = T(0.92D + 145) + NP$
200	$M = T(0.93D + 125) + NP$

where
M = mass of 1 m² of leaf in kg/m²;
T = thickness of masonry in metres (i.e. unplastered thickness);
D = density of of masonry units in kg/m³ (at 3% moisture content);
N = number of finished faces (if no finish N = 0, if finish on one side only N = 1, if finish on both sides N = 2);
P = mass of 1 m² wall finish in kg/m² (see top of next column).

Finishes	
Mass of plaster (assumed thickness 13 mm)	
Cement render	29 kg/m²
Gypsum	17 kg/m²
Lightweight	10 kg/m²
Plasterboard	10 kg/m²

There is no set definition of 'dense' when blockwork is used in 'dense concrete masonry'. The term should mean 2000+ kg/m³. Forticrete's 2200 kg/m³ density approaches the 2360 kg/m³ of reinforced *in situ* concrete. Some data for Edenhall blocks:

Thickness (mm)	'Evalite' blocks 1400 kg/m³		'Evalast' blocks 2000kg/m³	
	Hollow (dB)	Solid (dB)	Hollow (dB)	Solid (dB)
75	–	39	–	43
90	–	40	–	43
100	–	41	–	43
140	41	43	44	45
150	42	44	44	46
190	43	45	46	47
200	43	45	46	48
215	44	46	47	48

Values are for single-leaf plastered work over a frequency range of 100–3150 Hz.
In theory the average sound reduction index will increase by 6 dB/doubling of surface mass. In practice it is ≤ 5 dB/doubling. For thin materials, e.g. glass, a rate of 4 dB/doubling is adversely affected by coincidence resonance:

$$f_c = \frac{12000}{d} \quad \text{where } f_c \text{ is critical frequency and } d \text{ is the}$$

glass thickness. At the critical frequency, performance drops markedly (5–10 dB).

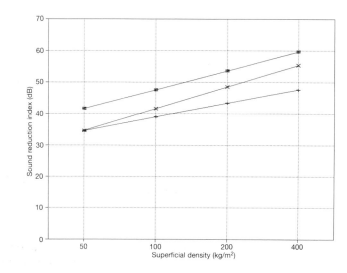

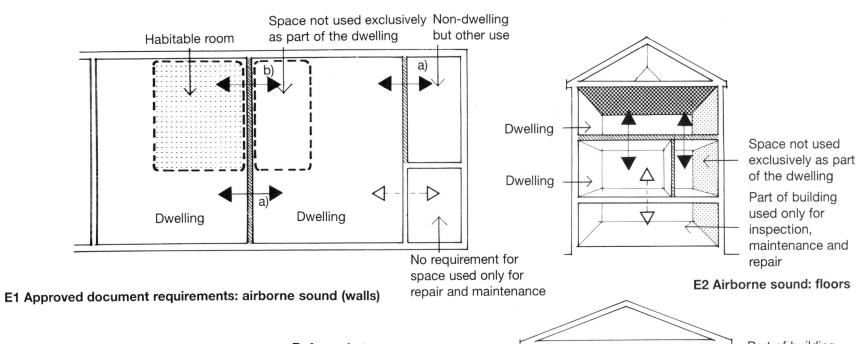

Habitable room

Space not used exclusively as part of the dwelling

Non-dwelling but other use

b)

a)

a)

Dwelling

Dwelling

No requirement for space used only for repair and maintenance

E1 Approved document requirements: airborne sound (walls)

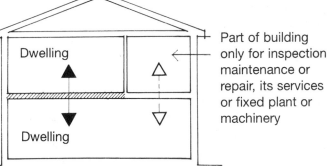

Dwelling

Dwelling

Space not used exclusively as part of the dwelling

Part of building used only for inspection, maintenance and repair

E2 Airborne sound: floors

Refuse chutes

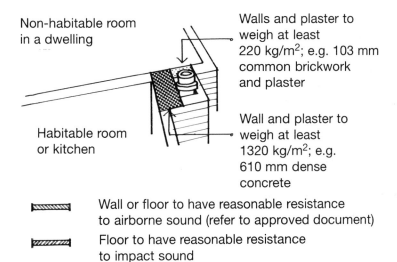

Non-habitable room in a dwelling

Habitable room or kitchen

Walls and plaster to weigh at least 220 kg/m^2; e.g. 103 mm common brickwork and plaster

Wall and plaster to weigh at least 1320 kg/m^2; e.g. 610 mm dense concrete

Wall or floor to have reasonable resistance to airborne sound (refer to approved document)

Floor to have reasonable resistance to impact sound

Dwelling

Dwelling

Part of building only for inspection maintenance or repair, its services or fixed plant or machinery

E3 Impact sound: floors

Source: Building Regulations 1991 (amended 1992)

Housing

15

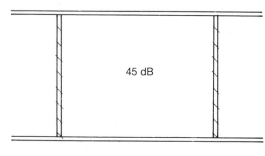

1. Basic standard for secondary school

Musical sounds clearly audible in adjacent rooms.
High risk of mutual disturbance.
Relatively cheap.

Walls: 100 mm medium density blockwork; or 115 mm brick plastered both sides; or dry-lined partition with 2 × 12.5 mm plasterboard on either side of 48 mm metal studs with mineral wool packing.

Floors: 100 mm dense concrete

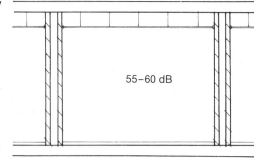

3. Good standard for university/college

Some musical sounds audible but not intrusive
Low risk of mutual disturbance
Care needed with ventilation and services to avoid downgrading sound reduction. Expensive

Walls: 100 mm dense blockwork plastered both sides, min. 150 mm cavity with mineral wool quilt

Floors: 25 mm chipboard raised floor on resilient battens; or 50 mm cement screed on resilient layer over 200–300 mm *in situ* concrete; or 25 mm plaster or two-layer plasterboard ceiling.

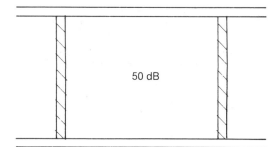

2. Good standard for secondary school

Musical sounds audible in adjacent rooms
Reduced but significant risk of mutual disturbance
More expensive

Walls: 200 mm solid or 250 mm cavity brick or blockwork plastered both sides; or dry-lined partition with 2 × 12.5 m boards both sides of 146 mm studs with mineral wool in airspace.

Floors: 200 mm reinforced concrete

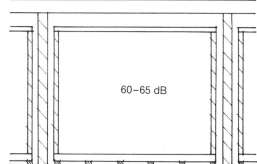

4. Excellent standard for university/college

Occasional sounds audible but not significant. Minimal risk of disturbance
Sophisticated servicing required
Very expensive

Outer box:
Walls: 230 mm brick or 200 mm dense concrete block rendered both sides
Floors: 300 mm *in situ* concrete
Inner box:
Walls: 100 mm medium density blockwork
Floors: 150 mm resiliently supported concrete
Roof: 100 mm concrete/prescreeded woodwool slab
Airspaces: 100 mm minimum

Continuous noise
Maximum NR 30
Minimum NR 25

Source: Arup Acoustics

Typical average sound insulation and contructions

Space Designator	Room Descriptor	Key Activities	Shape, Floor area, Height, Volume, Dimensions Typical size and range	Surface Finishes	Reverberation Time/Seconds	Variable Acoustics
Practice/ group rooms	Individual or group practice up to 6 pupils	Individual and small group instrumental teaching and practice	Rectangular. Every other cross-wall preferably non-parallel. 8 m² × 2.7 m high range 6–15 m² 2.7–3 m high	Predominantly hard with floor carpet. Some sound absorbing walls and ceilings.	0.4–1.0	Desirable. Simple variation by use of curtains

Source: Draft D.E.S Design Note 17.

Music practice rooms

Roofs

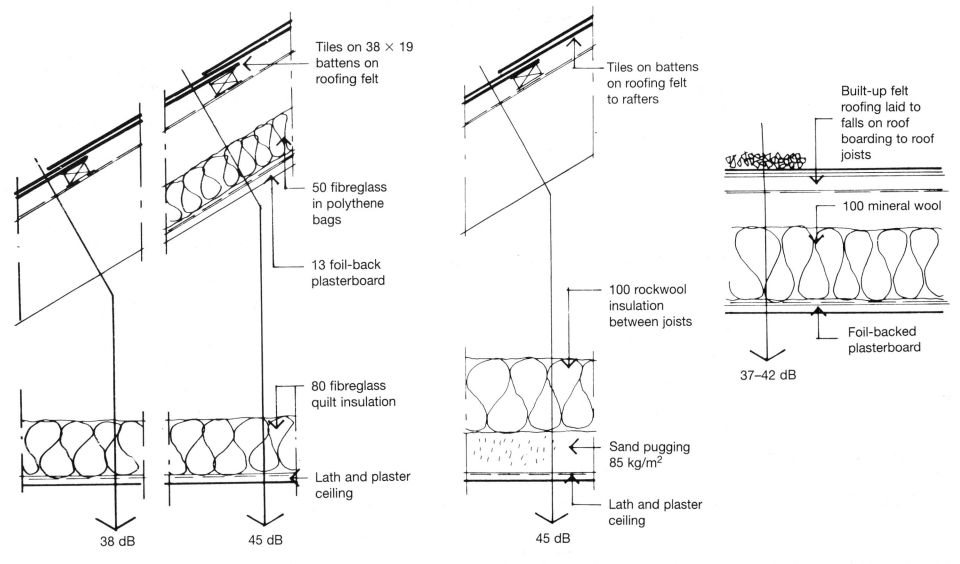

Tiles on 38 × 19 battens on roofing felt

50 fibreglass in polythene bags

13 foil-back plasterboard

80 fibreglass quilt insulation

Lath and plaster ceiling

38 dB

45 dB

Tiles on battens on roofing felt to rafters

100 rockwool insulation between joists

Sand pugging 85 kg/m²

Lath and plaster ceiling

45 dB

Built-up felt roofing laid to falls on roof boarding to roof joists

100 mineral wool

Foil-backed plasterboard

37–42 dB

Detailing guidance can be found in CIRIA Report 114 *Sound Control for Homes* by J. Miller.

Performance of typical constructions

Roofs

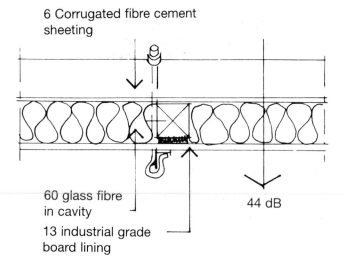

6 Corrugated fibre cement sheeting

60 glass fibre in cavity

13 industrial grade board lining

44 dB

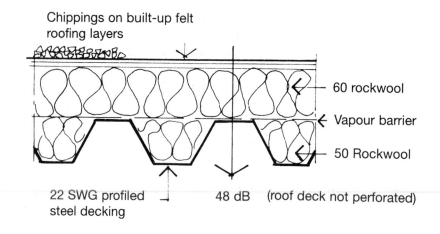

Chippings on built-up felt roofing layers

60 rockwool

Vapour barrier

50 Rockwool

22 SWG profiled steel decking   48 dB   (roof deck not perforated)

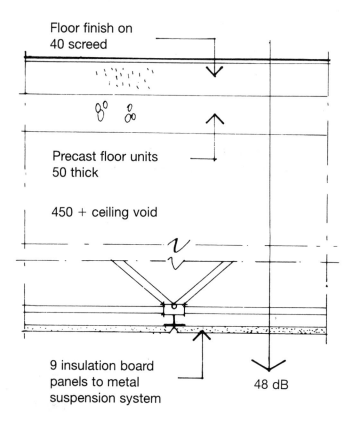

Floor finish on 40 screed

Precast floor units 50 thick

450 + ceiling void

9 insulation board panels to metal suspension system

48 dB

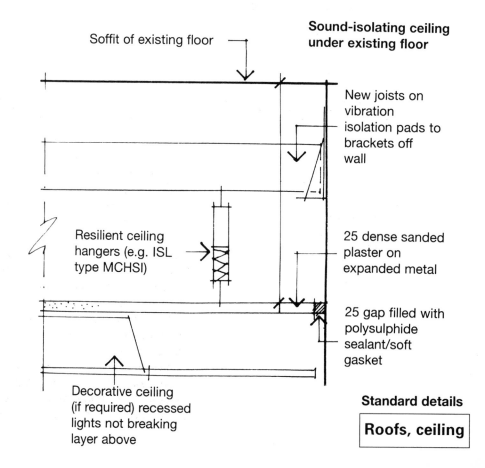

Soffit of existing floor

Sound-isolating ceiling under existing floor

New joists on vibration isolation pads to brackets off wall

Resilient ceiling hangers (e.g. ISL type MCHSI)

25 dense sanded plaster on expanded metal

25 gap filled with polysulphide sealant/soft gasket

Decorative ceiling (if required) recessed lights not breaking layer above

Standard details

Roofs, ceiling

18

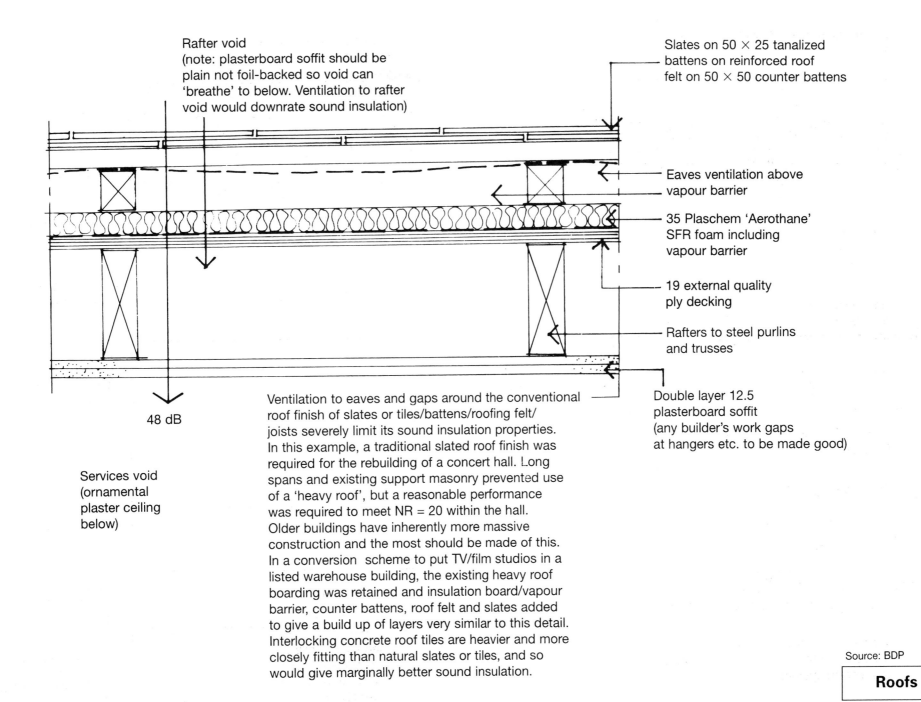

Rafter void
(note: plasterboard soffit should be plain not foil-backed so void can 'breathe' to below. Ventilation to rafter void would downrate sound insulation)

Slates on 50 × 25 tanalized battens on reinforced roof felt on 50 × 50 counter battens

Eaves ventilation above vapour barrier

35 Plaschem 'Aerothane' SFR foam including vapour barrier

19 external quality ply decking

Rafters to steel purlins and trusses

Double layer 12.5 plasterboard soffit (any builder's work gaps at hangers etc. to be made good)

48 dB

Services void (ornamental plaster ceiling below)

Ventilation to eaves and gaps around the conventional roof finish of slates or tiles/battens/roofing felt/ joists severely limit its sound insulation properties. In this example, a traditional slated roof finish was required for the rebuilding of a concert hall. Long spans and existing support masonry prevented use of a 'heavy roof', but a reasonable performance was required to meet NR = 20 within the hall. Older buildings have inherently more massive construction and the most should be made of this. In a conversion scheme to put TV/film studios in a listed warehouse building, the existing heavy roof boarding was retained and insulation board/vapour barrier, counter battens, roof felt and slates added to give a build up of layers very similar to this detail. Interlocking concrete roof tiles are heavier and more closely fitting than natural slates or tiles, and so would give marginally better sound insulation.

Source: BDP

Roofs

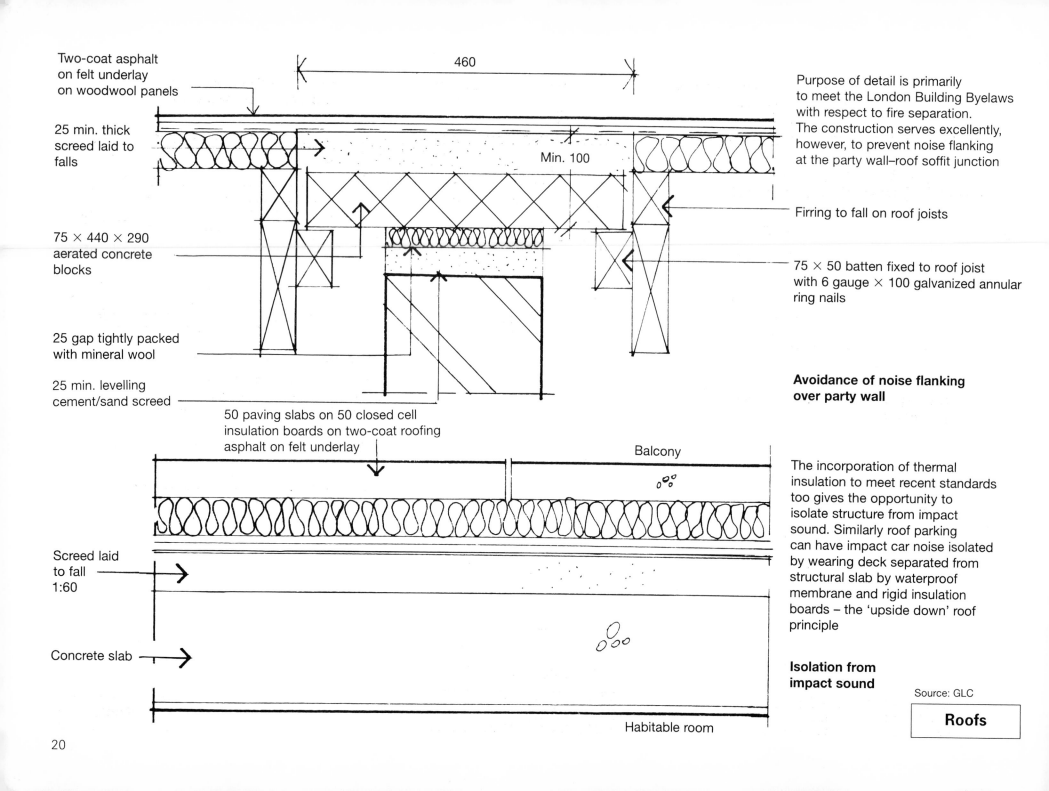

Two-coat asphalt
on felt underlay
on woodwool panels

460

Min. 100

Purpose of detail is primarily
to meet the London Building Byelaws
with respect to fire separation.
The construction serves excellently,
however, to prevent noise flanking
at the party wall–roof soffit junction

25 min. thick
screed laid to
falls

Firring to fall on roof joists

75 × 440 × 290
aerated concrete
blocks

75 × 50 batten fixed to roof joist
with 6 gauge × 100 galvanized annular
ring nails

25 gap tightly packed
with mineral wool

**Avoidance of noise flanking
over party wall**

25 min. levelling
cement/sand screed

50 paving slabs on 50 closed cell
insulation boards on two-coat roofing
asphalt on felt underlay

Balcony

Screed laid
to fall
1:60

The incorporation of thermal
insulation to meet recent standards
too gives the opportunity to
isolate structure from impact
sound. Similarly roof parking
can have impact car noise isolated
by wearing deck separated from
structural slab by waterproof
membrane and rigid insulation
boards – the 'upside down' roof
principle

Concrete slab

**Isolation from
impact sound**

Source: GLC

Habitable room

Roofs

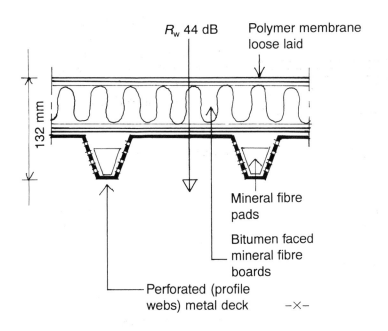

R_w 44 dB Polymer membrane loose laid

132 mm

Mineral fibre pads

Bitumen faced mineral fibre boards

Perforated (profile webs) metal deck $-\times-$

Lightweight roof system 'Superalpha' by Axter Ltd.

Surface mass 25 kg/m^2.

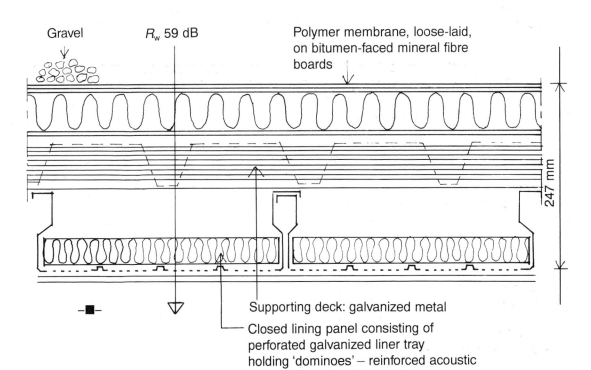

Gravel R_w 59 dB Polymer membrane, loose-laid, on bitumen-faced mineral fibre boards

247 mm

Supporting deck: galvanized metal

Closed lining panel consisting of perforated galvanized liner tray holding 'dominoes' – reinforced acoustic blocks (glass fibre faced mineral fibre mat and loose-laid galvanized metal sheet).

Roof system 'Thermoson A' by Axter Ltd.

Surface mass 141 kg/m^2.

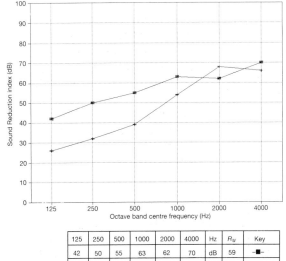

125	250	500	1000	2000	4000	Hz	R_w	Key
42	50	55	63	62	70	dB	59	–■–
26	32	39	54	68	66	dB	44	–×–

125	250	500	1000	2000	4000	Hz	Key
0.52	0.57	0.83	0.88	0.82	0.62	α	–■–
0.37	0.70	0.85	0.82	0.60	0.38	α	–×–

Roofs

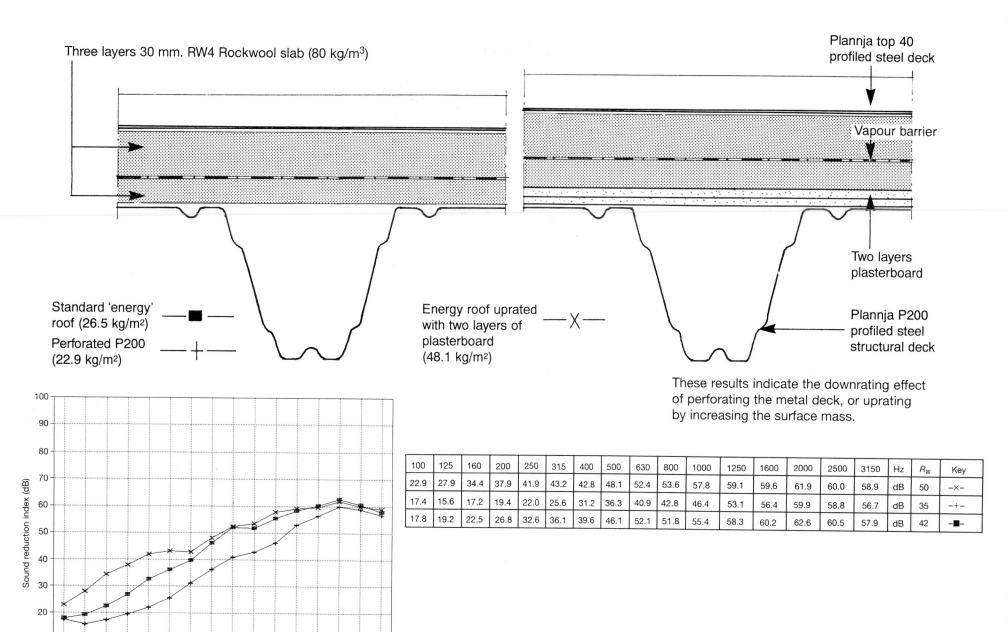

Three layers 30 mm. RW4 Rockwool slab (80 kg/m³)

Plannja top 40 profiled steel deck

Vapour barrier

Two layers plasterboard

Plannja P200 profiled steel structural deck

Standard 'energy' roof (26.5 kg/m²) ──■──

Perforated P200 (22.9 kg/m²) ──+──

Energy roof uprated with two layers of plasterboard (48.1 kg/m²) ──X──

These results indicate the downrating effect of perforating the metal deck, or uprating by increasing the surface mass.

100	125	160	200	250	315	400	500	630	800	1000	1250	1600	2000	2500	3150	Hz	R_w	Key
22.9	27.9	34.4	37.9	41.9	43.2	42.8	48.1	52.4	53.6	57.8	59.1	59.6	61.9	60.0	58.9	dB	50	─X─
17.4	15.6	17.2	19.4	22.0	25.6	31.2	36.3	40.9	42.8	46.4	53.1	56.4	59.9	58.8	56.7	dB	35	─+─
17.8	19.2	22.5	26.8	32.6	36.1	39.6	46.1	52.1	51.8	55.4	58.3	60.2	62.6	60.5	57.9	dB	42	─■─

Source: Plannja Ltd/ University of Salford

Roofs

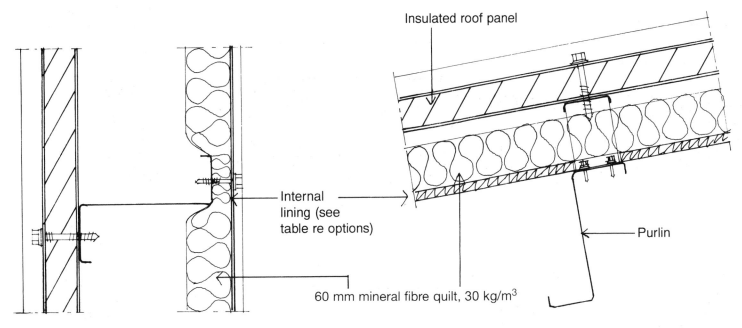

Insulated roof panel

Internal lining (see table re options)

60 mm mineral fibre quilt, 30 kg/m³

Purlin

Wall application

Roof application

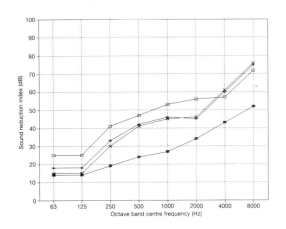

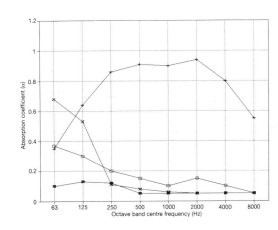

A popular cladding material is the double metal skin panel with a core of rigid lightweight thermal insulation. Insulated panels on their own have low sound insulation values but panel/airgap/quilt/ liner cladding has much improved properties.

Perforating the liner transforms the absorption characteristic without a great loss of sound insulation.

Construction method	63	125	250	500	1000	2000	4000	8000	Hz	R_W	Key
Insulated panel	14	14	19	24	27	34	43	52	dB	27	—■—
a - 0.4 mm profiled steel liner	18	18	33	42	46	45	60	75	dB	42	—+—
b - 0.4 mm profiled perforated liner	15	15	30	41	45	46	61	76	dB	40	—×—
c - 12 mm board (900 kg/m³)	25	25	41	47	53	56	57	72	dB	49	—□—

Construction method	63	125	250	500	1000	2000	4000	8000	Hz	Key
Insulated panel	0.10	0.13	0.12	0.05	0.05	0.05	0.05	0.05	α	—■—
a - 0.4 mm profiled steel liner	0.68	0.53	0.11	0.08	0.06	0.05	0.05	0.05	α	—×—
b - 0.4 mm profiled perforated steel liner	0.35	0.64	0.86	0.91	0.90	0.94	0.80	0.55	α	—+—
c - 12 mm board	0.37	0.30	0.20	0.15	0.10	0.15	0.10	0.05	α	—□—

Source: Kingspan Insulated Panels

Roof, wall cladding

23

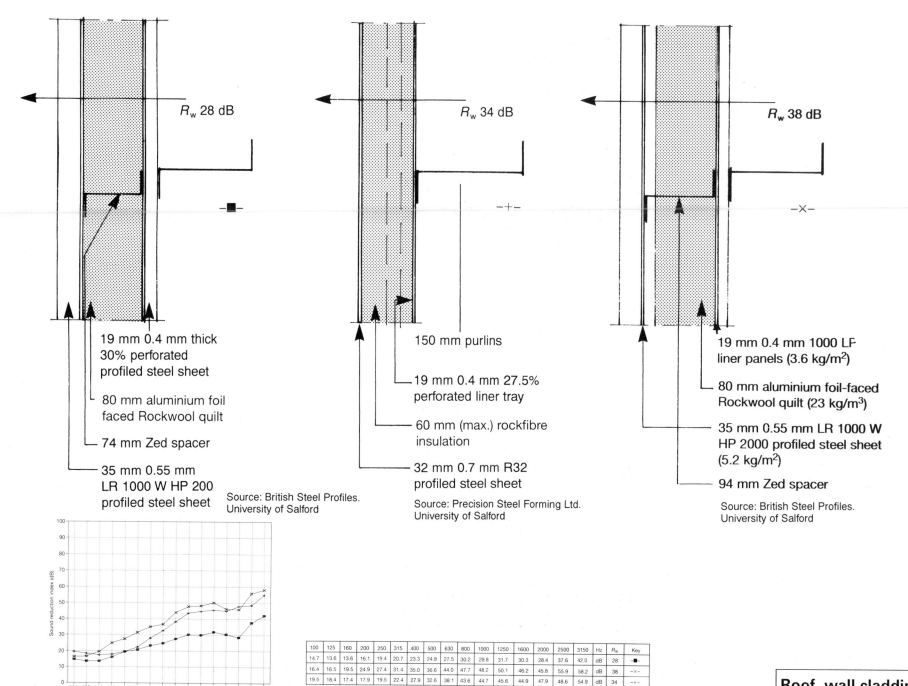

R_w 28 dB

R_w 34 dB

R_w 38 dB

-■-

-+-

-×-

19 mm 0.4 mm thick
30% perforated
profiled steel sheet

80 mm aluminium foil
faced Rockwool quilt

74 mm Zed spacer

35 mm 0.55 mm
LR 1000 W HP 200
profiled steel sheet

Source: British Steel Profiles.
University of Salford

150 mm purlins

19 mm 0.4 mm 27.5%
perforated liner tray

60 mm (max.) rockfibre
insulation

32 mm 0.7 mm R32
profiled steel sheet

Source: Precision Steel Forming Ltd.
University of Salford

19 mm 0.4 mm 1000 LF
liner panels (3.6 kg/m²)

80 mm aluminium foil-faced
Rockwool quilt (23 kg/m³)

35 mm 0.55 mm LR 1000 W
HP 2000 profiled steel sheet
(5.2 kg/m²)

94 mm Zed spacer

Source: British Steel Profiles.
University of Salford

100	125	160	200	250	315	400	500	630	800	1000	1250	1600	2000	2500	3150	Hz	R_w	Key
14.7	13.6	13.6	16.1	19.4	20.7	23.3	24.8	27.5	30.2	29.8	31.7	30.3	28.4	37.6	42.0	dB	28	-■-
16.4	16.5	19.5	24.9	27.4	31.4	35.0	36.6	44.0	47.7	48.2	50.1	46.2	45.8	55.9	58.2	dB	38	-×-
19.5	18.4	17.4	17.9	19.5	22.4	27.9	32.6	38.1	43.6	44.7	45.6	44.9	47.9	48.6	54.9	dB	34	-+-

Roof, wall cladding

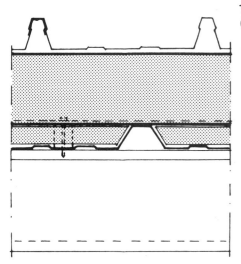

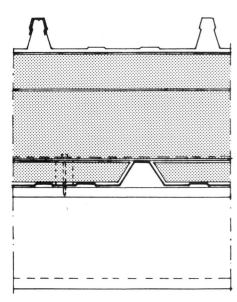

1 Sound roof – 37 decibel
(18.5 kg/m²)

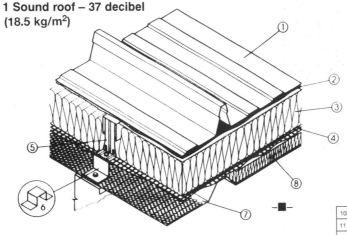

2 Sound roof – 42 decibel
(26.25 kg/m²)

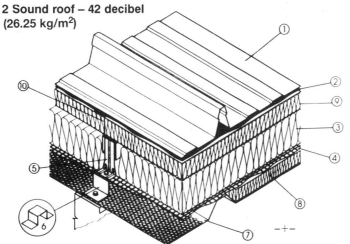

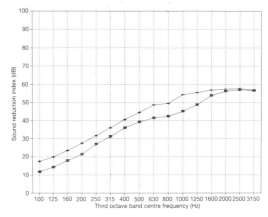

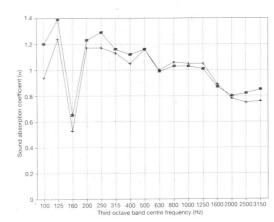

100	125	160	200	250	315	400	500	630	800	1000	1250	1600	2000	2500	3150	Hz	R_W	Key	
11.7	14.3	17.8	21.3	27.0	31.2	36.0	39.1	41.3	42.4	45.1	48.8	53.9	56.2	57.1	56.6	dB	37	–■–	1
17.6	19.9	23.5	27.5	31.6	36.0	40.5	44.4	48.7	49.6	54.3	55.5	56.9	57.3	57.7	56.7	dB	42	–+–	2

100	125	160	200	250	315	400	500	630	800	1000	1250	1600	2000	2500	3150	Hz	Key
0.94	1.24	0.53	1.17	1.17	1.13	1.05	1.16	1.00	1.06	1.05	1.05	0.89	0.78	0.75	0.76	α	–+–
1.2	1.39	0.65	1.23	1.29	1.16	1.12	1.16	0.99	1.03	1.03	1.01	0.87	0.80	0.82	0.85	α	–■–

The roofs offer both good sound insulation for modest weight and sound absorption. The high density quilt in the 42 dB version is an effective addition.

1 SpeedDeck in steel for full performance and in steel or aluminium where absorption performance only is required.
2 Breather membrane SD 100.
3 100 mm 33 kg/m³ rock fibre – packed tightly up to and under IsoBar. Avoid any gaps.
4 StramCheck, all laps sealed using using butyl strip. Seal for continuity over junctions and at penetrations.
5 IsoBar spacer incorporating an integral foam pad selector.
6 Top hat stool.
7 Pan perforated StramLiner.
8 Tissue faced Stramit acoustic batts in each trough. Tissue face against the perforations to control dust fall.
9 50 mm 140 kg/m³ rock fibre (SoundRoof 42 Decibel only). Packed closely into spacer.
10 Zed Spacer (SoundRoof 42 Decibel only). Positioned over IsoBar with 50 mm insulation packed under.

Source: Stramit Industries Ltd/ Sound Research Laboratories Ltd.

Roofing

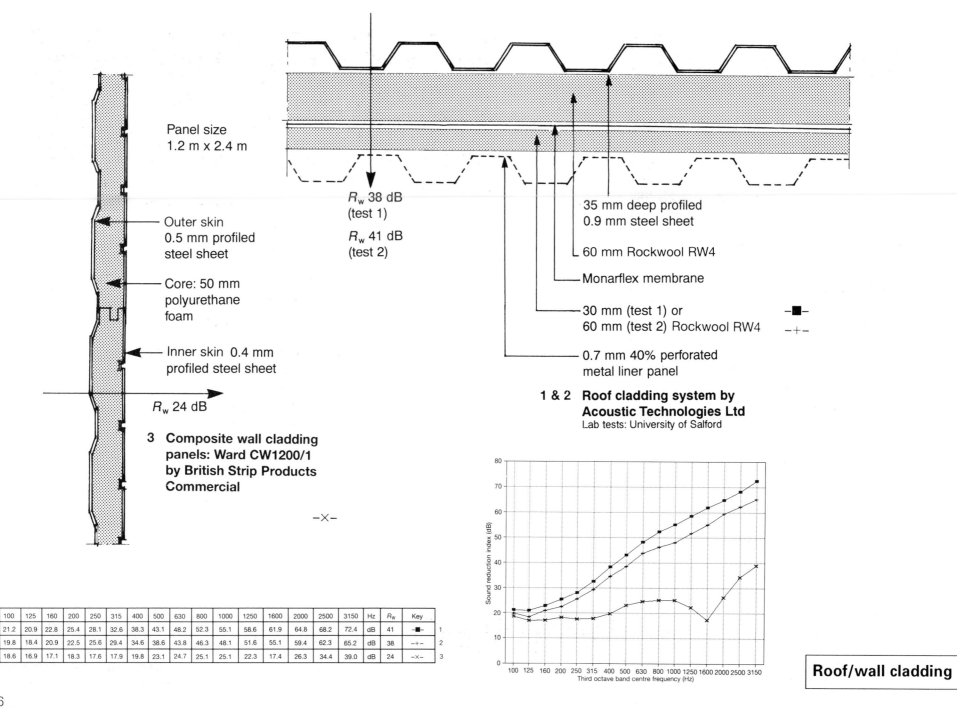

Panel size
1.2 m x 2.4 m

Outer skin
0.5 mm profiled
steel sheet

Core: 50 mm
polyurethane
foam

Inner skin 0.4 mm
profiled steel sheet

R_w 24 dB

**3 Composite wall cladding
panels: Ward CW1200/1
by British Strip Products
Commercial**

R_w 38 dB
(test 1)

R_w 41 dB
(test 2)

35 mm deep profiled
0.9 mm steel sheet

60 mm Rockwool RW4

Monarflex membrane

30 mm (test 1) or
60 mm (test 2) Rockwool RW4

0.7 mm 40% perforated
metal liner panel

**1 & 2 Roof cladding system by
Acoustic Technologies Ltd**
Lab tests: University of Salford

100	125	160	200	250	315	400	500	630	800	1000	1250	1600	2000	2500	3150	Hz	R_w	Key	
21.2	20.9	22.8	25.4	28.1	32.6	38.3	43.1	48.2	52.3	55.1	58.6	61.9	64.8	68.2	72.4	dB	41	-■-	1
19.8	18.4	20.9	22.5	25.6	29.4	34.6	38.6	43.8	46.3	48.1	51.6	55.1	59.4	62.3	65.2	dB	38	-+-	2
18.6	16.9	17.1	18.3	17.6	17.9	19.8	23.1	24.7	25.1	25.1	22.3	17.4	26.3	34.4	39.0	dB	24	-×-	3

Roof/wall cladding

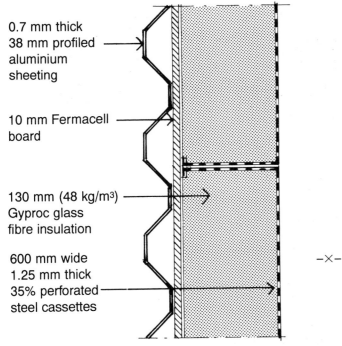

0.7 mm thick
38 mm profiled
aluminium
sheeting

10 mm Fermacell
board

130 mm (48 kg/m³)
Gyproc glass
fibre insulation

600 mm wide
1.25 mm thick
35% perforated
steel cassettes

**Cladding construction used
on a power station**

−×−

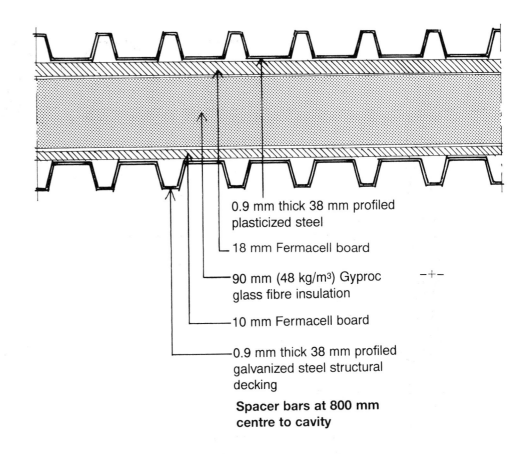

0.9 mm thick 38 mm profiled
plasticized steel

18 mm Fermacell board

90 mm (48 kg/m³) Gyproc
glass fibre insulation

10 mm Fermacell board

0.9 mm thick 38 mm profiled
galvanized steel structural
decking

−+−

**Spacer bars at 800 mm
centre to cavity**

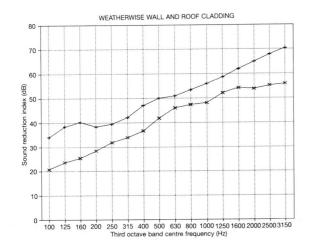

WEATHERWISE WALL AND ROOF CLADDING

Sound reduction index (dB)

Third octave band centre frequency (Hz)

100	125	160	200	250	315	400	500	630	800	1000	1250	1600	2000	2500	3150	Hz	R_w	Key
34.1	38.4	40.3	38.3	39.5	42.2	47.1	50.1	50.9	53.4	56.0	58.7	62.0	65.0	67.9	70.4	dB	53	−+−
20.8	23.7	25.4	28.4	31.9	34.0	36.6	41.8	46.1	47.3	48.1	52.1	54.2	53.8	55.2	55.8	dB	43	−×−

Source: Weather Wise Ltd/
University of Salford

Roof and wall cladding

Ceilings

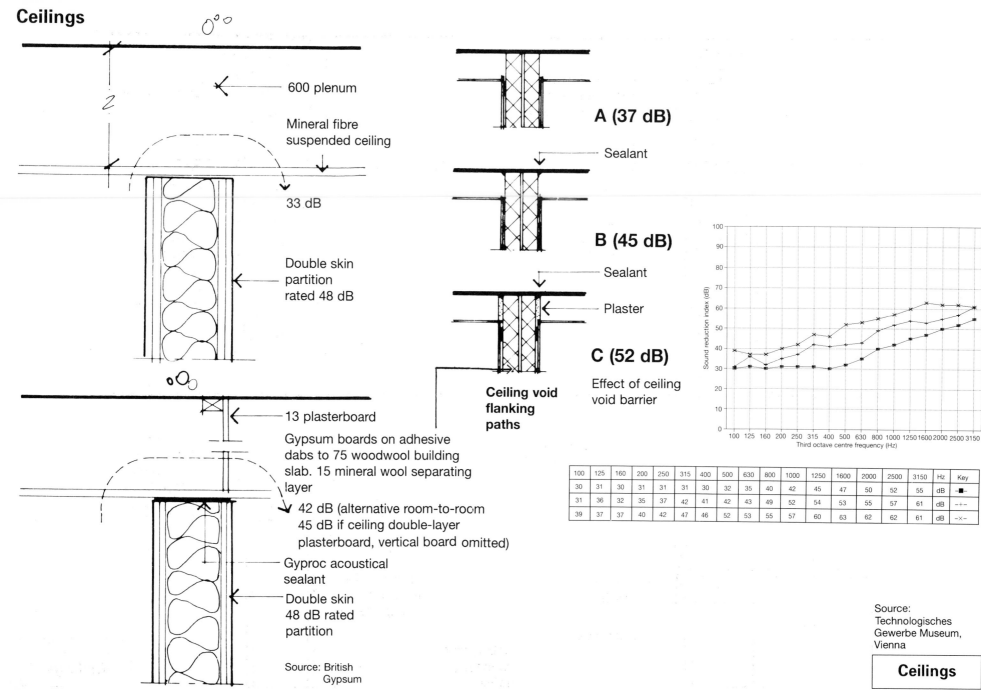

600 plenum

Mineral fibre
suspended ceiling

33 dB

Double skin
partition
rated 48 dB

13 plasterboard

Gypsum boards on adhesive
dabs to 75 woodwool building
slab. 15 mineral wool separating
layer

42 dB (alternative room-to-room
45 dB if ceiling double-layer
plasterboard, vertical board omitted)

Gyproc acoustical
sealant

Double skin
48 dB rated
partition

Source: British
Gypsum

A (37 dB)

Sealant

B (45 dB)

Sealant

Plaster

C (52 dB)

Effect of ceiling
void barrier

**Ceiling void
flanking
paths**

100	125	160	200	250	315	400	500	630	800	1000	1250	1600	2000	2500	3150	Hz	Key
30	31	30	31	31	31	30	32	35	40	42	45	47	50	52	55	dB	–■–
31	36	32	35	37	42	41	42	43	49	52	54	53	55	57	61	dB	–+–
39	37	37	40	42	47	46	52	53	55	57	60	63	62	62	61	dB	–×–

Source:
Technologisches
Gewerbe Museum,
Vienna

Ceilings

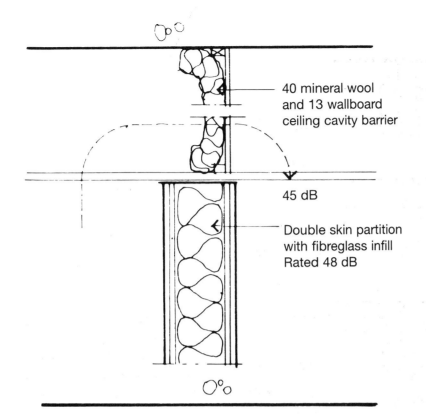

40 mineral wool and 13 wallboard ceiling cavity barrier

45 dB

Double skin partition with fibreglass infill Rated 48 dB

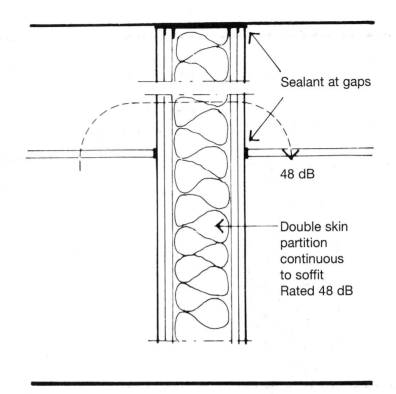

Sealant at gaps

48 dB

Double skin partition continuous to soffit Rated 48 dB

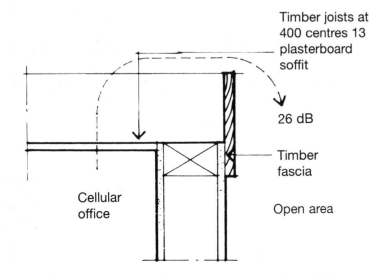

Timber joists at 400 centres 13 plasterboard soffit

26 dB

Timber fascia

Cellular office

Open area

Ceiling void flanking paths

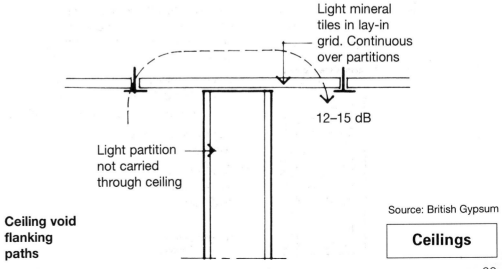

Light mineral tiles in lay-in grid. Continuous over partitions

12–15 dB

Light partition not carried through ceiling

Source: British Gypsum

Ceilings

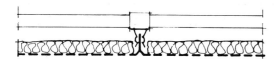

Perforated metal tiles clipped
to support framing, 25 proprietary
pads – density 64 kg/m^2

Sound absorption:
0.20 0.55 0.80 0.80 0.80 0.75

Sound attenuation (room to room)
32 dB (40 dB for solid face tile)

Linear air diffuser

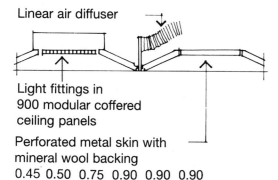

Light fittings in
900 modular coffered
ceiling panels

Perforated metal skin with
mineral wool backing
0.45 0.50 0.75 0.90 0.90 0.90

Metal deck cladding
or roof finish spacer

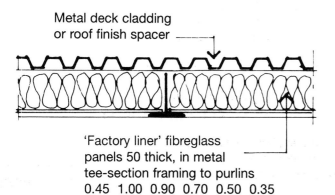

'Factory liner' fibreglass
panels 50 thick, in metal
tee-section framing to purlins
0.45 1.00 0.90 0.70 0.50 0.35

Varying thicknesses of
mineral wool on
lightweight ceiling

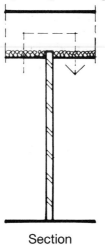

Section

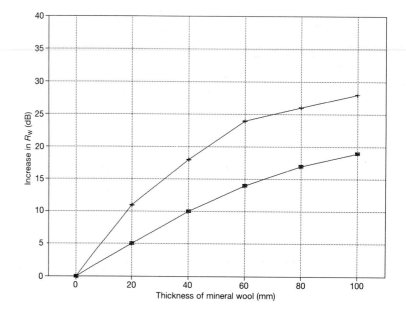

Thickness (mm)		20	40	60	80	100		Key
1.	Airtight ceilings (R_W)	5	10	14	17	19	dB	-■-
2.	Suspended proprietary ceilings – no airtight joints	11	18	24	26	28	dB	-+-

Reducing flanking via ceiling tiles

Source: Dr Lang, Vienna

Ceilings

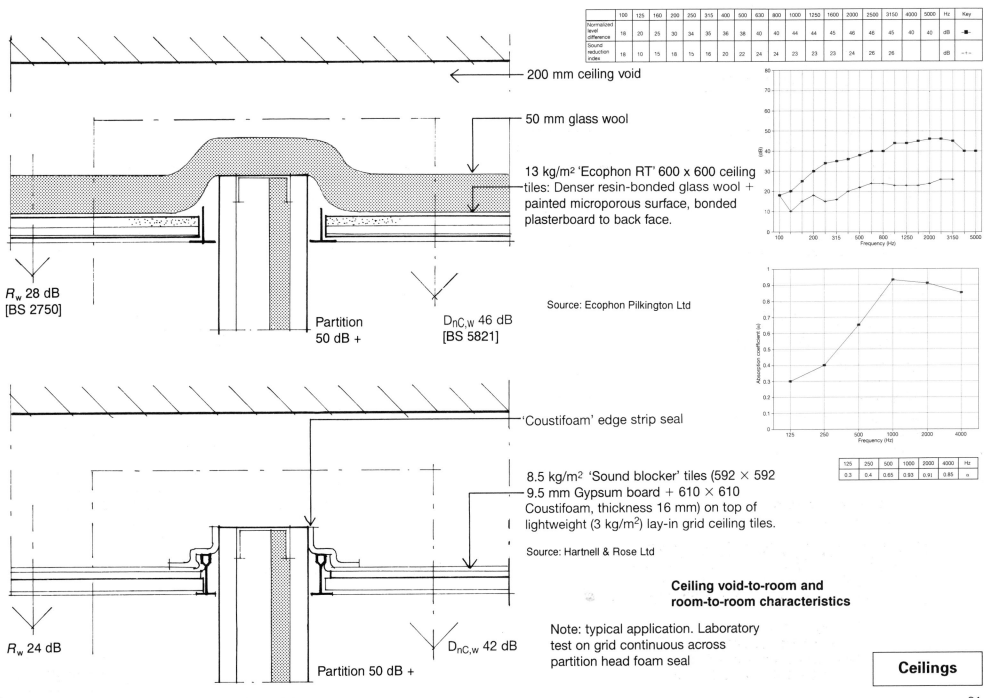

	100	125	160	200	250	315	400	500	630	800	1000	1250	1600	2000	2500	3150	4000	5000	Hz	Key
Normalized level difference	18	20	25	30	34	35	36	38	40	40	44	44	45	46	46	45	40	40	dB	–■–
Sound reduction index	18	10	15	18	15	16	20	22	24	24	23	23	23	24	26	26			dB	–+–

200 mm ceiling void

50 mm glass wool

13 kg/m^2 'Ecophon RT' 600 x 600 ceiling tiles: Denser resin-bonded glass wool + painted microporous surface, bonded plasterboard to back face.

Source: Ecophon Pilkington Ltd

R_w 28 dB
[BS 2750]

Partition
50 dB +

$D_{nC,w}$ 46 dB
[BS 5821]

'Coustifoam' edge strip seal

8.5 kg/m^2 'Sound blocker' tiles (592 × 592 9.5 mm Gypsum board + 610 × 610 Coustifoam, thickness 16 mm) on top of lightweight (3 kg/m^2) lay-in grid ceiling tiles.

Source: Hartnell & Rose Ltd

R_w 24 dB

$D_{nC,w}$ 42 dB

Partition 50 dB +

125	250	500	1000	2000	4000	Hz
0.3	0.4	0.65	0.93	0.91	0.85	α

Ceiling void-to-room and room-to-room characteristics

Note: typical application. Laboratory test on grid continuous across partition head foam seal

Ceilings

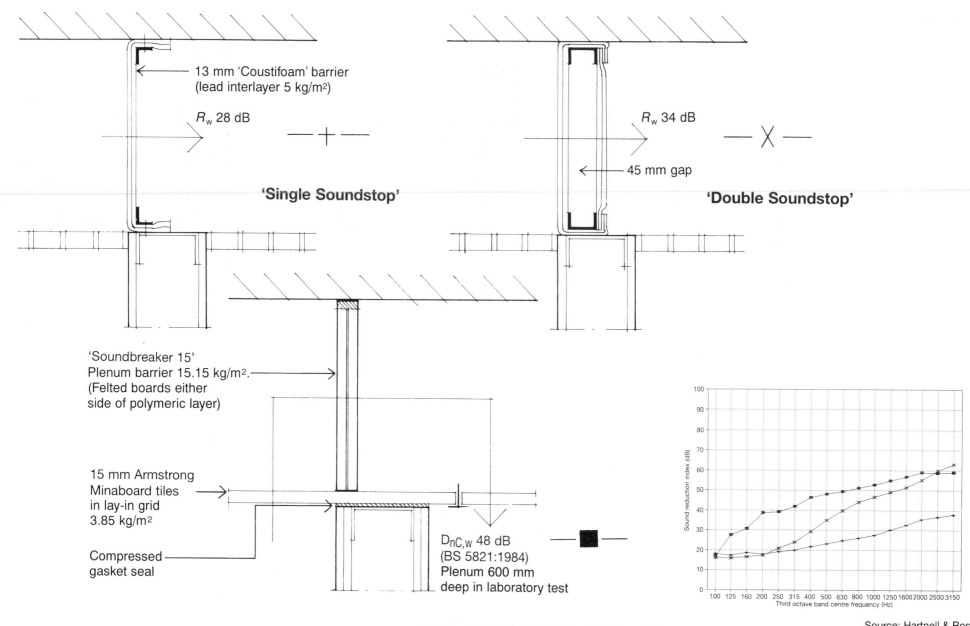

13 mm 'Coustifoam' barrier
(lead interlayer 5 kg/m²)

R_w 28 dB

— + —

'Single Soundstop'

R_w 34 dB

— X —

← 45 mm gap

'Double Soundstop'

'Soundbreaker 15'
Plenum barrier 15.15 kg/m².
(Felted boards either
side of polymeric layer)

15 mm Armstrong
Minaboard tiles
in lay-in grid
3.85 kg/m²

Compressed
gasket seal

$D_{nC,w}$ 48 dB
(BS 5821:1984)
Plenum 600 mm
deep in laboratory test

100	125	160	200	250	315	400	500	630	800	1000	1250	1600	2000	2500	3150	Hz	R_w	Key
17.1	27.5	30.7	38.6	39.1	41.8	46.3	48.1	49.3	51.2	52.8	54.8	56.7	59.0	58.6	59.0	dB		–■–
18.1	17.3	18.7	17.9	19.2	19.9	21.7	23.1	24.7	26.0	27.5	30.1	32.6	35.4	36.7	37.8	dB	28	–+–
16.1	16.0	16.5	17.3	20.9	24.0	29.2	34.9	39.8	44.1	46.6	49.1	51.5	55.2	59.8	63.0	dB	34	–×–

Source: Hartnell & Rose
Ltd/British Gypsum Ltd

Ceiling barriers

Partitions

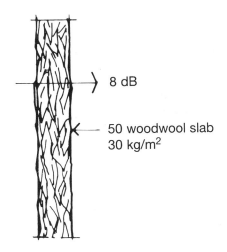

→ 8 dB

50 woodwool slab
30 kg/m²

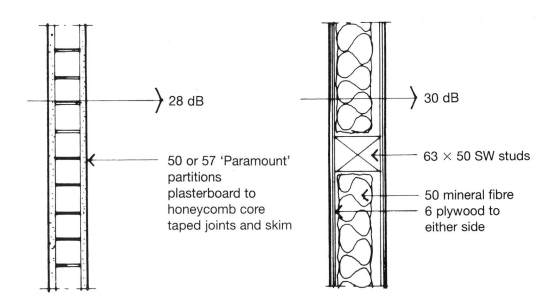

→ 28 dB

50 or 57 'Paramount'
partitions
plasterboard to
honeycomb core
taped joints and skim

→ 30 dB

63 × 50 SW studs

50 mineral fibre
6 plywood to
either side

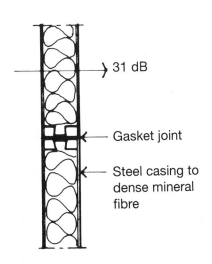

→ 31 dB

Gasket joint

Steel casing to
dense mineral
fibre

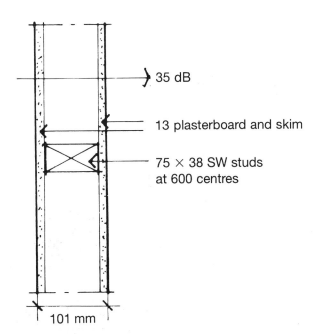

→ 35 dB

13 plasterboard and skim

75 × 38 SW studs
at 600 centres

101 mm

Partitions

Standard details

33

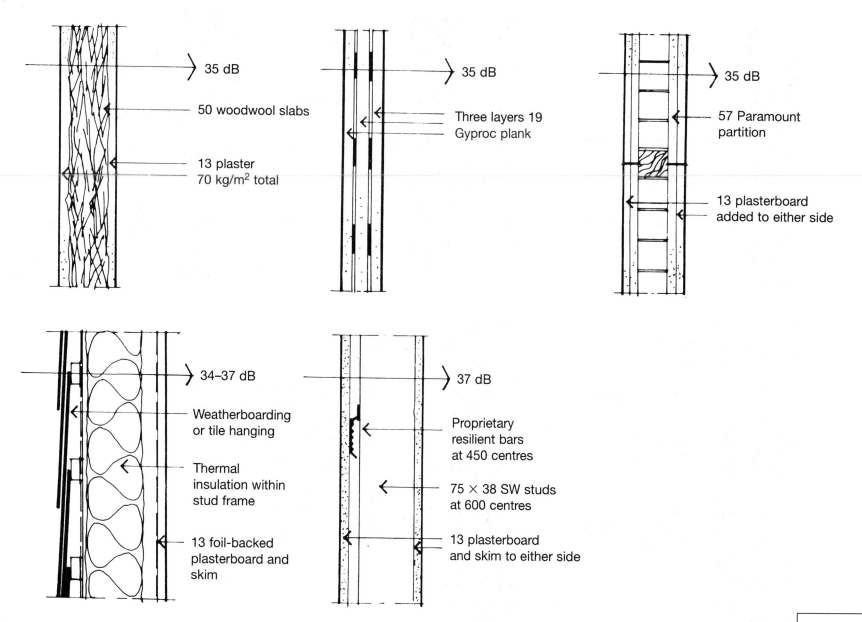

35 dB

50 woodwool slabs

13 plaster
70 kg/m² total

35 dB

Three layers 19
Gyproc plank

35 dB

57 Paramount
partition

13 plasterboard
added to either side

34–37 dB

Weatherboarding
or tile hanging

Thermal
insulation within
stud frame

13 foil-backed
plasterboard and
skim

37 dB

Proprietary
resilient bars
at 450 centres

75 × 38 SW studs
at 600 centres

13 plasterboard
and skim to either side

Partitions

Standard details

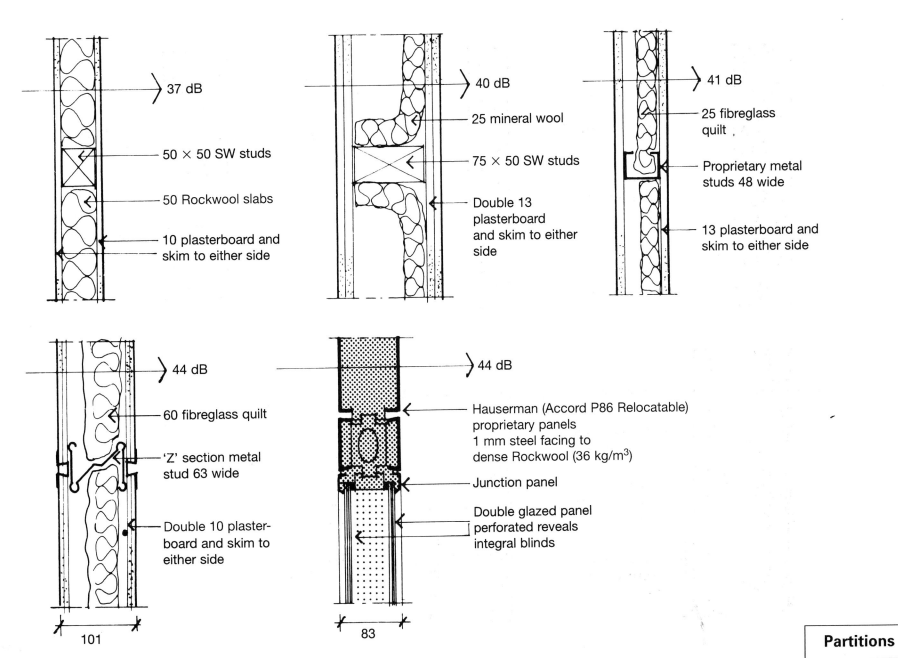

37 dB

50 × 50 SW studs

50 Rockwool slabs

10 plasterboard and skim to either side

40 dB

25 mineral wool

75 × 50 SW studs

Double 13 plasterboard and skim to either side

41 dB

25 fibreglass quilt

Proprietary metal studs 48 wide

13 plasterboard and skim to either side

44 dB

60 fibreglass quilt

'Z' section metal stud 63 wide

Double 10 plasterboard and skim to either side

101

44 dB

Hauserman (Accord P86 Relocatable) proprietary panels 1 mm steel facing to dense Rockwool (36 kg/m^3)

Junction panel

Double glazed panel perforated reveals integral blinds

83

Partitions

Standard details

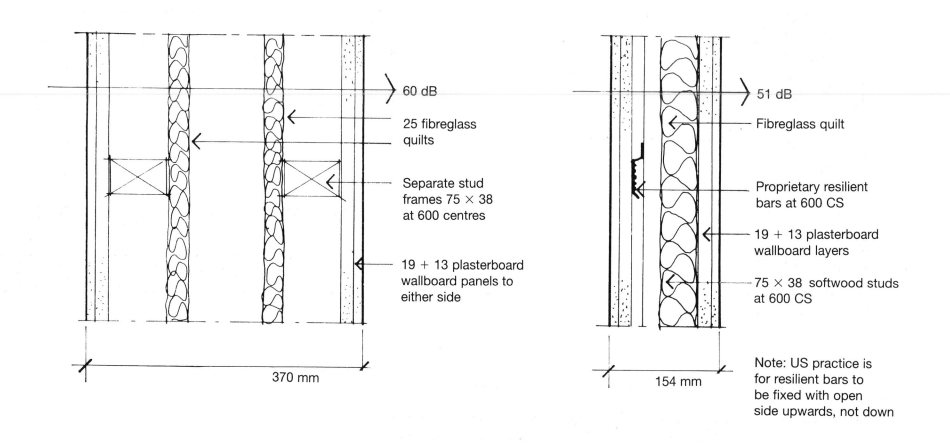

60 dB

25 fibreglass
quilts

Separate stud
frames 75 × 38
at 600 centres

19 + 13 plasterboard
wallboard panels to
either side

370 mm

51 dB

Fibreglass quilt

Proprietary resilient
bars at 600 CS

19 + 13 plasterboard
wallboard layers

75 × 38 softwood studs
at 600 CS

154 mm

Note: US practice is
for resilient bars to
be fixed with open
side upwards, not down

Partitions

Standard details

36

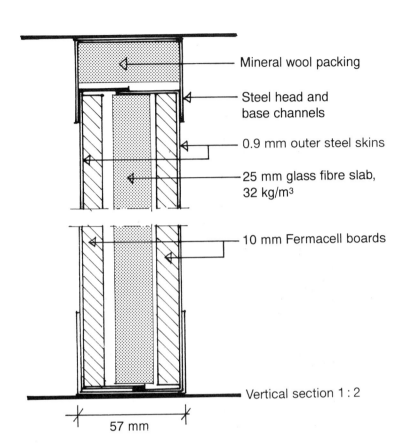

— Mineral wool packing

— Steel head and base channels

— 0.9 mm outer steel skins

— 25 mm glass fibre slab, 32 kg/m³

— 10 mm Fermacell boards

Vertical section 1 : 2

57 mm

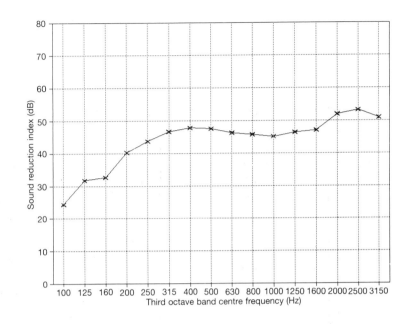

100	125	160	200	250	315	400	500	630	800	1000	1250	1600	2000	2500	3150	Hz	R_W
24.4	31.8	32.6	40.3	43.8	46.7	47.9	47.6	46.3	45.8	45.1	46.4	47.1	52.0	53.3	51.0	dB	48.0

Post upright with central spacer

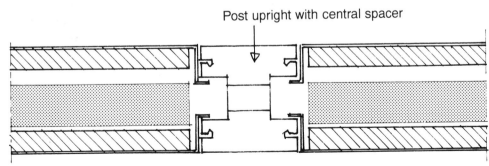

Horizontal section 1 : 2

Source: Keysan Ltd/
University of Salford

Partitions

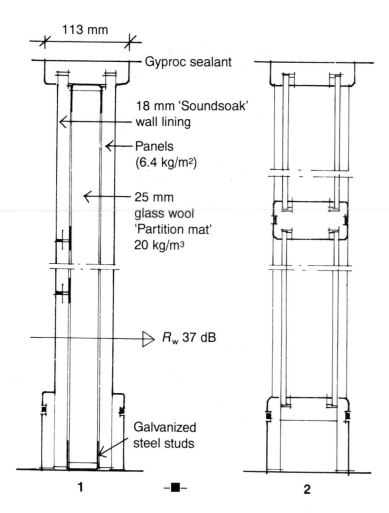

113 mm

— Gyproc sealant

— 18 mm 'Soundsoak' wall lining

— Panels (6.4 kg/m²)

— 25 mm glass wool 'Partition mat' 20 kg/m³

R_w 37 dB

Galvanized steel studs

1   —■—   2

— 12.7 mm plasterboard panels

R_w 43 dB

3

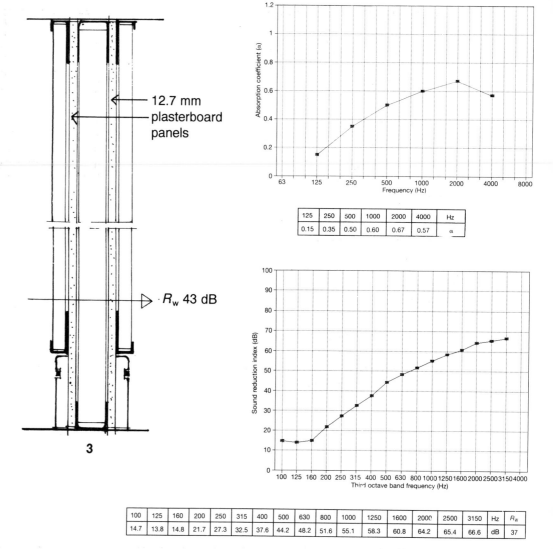

125	250	500	1000	2000	4000	Hz
0.15	0.35	0.50	0.60	0.67	0.57	α

100	125	160	200	250	315	400	500	630	800	1000	1250	1600	2000	2500	3150	Hz	R_w
14.7	13.8	14.8	21.7	27.3	32.5	37.6	44.2	48.2	51.6	55.1	58.3	60.8	64.2	65.4	66.6	dB	37

'Tenon Scion Soundsoak' is a partitioning system that combines reasonable sound insulation between cellular offices, with very useful wall sound absorption with pinboard capability. The best meeting rooms have sound-reflecting ceilings, and sound-absorbing wall finishes.

Source: Armstrong Tenon Partition Systems Ltd/ British Gypsum Ltd

Partitions

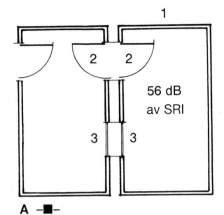

A −■−

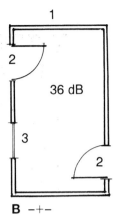

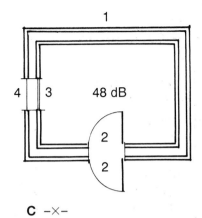

B −+−

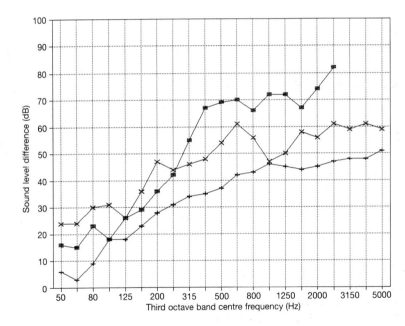

C −×−

56 dB
av SRI

36 dB

48 dB

1   100 mm thick enclosure panels:
    mild steel skins with mineral
    wool core
2   2 m x 1 m steel doors with seals
3   Double glazed window
4   Single glazed window

Field performance measurements by BBC on
examples of vocal booth (C) and control
rooms. Partitions are demountable and full
height, i.e. common floor and ceiling
to rest of room.

50	63	80	100	125	160	200	250	315	400	500	630	800	1k	1250	1600	2k	2500	3150	4k	5k	Hz	Av. SRI	Key
16	15	23	18	26	29	36	42	55	67	69	70	66	72	72	67	74	82	--	--	--	dB	56	−■−
6	3	9	18	18	23	28	31	34	35	37	42	43	46	45	44	45	47	48	48	51	dB	36	−+−
24	24	30	31	26	36	47	44	46	48	54	61	56	47	50	58	56	61	59	61	59	dB	48	−×−

Partitions

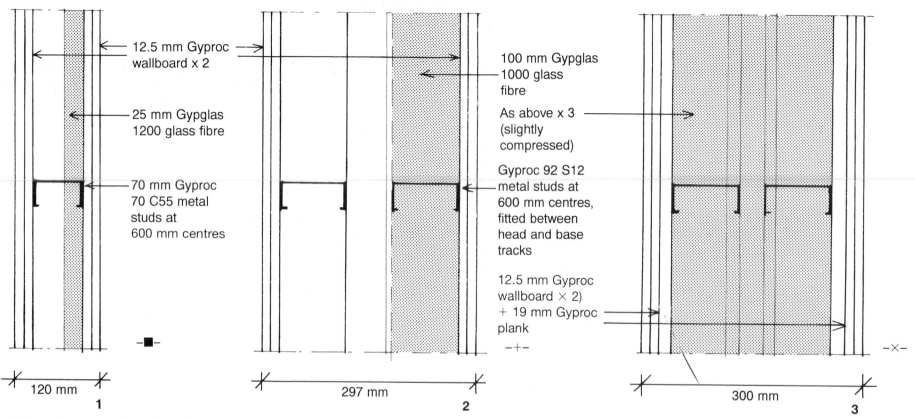

12.5 mm Gyproc wallboard x 2

25 mm Gypglas 1200 glass fibre

70 mm Gyproc 70 C55 metal studs at 600 mm centres

100 mm Gypglas 1000 glass fibre

As above x 3 (slightly compressed)

Gyproc 92 S12 metal studs at 600 mm centres, fitted between head and base tracks

12.5 mm Gyproc wallboard × 2) + 19 mm Gyproc plank

120 mm

1

297 mm

2

300 mm

3

High performance plasterboard assemblies have been used successfully over 20 years in cinema multiplexes. High standards of workmanship, edge sealing, and attention to junction detailing are required to realise the laboratory test results in practice.

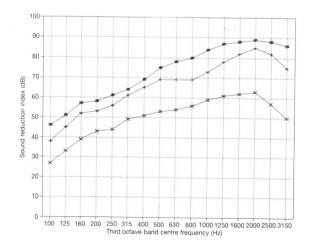

Source: British Gypsum

Partitions

100	125	160	200	250	315	400	500	630	800	1000	1250	1600	2000	2500	3150	Hz	Rw	Key
27	33	39	43	44	49	51	53	54	56	59	61	62	63	57	50	dB	53	-■-
38	45	52	53	56	61	65	69	69	69	73	78	82	85	82	75	dB	67	-+-
46	51	57	58	61	64	69	75	78	80	84	87	88	89	88	86	dB	72	-×-

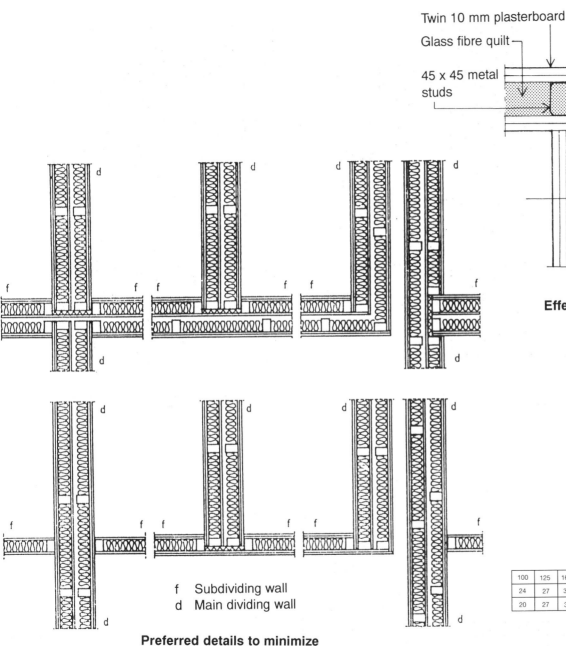

f Subdividing wall
d Main dividing wall

Preferred details to minimize flanking of main dividing walls

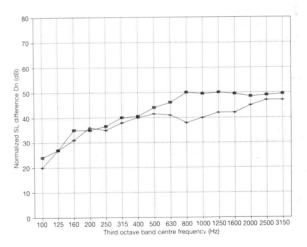

Twin 10 mm plasterboard

Glass fibre quilt

45 x 45 metal studs

$D_{n.T.w}$ 42 dB

1 —+—

$D_{n.T.w}$ 46 dB

2 —■—

Effect of continuity at junctions

100	125	160	200	250	315	400	500	630	800	1000	1250	1600	2000	2500	3150	Hz	Key
24	27	35	35	36.5	40	40.5	44	46	50	49.5	50	49.5	48.5	49	49.5	dB	-■-
20	27	31	36	35	38	40	41.5	41	38	40	42	42	45	47	47	dB	-+-

Source: Dr Lang, Vienna

Partition junctions

41

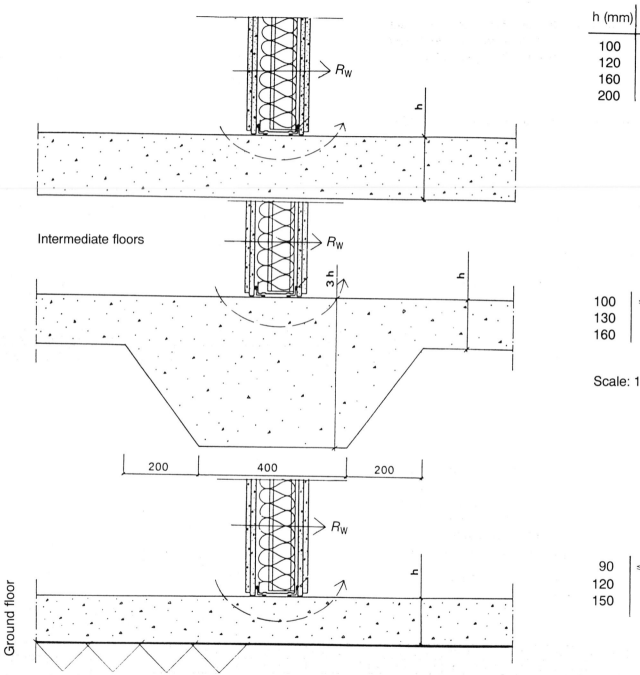

h (mm)	R_W (dB)
100	44
120	48
160	52
200	55

These results show the downrating effects of flanking sound at the partition–floor junction. Not only does the noise excite the common floor structure more easily in a thinner floor, but also the floor will deflect more easily and open up the base seal at mid-spans.

Intermediate floors

100	≤48
130	52
160	55

Scale: 1:10

Such flanking effects can explain the variance of field ($D'_{nT,w}$) and laboratory ($D_{nT,w}$) measurements.

Ground floor

90	≤48
120	52
150	55

Source: Gyproc

Partition junctions

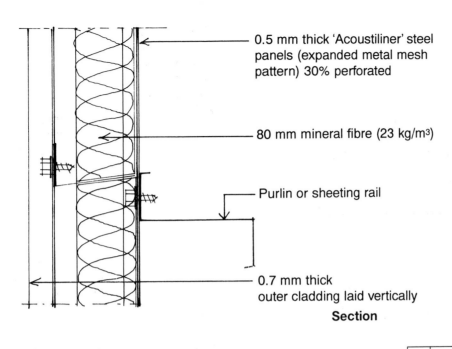

0.5 mm thick 'Acoustiliner' steel panels (expanded metal mesh pattern) 30% perforated

80 mm mineral fibre (23 kg/m³)

Purlin or sheeting rail

0.7 mm thick outer cladding laid vertically

Section

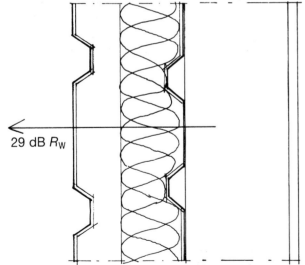

29 dB R_W

Lining panel system by European Profiles Ltd for use in industrial buildings to control reverberant sound pressure levels, or in TV production studios.

Plan

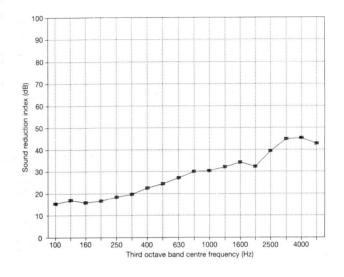

100	125	160	200	250	315	400	500	630	800	1000	1250	1600	2000	2500	3150	4000	5000	Hz	R_w
15.3	16.9	15.7	16.6	18.4	19.6	22.5	24.4	27.2	30.0	30.3	32.1	34.2	32.3	39.3	44.7	45.2	42.6	dB	29

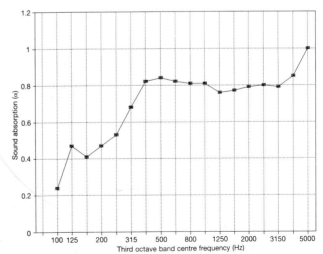

100	125	160	200	250	315	400	500	630	800	1000	1250	1600	2000	2500	3150	4000	5000	Hz
0.24	0.47	0.41	0.47	0.53	0.68	0.82	0.84	0.82	0.81	0.81	0.76	0.77	0.79	0.80	0.79	0.85	1.00	α

Acoustic lining system

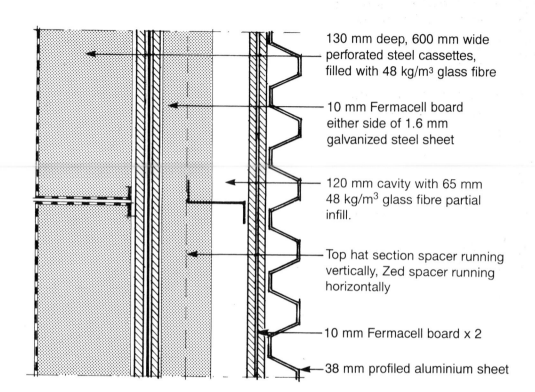

130 mm deep, 600 mm wide perforated steel cassettes, filled with 48 kg/m³ glass fibre

10 mm Fermacell board either side of 1.6 mm galvanized steel sheet

120 mm cavity with 65 mm 48 kg/m³ glass fibre partial infill.

Top hat section spacer running vertically, Zed spacer running horizontally

10 mm Fermacell board x 2

38 mm profiled aluminium sheet

Wall cladding developed for high sound insulation for a power station, combined with sound absorbing inner face to reduce reverberant sound pressure levels. Overall surface mass 95 kg/m².

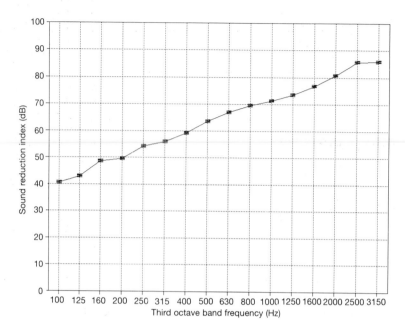

100	125	160	200	250	315	400	500	630	800	1000	1250	1600	2000	2500	3150	Hz	R_w
40.6	42.9	48.5	49.5	54.1	56.0	59.1	63.6	67.0	69.5	71.3	73.6	76.7	80.7	85.7	85.9	dB	64

Source: Weatherwise Ltd/
University of Salford

Wall cladding

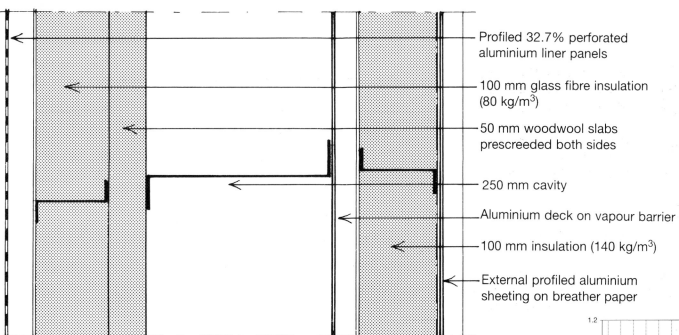

- Profiled 32.7% perforated aluminium liner panels
- 100 mm glass fibre insulation (80 kg/m³)
- 50 mm woodwool slabs prescreeded both sides
- 250 mm cavity
- Aluminium deck on vapour barrier
- 100 mm insulation (140 kg/m³)
- External profiled aluminium sheeting on breather paper

High performance wall construction for a power station

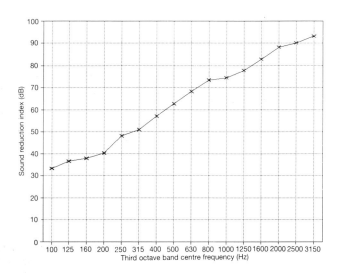

100	125	160	200	250	315	400	500	630	800	1000	1250	1600	2000	2500	3150	R_w	Hz
33.4	36.5	37.8	40.3	48.1	51.0	57.1	62.6	68.3	73.3	74.3	77.7	82.8	88.2	90.2	93.2	58	dB

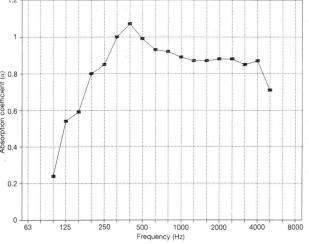

100	125	160	200	250	315	400	500	630	800	1000	1250	1600	2000	2500	3150	4000	5000	Hz
0.24	0.54	0.59	0.80	0.85	1.00	1.07	0.99	0.93	0.92	0.89	0.87	0.87	0.88	0.88	0.85	0.87	0.71	α

Source: Sandy Brown Associates/ University of Salford

Wall cladding

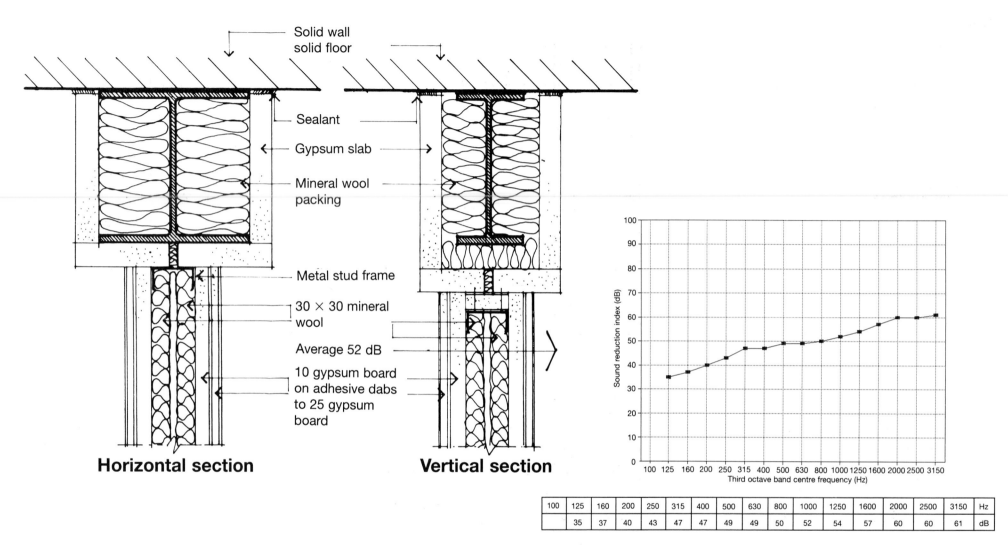

Solid wall
solid floor

Sealant

Gypsum slab

Mineral wool
packing

Metal stud frame

30 × 30 mineral
wool

Average 52 dB

10 gypsum board
on adhesive dabs
to 25 gypsum
board

Horizontal section

Vertical section

100	125	160	200	250	315	400	500	630	800	1000	1250	1600	2000	2500	3150	Hz
	35	37	40	43	47	47	49	49	50	52	54	57	60	60	61	dB

**Junctions to
structural
steelwork**

Source: Dr Lang
Technologisches
Gewerbe Museum,
Vienna

Partitions

46

Walls

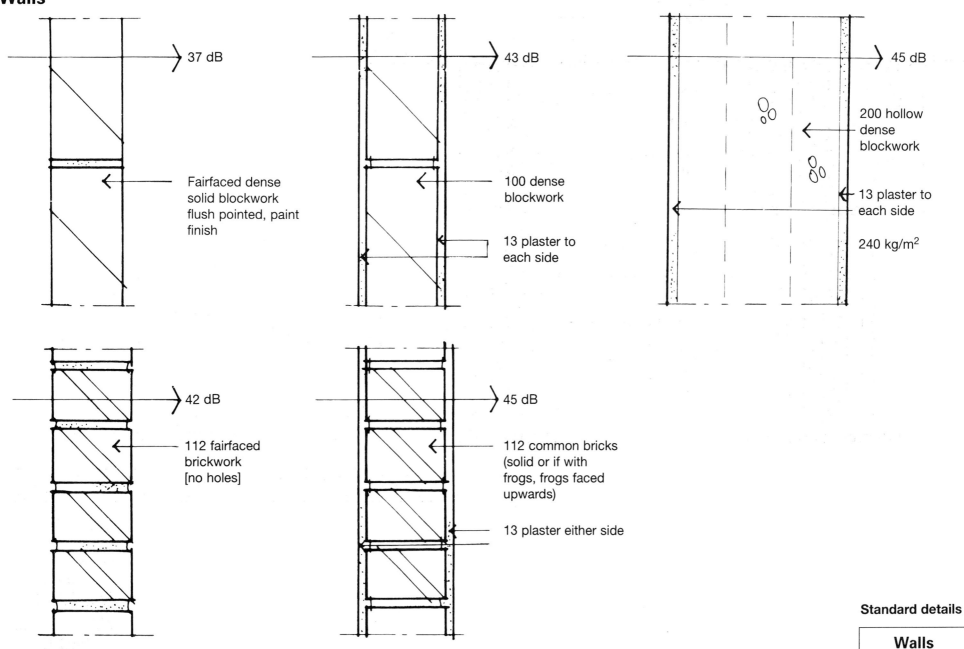

37 dB

Fairfaced dense solid blockwork flush pointed, paint finish

43 dB

100 dense blockwork

13 plaster to each side

45 dB

200 hollow dense blockwork

13 plaster to each side

240 kg/m²

42 dB

112 fairfaced brickwork [no holes]

45 dB

112 common bricks (solid or if with frogs, frogs faced upwards)

13 plaster either side

Standard details

Walls

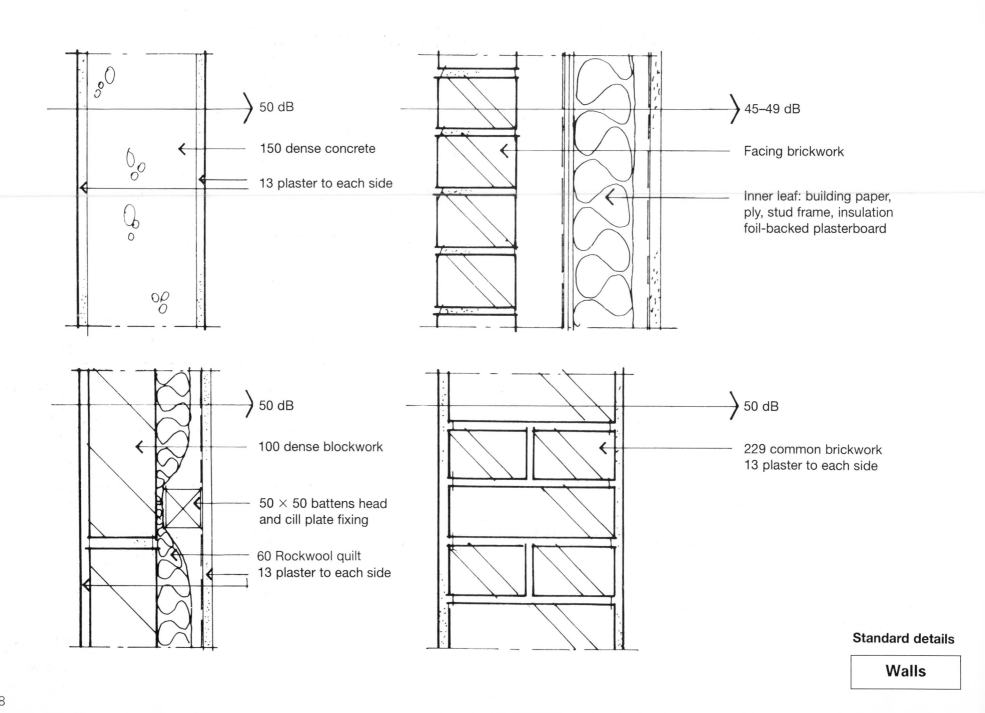

50 dB

150 dense concrete

13 plaster to each side

45–49 dB

Facing brickwork

Inner leaf: building paper,
ply, stud frame, insulation
foil-backed plasterboard

50 dB

100 dense blockwork

50 × 50 battens head
and cill plate fixing

60 Rockwool quilt
13 plaster to each side

50 dB

229 common brickwork
13 plaster to each side

Standard details

Walls

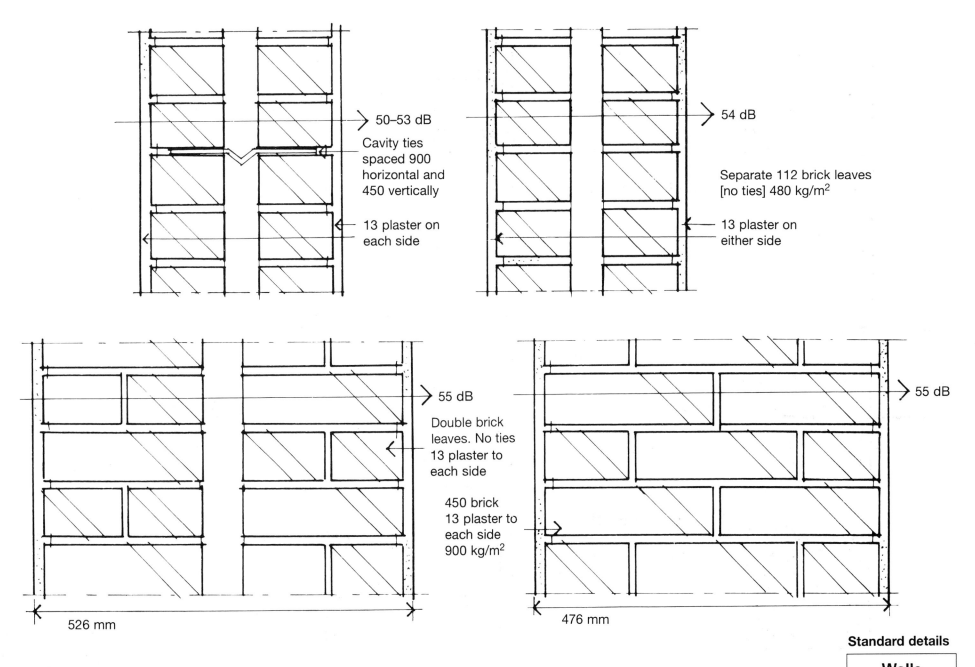

> 50–53 dB

Cavity ties spaced 900 horizontal and 450 vertically

13 plaster on each side

> 54 dB

Separate 112 brick leaves [no ties] 480 kg/m²

13 plaster on either side

> 55 dB

Double brick leaves. No ties 13 plaster to each side

450 brick 13 plaster to each side 900 kg/m²

526 mm

> 55 dB

476 mm

Standard details

Walls

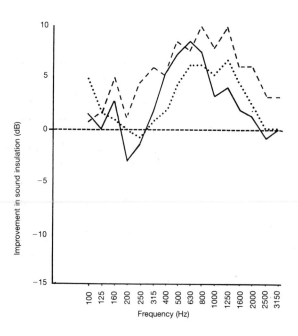

Key	External wall lining	Separating wall lining
——	1 Layer 9.5 mm plasterboard	1 Layer 9.5 mm plasterboard
– – –	1 Layer 9.5 mm plasterboard	2 Layers 9.5 mm plasterboard
·········	12.5 mm lightweight plaster	12.5 mm lightweight plaster

Improvement in sound insulation provided by various wall linings (source: CIRIA)

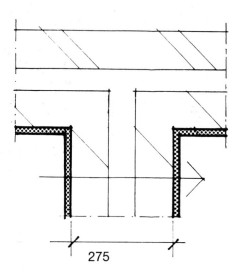

275

Party walls

As well as the mass of separating and external walls the following aspects affect the sound insulation through the operating walls

1. Ties. Absence of ties considerably improves the sound insulation. Butterfly ties preferable to strip ties.

2. Cavity insulation. 60–70 kg/m³ mineral wool lining to separating wall cavity improves sound insulation by impeding sound tracking across the cavity. (Must be loosely placed in cavity.)

3. Joist direction. Joists parallel to separating walls have in tests given consistently higher sound insulation than joists perpendicular to separating wall.

4. Joist tightness. Rather than 'loose' pockets at joist ends, consider use of joist hangers to allow the wall integrity to be maintained.

5. Dry lining. The effect of wall finishes is shown on the left. Two layers to separating wall are necessary to improve on plaster. One layer can actually reduce sound insulation at some frequencies because of resonance.

Walls

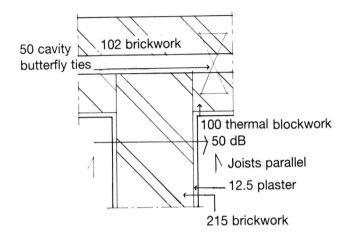

50 cavity butterfly ties

102 brickwork

100 thermal blockwork
→ 50 dB
Joists parallel
12.5 plaster

215 brickwork

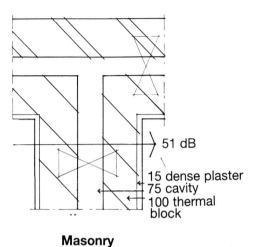

51 dB

15 dense plaster
75 cavity
100 thermal block

Masonry party walls
Scale 1 : 10

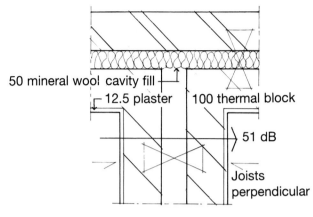

50 mineral wool cavity fill
12.5 plaster   100 thermal block
→ 51 dB
Joists perpendicular

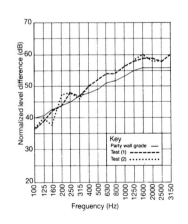

Frequency (Hz)	Test results (dB)	
	(1)	(2)
100	36	36
125	39	40
160	42	38
200	44	47
250	48	48
315	47	46
400	50	50
500	52	52
630	54	54
800	54	54
1000	56	56
1250	58	58
1600	59	60
2000	59	59
2500	58	58
3150	60	60
Average insulation	51	51
BS 5821: 1980 Standardized weighted level difference (D$_{nT,w}$)	55	55

Key
Party wall grade ——
Test (1) ————
Test (2) ··········

Normalized level difference (dB) vs Frequency (Hz)

Frequency (Hz)	Test results (dB)	
	(1)	(2)
100	40	39
125	42	40
160	42	41
200	43	42
250	47	46
315	48	48
400	49	49
500	54	53
630	56	55
800	56	55
1000	58	56
1250	58	56
1600	59	57
2000	59	59
2500	58	58
3150	58	58
Average insulation	52	50
BS 5821: 1980 Standardized weighted level difference (D$_{nT,w}$)	56	55

Key
Party wall grade ——
Test (1) ————
Test (2) ··········

Normalized level difference (dB) vs Frequency (Hz)

Frequency (Hz)	Test results (dB)	
	(1)	(2)
100	31	30
125	38	38
160	42	44
200	44	44
250	46	44
315	47	47
400	48	48
500	52	51
630	54	55
800	56	56
1000	58	58
1250	59	59
1600	60	60
2000	58	58
2500	57	57
3150	58	58
Average insulation	50	51
BS 5821: 1980 Standardized weighted level difference (D$_{nT,w}$)	55	55

Key
Party wall grade ——
Test (1) ————
Test (2) ··········

Normalized level difference (dB) vs Frequency (Hz)

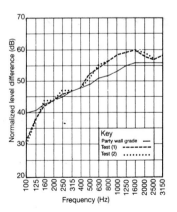

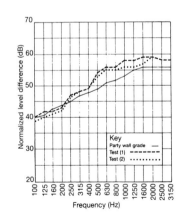

Source: CIRIA

Walls

	440 × 215 × 100	
Dense solid	440 × 215 × 100 laid flat	
	440 × 215 × 140	
	100/50/100	
	440 × 215 × 100	
Dense hollow/cellular	440 × 215 × 100	
	440 × 215 × 215	
	100/50/100	
	440 × 215 × 100	
Lightweight	440 × 215 × 100 laid flat	
	440 × 215 × 140	
	100/50/100	

Weight (kg/m²)	Plaster type	R_w(dB)
210	Fairfaced (–)	49
234	Lightweight (L)	50
258	Dense (D)	51
234	Drylined (Y)	50
448	–	56
472	L	57
496	D	58
472	Y	56
280	–	52
304	L	53
328	D	53
304	Y	53
420	–	56
444	L	57
468	D	58
444	Y	56
190	–	48
214	L	49
238	D	50
214	Y	49
214	–	49
238	L	50
262	D	51
238	Y	50
270	–	51
294	L	52
318	D	53
294	Y	52
380	–	54
404	L	54
428	D	55
404	Y	54
155	–	46
179	L	47
203	D	48
179	Y	47
344	–	54
368	L	54
392	D	55
368	Y	54
233	–	50
257	L	51
282	D	52
257	Y	51
310	–	53
334	L	54 (D_{nTW} 58 dB)
358	D	54
334	Y	54

(mean SRI values typically 3 dB less)

Typical sound absorption for different block types

Density (kg/m³)	OBCF (Hz)					
	125	250	500	1k	2k	4k
1550	0.25	0.25	0.20	0.30	0.40	0.45
2000	0.20	0.20	0.20	0.15	0.20	0.25
2100	0.15	0.15	0.10	0.15	0.30	0.35
1293 (slotted hollow)	0.60	0.60	0.50	0.50	0.50	0.55

Blockwork characteristics

Besides blockwork density, the trade-off of weight with total wall thickness may be seen. Hollow blocks of dense concrete are still slightly better for thin blocks, than lightweight, but worse for thicker blocks. A comprehensive specification is acoustic performance, block density, thickness/surface mass, 'solid no voids', and both faces plastered.

Source: Lignacite/Lignacrete, AIRO Ltd

Based on laboratory tests except cavity wall values which are estimated from test values.

Sound insulation

Walls

Wall Type 1: solid masonry

A   Brick plastered on both faces   (minimum mass 375 kg/m^2)
B   Concrete block plastered on both faces   (minimum mass 415 kg/m^2)
C   Brick with plasterboard on both faces   (minimum mass 375 kg/m^2)
D   Concrete block with plasterboard on both faces   (minimum mass 415 kg/m^2)
E   Concrete *in situ* or large panel and plaster   (minimum mass 415 kg/m^2)

Notes

(i)   Type D was not included in the 1985 edition.

(ii)   There is no specific mention of workmanship affecting plasterboard. The sound insulation will suffer if workmanship is poor and we recommend that boards should be close-cut (gaps of not more than 2 mm between panels) and gaps filled to the full depth of the plasterboard. Gaps and holes, e.g. for wiring and electrical sockets, should be kept to a minimum and filled with plaster or mastic.

(iii)   'Any normal fixing method' for fixing plasterboard is permitted. This is usually on softwood battens but proprietary fixing methods (e.g. metal studs and channels) are equally permissible. In general, sound insulation increases with the depth of the airspace between the plasterboard and the masonry.

The densities of concrete and brick are minima. There is no specific mention of hollow block; it is assumed that dense hollow block would be permissible if the mass requirement were met. Other forms of lightweight block are not permitted.

Wall Type 2: cavity masonry

Three approved constructions are illustrated as suitable for all cases:

A   Two leaves of brick 13 mm plaster on both room faces, 50 mm cavity. Total minimum mass 415 kg/m^2.
B   Two leaves of concrete block, 13 mm plaster on both room faces, 50 mm cavity. Total minimum mass 415 kg/m^2.
C   Two leaves of lightweight aggregate block, plastered or dry lined on both room faces. Minimum total mass 300 kg/m^2. 75 mm cavity.

Two further constructions are listed as suitable where there is a step or stagger or 300 mm between the two rooms:

D   Two leaves of concrete block, 50 mm cavity, 12.5 mm plasterboard on both faces, minimum mass of masonry 415 kg/m^2.
E   Two leaves of lightweight aggregate concrete block, 75 mm cavity, plastered or dry lined on both faces. Mass including finish 250 kg/m^2.

Wall Type 3: masonry between isolated panels

Four masonry cores and two isolated panel types are listed. Any combination of core and panels is permissible:

Cores: A: Single leaf brick, minimum mass 300 kg/m^2.
       B: Single leaf concrete block, minimum mass 300 kg/m^2.
       C: Lightweight concrete block, maximum density 1600 kg/m^3, mass 160 kg/m^2.
       D: Cavity brickwork or blockwork of any mass connected by butterfly ties only across a cavity of at least 50 mm.

Panels: E: Two sheets of plasterboard joined by a cellular core.
        F: Two sheets of plasterboard with staggered joints.

Notes:

(i)   The panels should be supported only at the floor and ceiling, not tied to the masonry core. There are other combinations of masonry cores and wall linings which may meet the requirements using resilient studs between the core and lining.

Wall type 4: timber framed walls

Two approved constructions are shown:

A Two leaves of plasterboard, each of 30 mm, separated by 200 mm on independent frames, cavity containing mineral wool.

B Two leaves of plasterboard, each of 30 mm, one each side of a masonry core, mineral wool in cavity on one side. There must be a minimum of 200 mm between the leaves (irrespective of the thickness of the core) and the frame on at least one side must be independent of the core.

Notes

(i) The required thickness of the mineral wool depends on the fixing method: 25 mm if suspended freely, 50 mm total if fixed to one or both frames. There is little advantage in using more mineral wool than this or in exceeding the specified density ($10\ kg/m^3$).

There are proprietary constructions that may meet the Requirements using metal rather than timber frames.

The quality of workmanship, detailing or (preferably) absence of penetrations such as power points and details such as staggered joints between plasterboard panels are of great importance in this type of construction.

Building airborne sound requirements in dB ($D'_{nT,w}$)

Individual & conversion	Mean	
49	Tests on up to 4 pairs of rooms	53
	Tests on 8 pairs of rooms	52

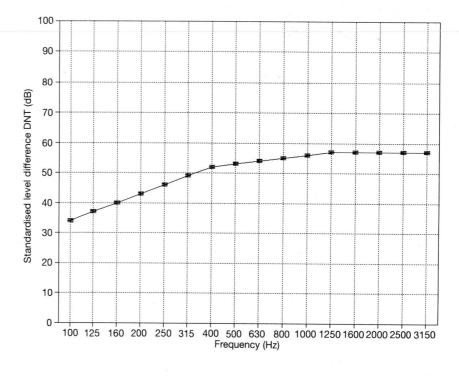

100	125	160	200	250	315	400	500	630	800	1000	1250	1600	2000	2500	3150	Hz	D_nT_w
34	37	40	43	46	49	52	53	54	55	56	57	57	57	57	57	dB	53

Party walls

Summary notes on Building Regulations Part E 1991 (amd. 1992)

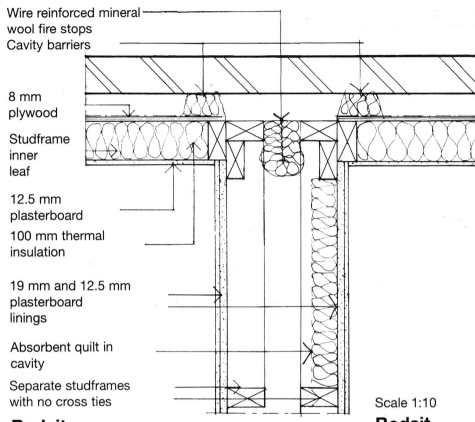

Wire reinforced mineral wool fire stops
Cavity barriers

8 mm plywood

Studframe inner leaf

12.5 mm plasterboard

100 mm thermal insulation

19 mm and 12.5 mm plasterboard linings

Absorbent quilt in cavity

Separate studframes with no cross ties

Scale 1:10

Bedsit

Bedsit

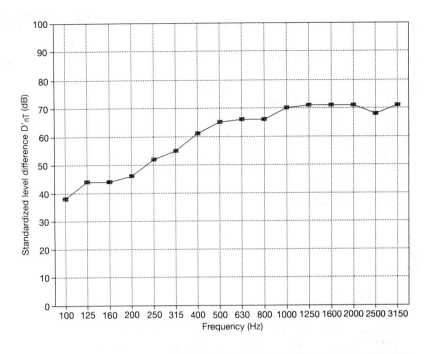

100	125	160	200	250	315	400	500	630	800	1000	1250	1600	2000	2500	3150	Hz	D'$_{nT,w}$
38	44	44	46	52	55	61	65	66	66	70	71	71	71	68	71	dB	63

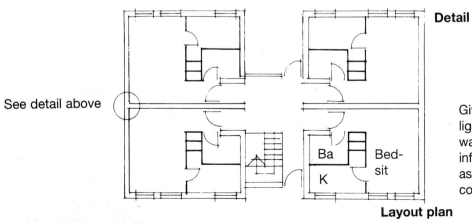

See detail above

Ba Bed-sit
K

Detail

Given careful construction lightweight party walls need not be inferior to masonry, as these tests on completed flats show.

Layout plan
Scale 1 : 20

Source: Wimpey Laboratories Ltd

Party walls

55

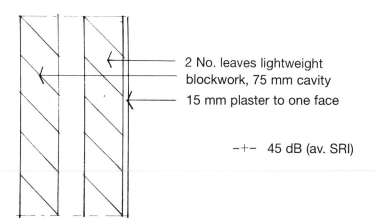

2 No. leaves lightweight blockwork, 75 mm cavity

15 mm plaster to one face

−+− 45 dB (av. SRI)

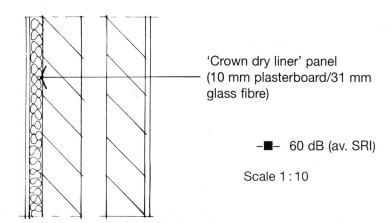

'Crown dry liner' panel (10 mm plasterboard/31 mm glass fibre)

−■− 60 dB (av. SRI)

Scale 1 : 10

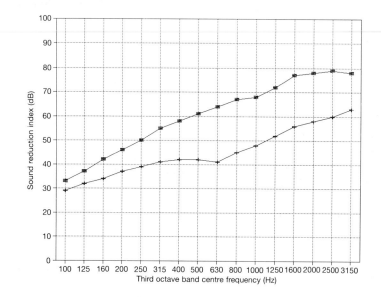

100	125	160	200	250	315	400	500	630	800	1000	1250	1600	2000	2500	3150	Hz	Key
33	37	42	46	50	55	58	61	64	67	68	72	77	78	79	78	dB	−■−
29	32	34	37	39	41	42	42	41	45	48	52	56	58	60	63	dB	−+−

Drylining cavity walls

Results from a test programme on this form of lining to upgrade masonry walls indicates:
1. Good improvement by lining one side only (to line both sides is of little additional benefit)
2. Adhesive rather than fixing of panels

Source: Pilkington Fibreglass
University of Salford
Dept. of Applied Acoustics

Walls

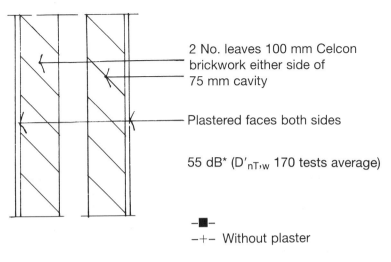

2 No. leaves 100 mm Celcon brickwork either side of 75 mm cavity

Plastered faces both sides

55 dB* ($D'_{nT,w}$ 170 tests average)

—■—
—+— Without plaster

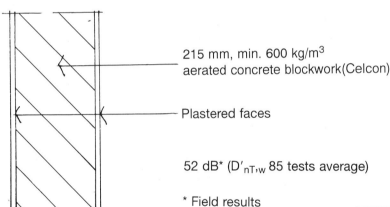

215 mm, min. 600 kg/m³ aerated concrete blockwork(Celcon)

Plastered faces

52 dB* ($D'_{nT,w}$ 85 tests average)

* Field results

Scale 1:10

Field tests of masonry walls

Results compare favourably with Table 2/ Section 3/Approved Document 'E', Building Regulations 1991 (amd. 1992), although these are not constructions specifically listed in the approved document, and minimum masses are much less than example approved wall constructions for party walls

AIRO have found that a 'correction factor' of 3 dB, applies for field results compared with laboratory

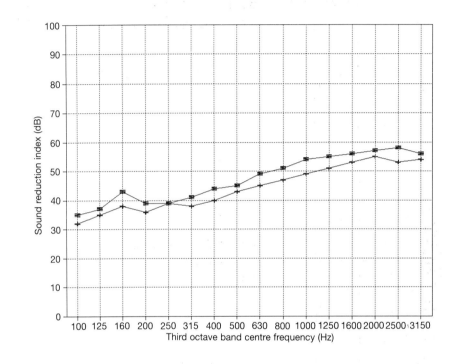

100	125	160	200	250	315	400	500	630	800	1000	1250	1600	2000	2500	3150	Hz	Key	
35	37	43	39	39	41	44	45	49	51	54	55	56	57	58	56	dB	—■—	With plaster
32	35	38	36	39	38	40	43	45	47	49	51	53	55	53	54	dB	—+—	Without plaster

Source: Celcon Ltd/AIRO Ltd

Walls

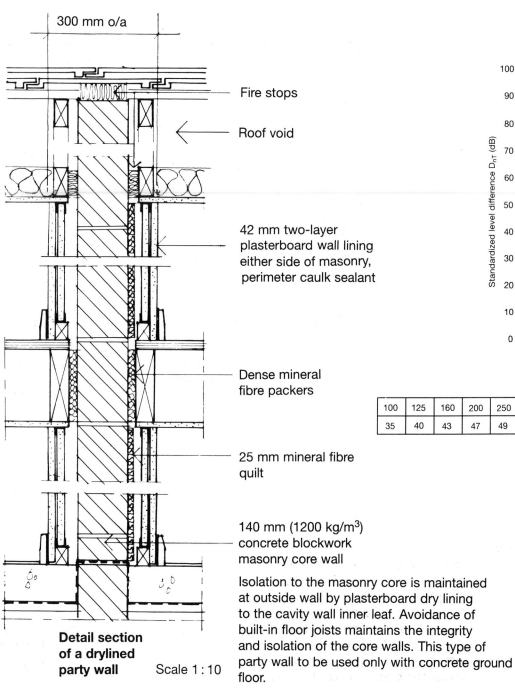

300 mm o/a

Fire stops

Roof void

42 mm two-layer
plasterboard wall lining
either side of masonry,
perimeter caulk sealant

Dense mineral
fibre packers

25 mm mineral fibre
quilt

140 mm (1200 kg/m³)
concrete blockwork
masonry core wall

Isolation to the masonry core is maintained
at outside wall by plasterboard dry lining
to the cavity wall inner leaf. Avoidance of
built-in floor joists maintains the integrity
and isolation of the core walls. This type of
party wall to be used only with concrete ground
floor.

**Detail section
of a drylined
party wall**   Scale 1 : 10

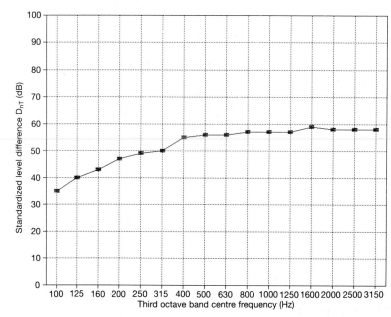

100	125	160	200	250	315	400	500	630	800	1000	1250	1600	2000	2500	3150	Hz	$D_{nT,w}$
35	40	43	47	49	50	55	56	56	57	57	57	59	58	58	58	dB	56

Source: The Cement and
Concrete Association/
Wimpey Laboratories Ltd

Walls

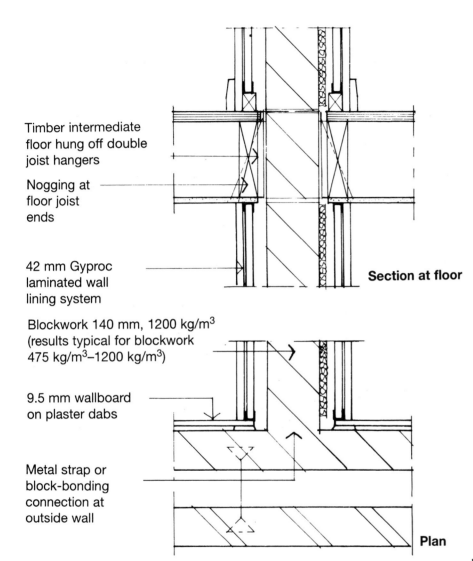

Timber intermediate floor hung off double joist hangers

Nogging at floor joist ends

42 mm Gyproc laminated wall lining system

Section at floor

Blockwork 140 mm, 1200 kg/m³ (results typical for blockwork 475 kg/m³–1200 kg/m³)

9.5 mm wallboard on plaster dabs

Metal strap or block-bonding connection at outside wall

Plan

Scale 1 : 10

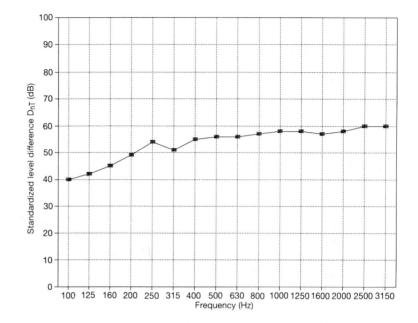

100	125	160	200	250	315	400	500	630	800	1000	1250	1600	2000	2500	3150	Hz	$D_{nT,w}$
40	42	45	49	54	51	55	56	56	57	58	58	57	58	60	60	dB	57

Joists perpendicular to party wall do not downgrade performance if supported off joist hangers from the face of the masonry corewall. Metal straps can also be used to provide structural lateral restraint of the intermediate floor across the party wall construction

Source: Cement and Concrete Association

Walls

59

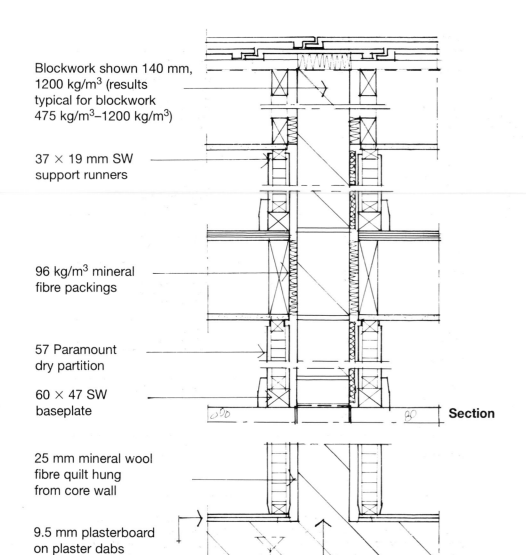

Blockwork shown 140 mm, 1200 kg/m³ (results typical for blockwork 475 kg/m³–1200 kg/m³)

37 × 19 mm SW support runners

96 kg/m³ mineral fibre packings

57 Paramount dry partition

60 × 47 SW baseplate

Section

25 mm mineral wool fibre quilt hung from core wall

9.5 mm plasterboard on plaster dabs

Metal strap or block-bonding connection at outside wall

Plan

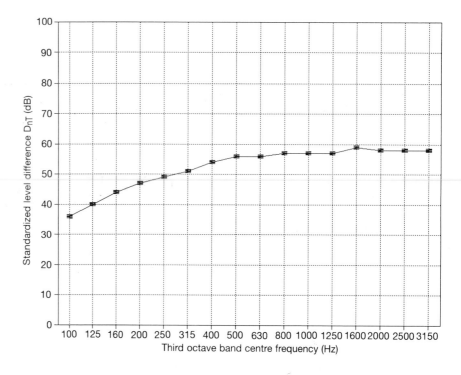

100	125	160	200	250	315	400	500	630	800	1000	1250	1600	2000	2500	3150	Hz	$D_{nT,w}$
36	40	44	47	49	51	54	56	56	57	57	57	59	58	58	58	dB	56

42 mm Gyproc laminated wall lining system can be used as an alternative to 57 mm Paramount dry partition and there is little to choose in performance terms between these two finishing methods

Source: Cement and Concrete Association

Walls

60

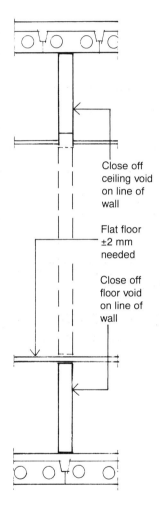

Close off
ceiling void
on line of
wall

Flat floor
±2 mm
needed

Close off
floor void
on line of
wall

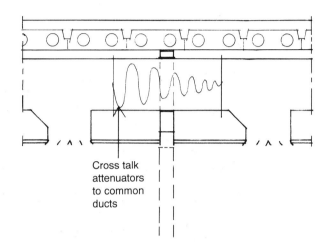

Cross talk
attenuators
to common
ducts

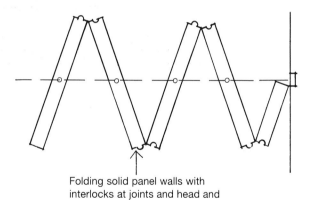

Folding solid panel walls with
interlocks at joints and head and
base seals better than concertina
type

Assessing performance needs

Resulting sound insulation	Required in building R'_w	Required in the lab R_w	Prerequisites to comply with requirements in building with reasonable certainty
Good sound insulation for loud speech	52 51 50 49 48	58 57 56 55 54	Acoustical experts be involved in the whole building process. The whole wall to be installed by trained people.
Moderate sound insulation for loud speech	47 46 45 44	53 52 51 50	Acoustical experts to be involved in the planning. The whole wall to be installed by trained people.
Good sound insulation for normal speech	43 42 41 40	49 48 47 46	General acoustical guidelines must be followed. Installation by trained people.
Moderate sound insulation for normal speech	39 38 37 36 35	45 44 43 42 41	General acoustical guidelines must be followed. Installation by trained people.
Moderate sound insulation with no special requirements	34 33 32 31 30	40 39 38 37 36	Joints to be sealed properly. Installation according to instructions.
Rather bad sound insulation	29 28 27 26 25	35 34 33 32 31	Installation according to instructions.
Bad sound insulation	24 23 22 21 20	27 26 25 24 23	Installation according to instructions.

Moving wall/folding partitions are often disappointing as installed compared to test results in laboratories; these may even be for panels alone and not total assembly.

The variance between laboratory test and field test results is suggested by German VDI standard to be 6–10 dB for high insulation mobile walls and 3–7 dB for low insulation.

Source: Swedish National Testing and Research Institute

Moving walls

61

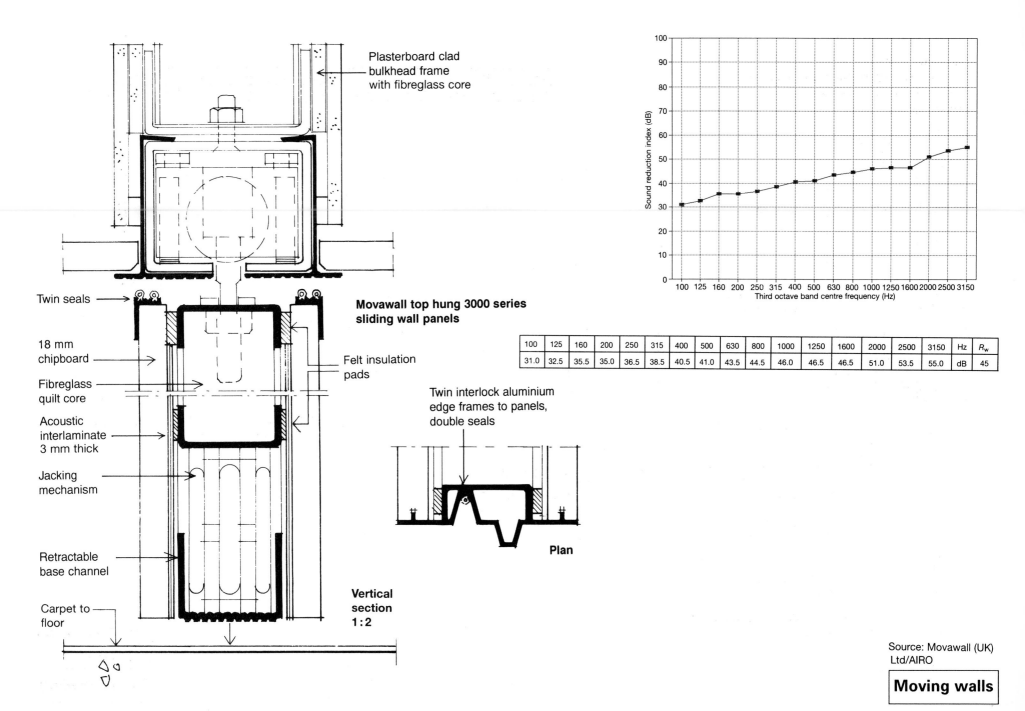

Plasterboard clad
bulkhead frame
with fibreglass core

**Movawall top hung 3000 series
sliding wall panels**

Twin seals

18 mm
chipboard

Felt insulation
pads

Fibreglass
quilt core

Acoustic
interlaminate
3 mm thick

Jacking
mechanism

Retractable
base channel

Carpet to
floor

**Vertical
section
1:2**

Twin interlock aluminium
edge frames to panels,
double seals

Plan

100	125	160	200	250	315	400	500	630	800	1000	1250	1600	2000	2500	3150	Hz	R_w
31.0	32.5	35.5	35.0	36.5	38.5	40.5	41.0	43.5	44.5	46.0	46.5	46.5	51.0	53.5	55.0	dB	45

Source: Movawall (UK)
Ltd/AIRO

Moving walls

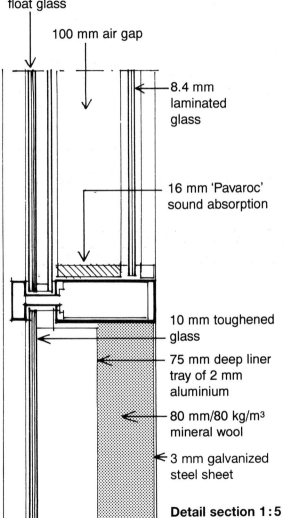

Double glazed unit:
10 mm Pilkingtons 'Antisun' toughened glass/16 mm air gap/6.4 mm laminated float glass

100 mm air gap

8.4 mm laminated glass

16 mm 'Pavaroc' sound absorption

10 mm toughened glass

75 mm deep liner tray of 2 mm aluminium

80 mm/80 kg/m³ mineral wool

3 mm galvanized steel sheet

Detail section 1 : 5

Test sample panel 1 : 50

Two glazed panels,
two opaque panels,
in framing system.

100	125	160	200	250	315	400	500	630	800	1000	1250	1600	2000	2500	3150	Hz	R_w
35.3	37.5	34.3	38.2	40.4	41.7	46.6	50.0	51.0	51.9	51.9	53.3	53.3	55.6	59.1	61.2	dB	51

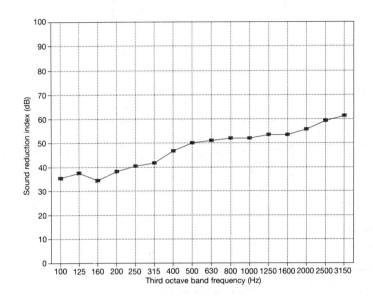

Source: Felix Construction SA/
University of Salford

Curtain walling

Floors

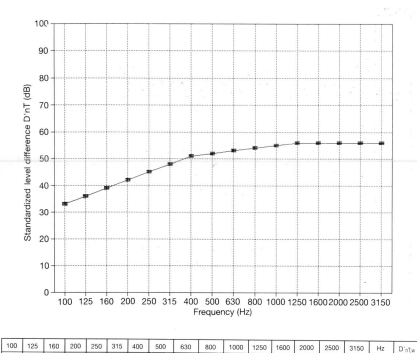

100	125	160	200	250	315	400	500	630	800	1000	1250	1600	2000	2500	3150	Hz	D'$_{nT,w}$
33	36	39	42	45	48	51	52	53	54	55	56	56	56	56	56	dB	52

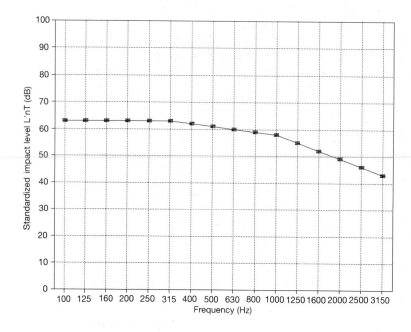

100	125	160	200	250	315	400	500	630	800	1000	1250	1600	2000	2500	3150	Hz	L'$_{nT,w}$
63	63	63	63	63	63	62	61	60	59	58	55	52	49	46	43	dB	61

–■– 1985 and 1991 Building Regulations (D'$_{nT}$ values)

Requirement in dB (D'$_{nT,w}$) for airborne sound

Individual and conversions	Mean	
48	Tests on up to 4 pairs of rooms	52
	⩾ Tests on 8 pairs of rooms	51

–■– 1985 and 1991 Building Regulations (L'$_{nT}$ values)

Requirement in dB (L'$_{nT,w}$) for impact sound

Individual and conversions	Mean	
65	Tests on up to 4 pairs of rooms	61
	⩾ Tests on 8 pairs of rooms	62

Single values taken
from reference
curve at 500 Hz

Sources:
BS 5821: Part 1&2 1984
ISO 717: 1982
Building Regulations
Part E

Party floors

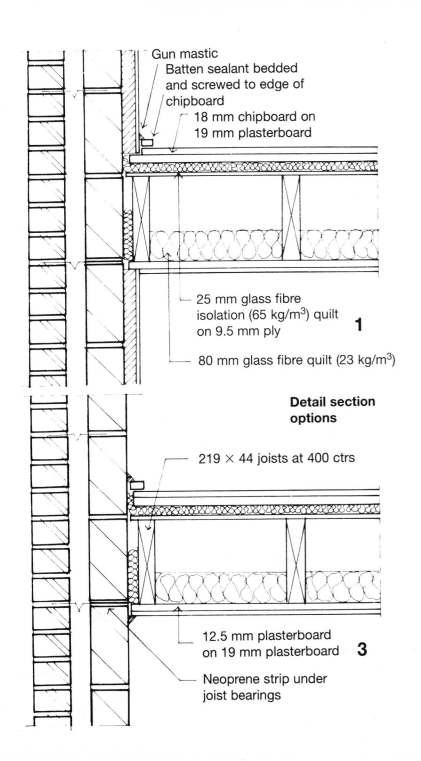

Gun mastic

Batten sealant bedded and screwed to edge of chipboard

18 mm chipboard on 19 mm plasterboard

1

25 mm glass fibre isolation (65 kg/m^3) quilt on 9.5 mm ply

80 mm glass fibre quilt (23 kg/m^3)

Detail section options

219 × 44 joists at 400 ctrs

12.5 mm plasterboard on 19 mm plasterboard **3**

Neoprene strip under joist bearings

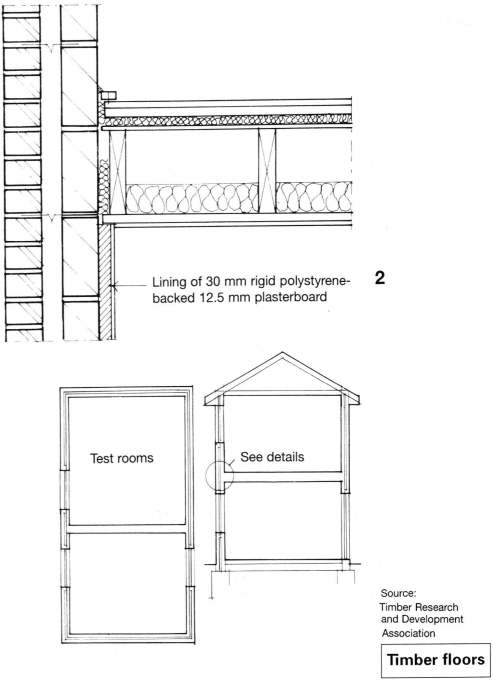

2

Lining of 30 mm rigid polystyrene-backed 12.5 mm plasterboard

Test rooms

See details

Source:
Timber Research and Development Association

Timber floors

65

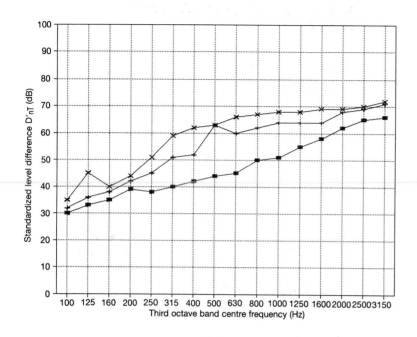

100	125	160	200	250	315	400	500	630	800	1000	1250	1600	2000	2500	3150	Hz	Key
30	33	35	39	38	40	42	44	45	50	51	55	58	62	65	66	dB	–■–
32	36	38	42	45	51	52	55	60	62	64	64	64	68	69	71	dB	–+–
35	45	40	44	51	59	62	63	66	67	68	68	69	69	70	72	dB	–×–

Airborne sound

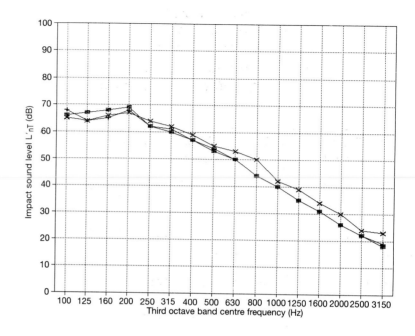

100	125	160	200	250	315	400	500	630	800	1000	1250	1600	2000	2500	3150	Hz	Key
66	67	68	69	62	60	57	53	50	44	40	35	31	26	22	18	dB	–■–
68	64	65	68	62	61	57	54	60	44	40	35	31	26	22	19	dB	–+–
65	64	66	67	64	62	59	55	53	50	42	39	34	30	24	23	dB	–×–

Impact sound

–×– Ground and first floor walls
     lined (see detail Section 1)

–+– Ground floor walls only lined (2)

–■– Walls unlined (3)

Dry lining improvements

The results show that dry linings to
both ground and first floors improved the
airborne sound insulation performance by
reducing flanking effects.
Laboratory tests to BS 2750:1980/ISO 140/
ASTM E90-75 show similar results except for
higher H.F. values

Source: Timber
Research and
Development
Association

Timber floors

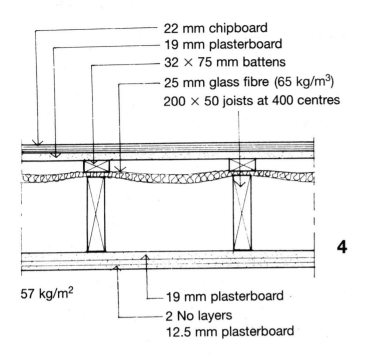

22 mm chipboard
19 mm plasterboard
32 × 75 mm battens
25 mm glass fibre (65 kg/m³)
200 × 50 joists at 400 centres

4

57 kg/m²

19 mm plasterboard
2 No layers
12.5 mm plasterboard

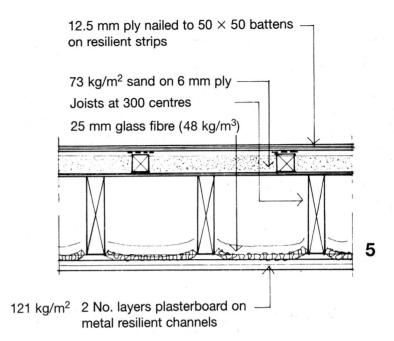

12.5 mm ply nailed to 50 × 50 battens
on resilient strips

73 kg/m² sand on 6 mm ply

Joists at 300 centres

25 mm glass fibre (48 kg/m³)

5

121 kg/m² 2 No. layers plasterboard on
metal resilient channels

Good timber floors should
include as features:
• substantial isolated floor deck
• stiff support frame of joists
• absorptive quilt in floor cavity
• substantial ceiling
Construction should not be over intricate
and unrealistic in workmanship required

Pugging (6) is favoured in Scottish construction
Electrical conduits can be run in the sand (5)

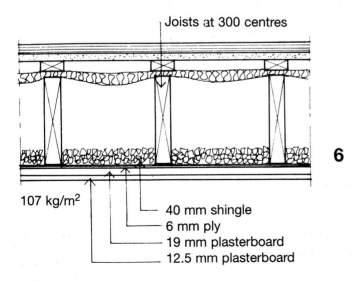

Joists at 300 centres

6

107 kg/m²

40 mm shingle
6 mm ply
19 mm plasterboard
12.5 mm plasterboard

Source: Timber
Research and
Development
Association

**Detail sections
options**

Timber floors

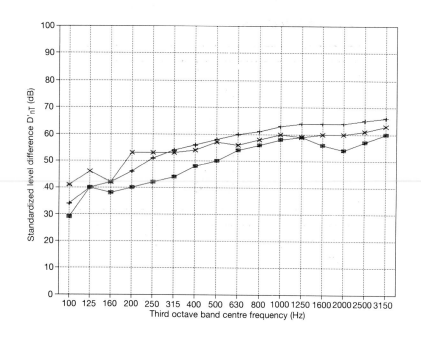

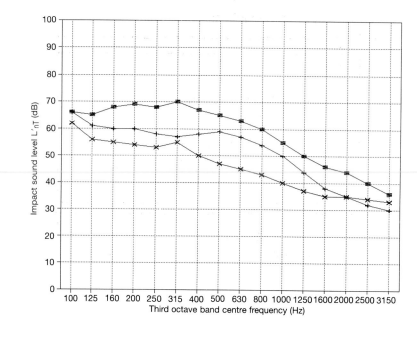

100	125	160	200	250	315	400	500	630	800	1000	1250	1600	2000	2500	3150	Hz	Key
29	40	38	40	42	44	48	50	54	56	58	59	56	54	57	60	dB	–■–
34	40	42	46	51	54	56	58	60	61	63	64	64	64	65	66	dB	–+–
41	46	42	53	53	53	54	57	56	58	60	59	60	60	61	63	dB	–×–

100	125	160	200	250	315	400	500	630	800	1000	1250	1600	2000	2500	3150	Hz	Key
66	65	68	69	68	70	67	65	63	60	55	50	46	44	40	36	dB	–■–
66	61	60	60	58	57	58	59	57	54	50	44	38	35	32	30	dB	–+–
62	56	55	54	53	55	50	47	45	43	40	37	35	35	34	33	dB	–×–

Detail section options

Key

–■– Floor construction as detail Section 4

–+– Floor construction as detail Section 5

–×– Floor construction as detail Section 6

Source: Timber
Research and
Development
Association

Timber floors

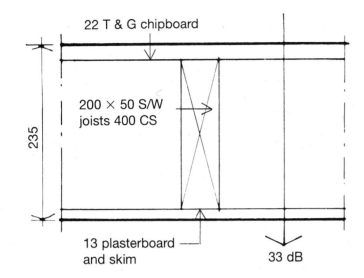

22 T & G chipboard

200 × 50 S/W
joists 400 CS

235

13 plasterboard
and skim

33 dB

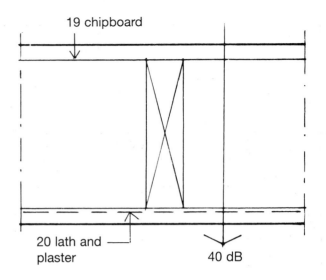

19 chipboard

20 lath and
plaster

40 dB

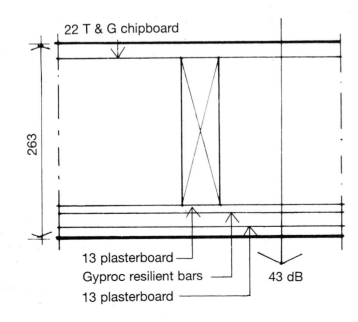

22 T & G chipboard

263

13 plasterboard

Gyproc resilient bars

13 plasterboard

43 dB

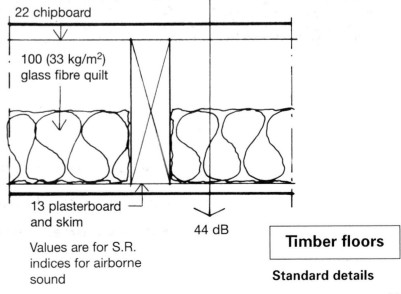

22 chipboard

100 (33 kg/m^2)
glass fibre quilt

13 plasterboard
and skim

44 dB

Values are for S.R.
indices for airborne
sound

Timber floors

Standard details

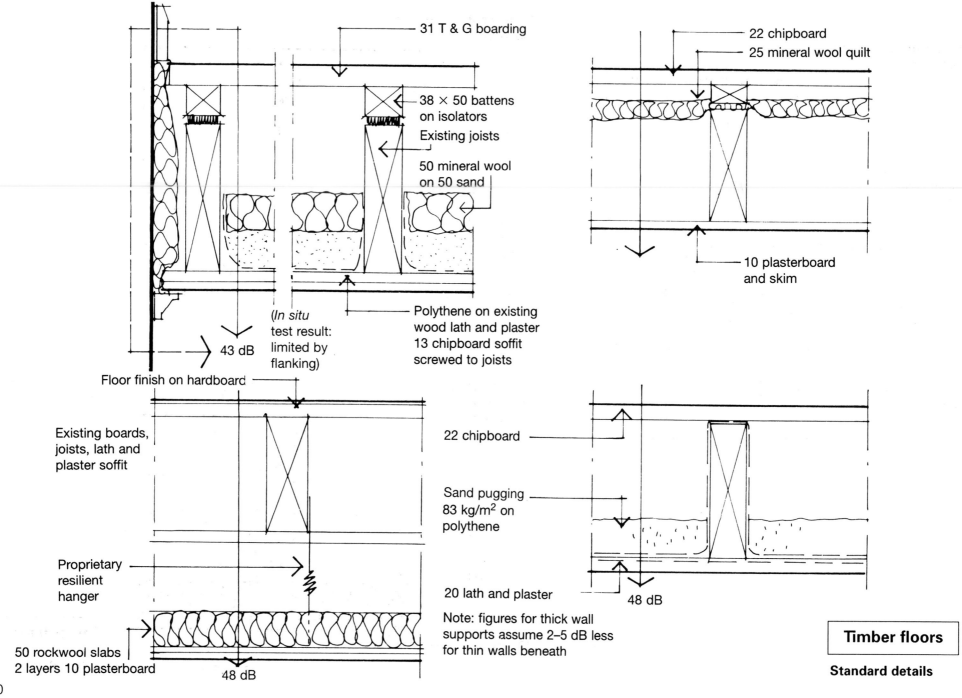

31 T & G boarding

38 × 50 battens on isolators

Existing joists

50 mineral wool on 50 sand

(In situ test result: limited by flanking)

43 dB

Polythene on existing wood lath and plaster 13 chipboard soffit screwed to joists

22 chipboard

25 mineral wool quilt

10 plasterboard and skim

Floor finish on hardboard

Existing boards, joists, lath and plaster soffit

Proprietary resilient hanger

50 rockwool slabs 2 layers 10 plasterboard

48 dB

22 chipboard

Sand pugging 83 kg/m² on polythene

20 lath and plaster

48 dB

Note: figures for thick wall supports assume 2–5 dB less for thin walls beneath

Timber floors

Standard details

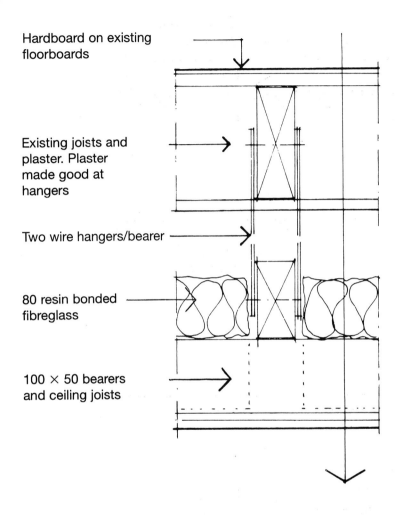

Hardboard on existing floorboards

Existing joists and plaster. Plaster made good at hangers

Two wire hangers/bearer

80 resin bonded fibreglass

100 × 50 bearers and ceiling joists

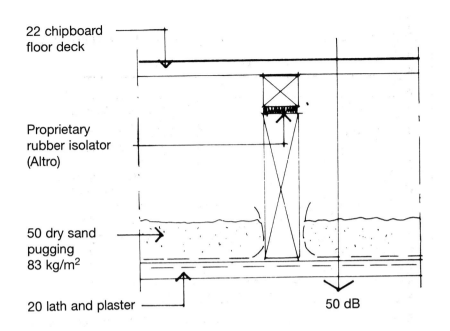

22 chipboard floor deck

Proprietary rubber isolator (Altro)

50 dry sand pugging 83 kg/m^2

20 lath and plaster

50 dB

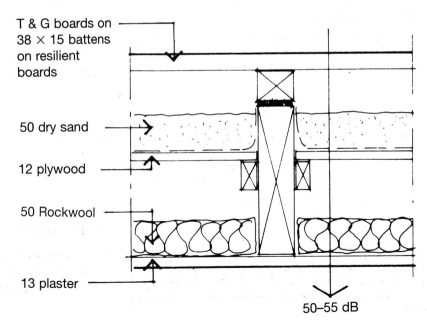

T & G boards on 38 × 15 battens on resilient boards

50 dry sand

12 plywood

50 Rockwool

13 plaster

50–55 dB

Timber floors

Standard details

71

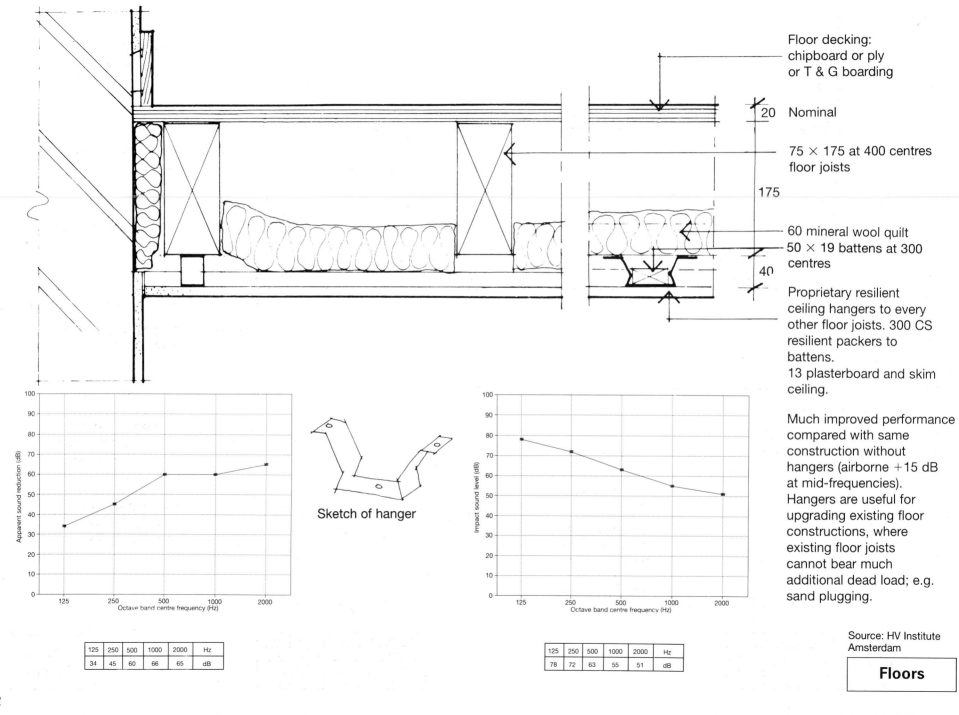

Floor decking:
chipboard or ply
or T & G boarding

20 Nominal

75 × 175 at 400 centres
floor joists

175

60 mineral wool quilt
50 × 19 battens at 300
centres

40

Proprietary resilient
ceiling hangers to every
other floor joists. 300 CS
resilient packers to
battens.
13 plasterboard and skim
ceiling.

Much improved performance
compared with same
construction without
hangers (airborne +15 dB
at mid-frequencies).
Hangers are useful for
upgrading existing floor
constructions, where
existing floor joists
cannot bear much
additional dead load; e.g.
sand plugging.

Sketch of hanger

125	250	500	1000	2000	Hz
34	45	60	66	65	dB

125	250	500	1000	2000	Hz
78	72	63	55	51	dB

Source: HV Institute
Amsterdam

Floors

72

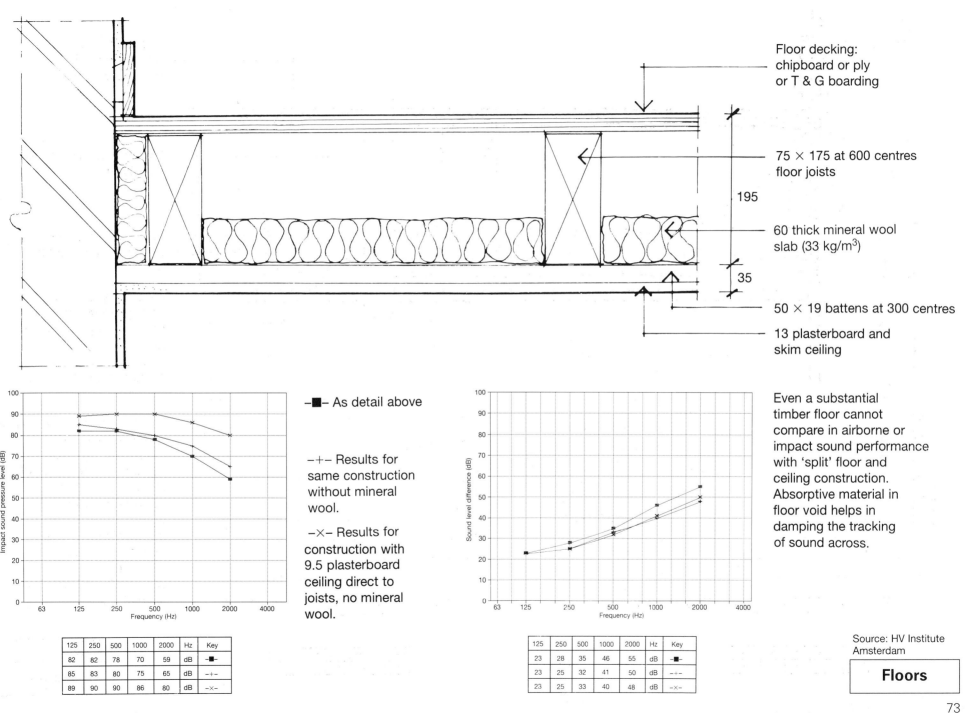

Floor decking: chipboard or ply or T & G boarding

75 × 175 at 600 centres floor joists

195

60 thick mineral wool slab (33 kg/m³)

35

50 × 19 battens at 300 centres

13 plasterboard and skim ceiling

–■– As detail above

–+– Results for same construction without mineral wool.

–×– Results for construction with 9.5 plasterboard ceiling direct to joists, no mineral wool.

Even a substantial timber floor cannot compare in airborne or impact sound performance with 'split' floor and ceiling construction. Absorptive material in floor void helps in damping the tracking of sound across.

125	250	500	1000	2000	Hz	Key
82	82	78	70	59	dB	–■–
85	83	80	75	65	dB	–+–
89	90	90	86	80	dB	–×–

125	250	500	1000	2000	Hz	Key
23	28	35	46	55	dB	–■–
23	25	32	41	50	dB	–+–
23	25	33	40	48	dB	–×–

Source: HV Institute Amsterdam

Floors

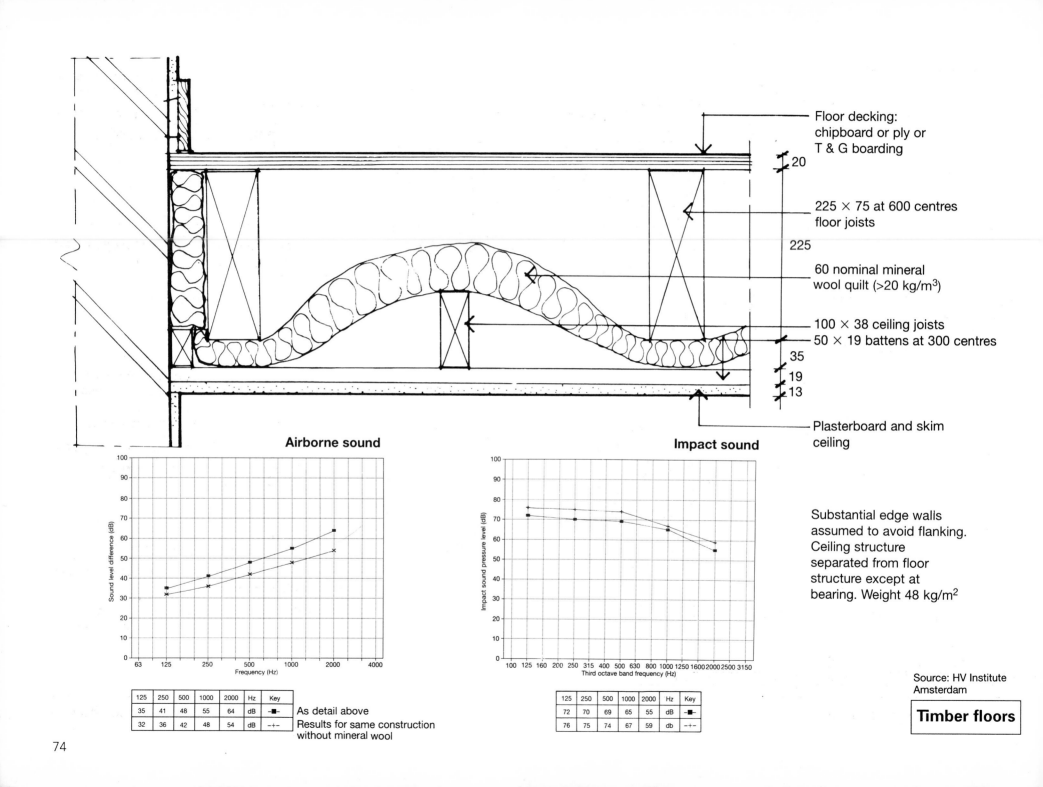

Floor decking:
chipboard or ply or
T & G boarding

20

225 × 75 at 600 centres
floor joists

225

60 nominal mineral
wool quilt (>20 kg/m³)

100 × 38 ceiling joists
50 × 19 battens at 300 centres

35
19
13

Plasterboard and skim
ceiling

Airborne sound

Sound level difference (dB)

Frequency (Hz)

Impact sound

Impact sound pressure level (dB)

Third octave band frequency (Hz)

Substantial edge walls
assumed to avoid flanking.
Ceiling structure
separated from floor
structure except at
bearing. Weight 48 kg/m²

125	250	500	1000	2000	Hz	Key
35	41	48	55	64	dB	–■–
32	36	42	48	54	dB	–+–

As detail above

Results for same construction
without mineral wool

125	250	500	1000	2000	Hz	Key
72	70	69	65	55	dB	–■–
76	75	74	67	59	db	–+–

Source: HV Institute
Amsterdam

Timber floors

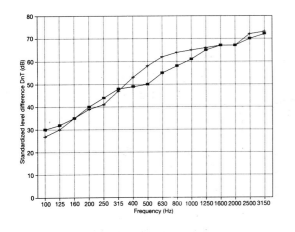

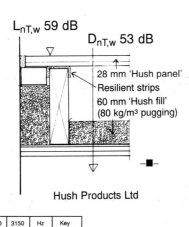

$L_{nT,w}$ 59 dB

$D_{nT,w}$ 53 dB

28 mm 'Hush panel'

Resilient strips

60 mm 'Hush fill'
(80 kg/m³ pugging)

Hush Products Ltd

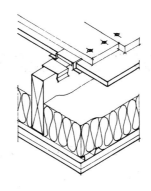

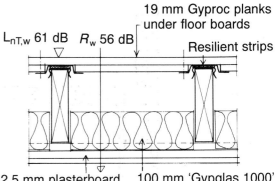

19 mm Gyproc planks under floor boards

$L_{nT,w}$ 61 dB R_w 56 dB

Resilient strips

12.5 mm plasterboard on 19 mm Gyproc plank

100 mm 'Gypglas 1000' glass wool on resilient bars

British Gypsum S.I. System

100	125	160	200	250	315	400	500	630	800	1000	1250	1600	2000	2500	3150	Hz	Key
30	32	35	40	44	48	49	50	55	58	61	65	67	68	70	72	dB	■
27	30	35	39	41	47	53	58	62	64	65	66	67	67	72	73	db	-+-

Airborne sound

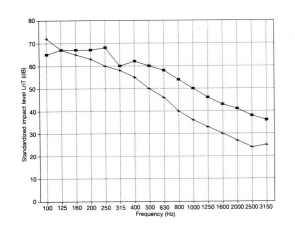

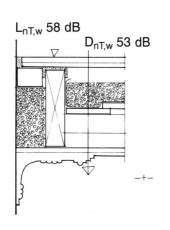

$L_{nT,w}$ 58 dB

$D_{nT,w}$ 53 dB

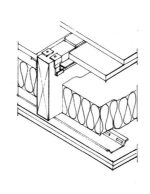

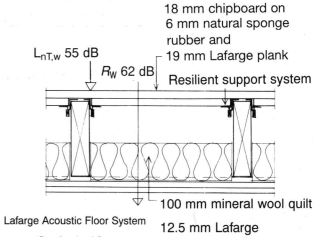

18 mm chipboard on 6 mm natural sponge rubber and 19 mm Lafarge plank

$L_{nT,w}$ 55 dB R_w 62 dB

Resilient support system

Lafarge Acoustic Floor System

Scale 1 : 10

100 mm mineral wool quilt

12.5 mm Lafarge wallboard on 19 mm planks to resilient bars

100	125	160	200	250	315	400	500	630	800	1000	1250	1600	2000	2500	3150	Hz	Key
65	67	67	67	68	60	62	60	58	54	50	46	43	41	38	36	dB	■
72	67	65	63	60	58	55	50	46	40	36	33	30	27	24	25	db	-+-

Impact sound

Timber floors

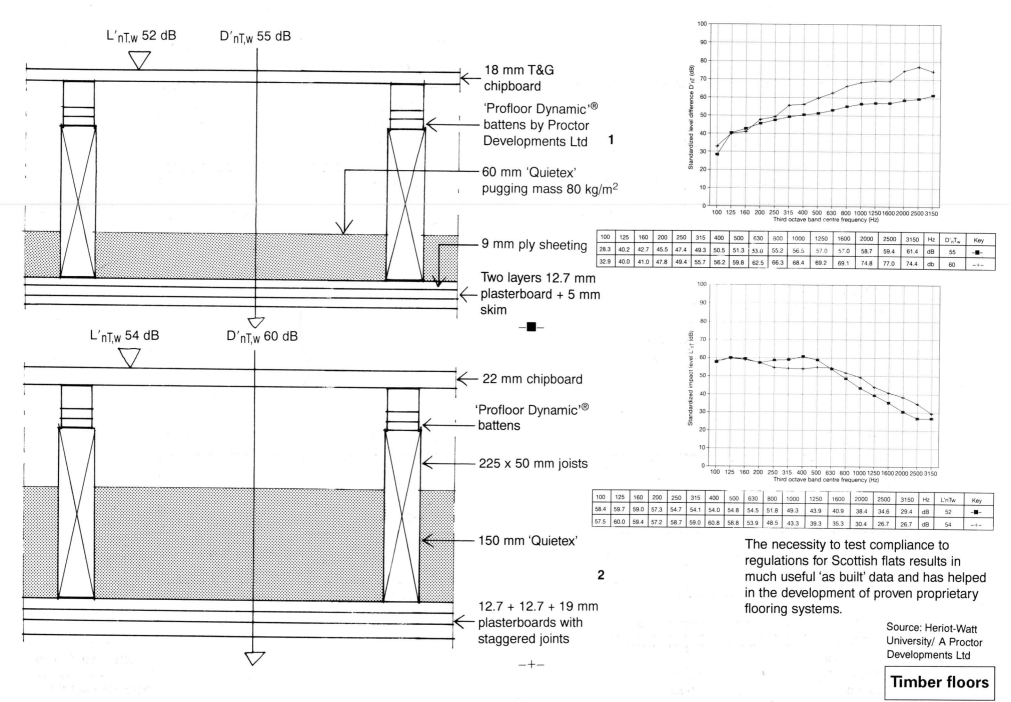

$L'_{nT,w}$ 52 dB $D'_{nT,w}$ 55 dB

1

18 mm T&G chipboard

'Profloor Dynamic'® battens by Proctor Developments Ltd

60 mm 'Quietex' pugging mass 80 kg/m²

9 mm ply sheeting

Two layers 12.7 mm plasterboard + 5 mm skim

—■—

$L'_{nT,w}$ 54 dB $D'_{nT,w}$ 60 dB

2

22 mm chipboard

'Profloor Dynamic'® battens

225 x 50 mm joists

150 mm 'Quietex'

12.7 + 12.7 + 19 mm plasterboards with staggered joints

—+—

100	125	160	200	250	315	400	500	630	800	1000	1250	1600	2000	2500	3150	Hz	D'nTw	Key
28.3	40.2	42.7	45.5	47.4	49.3	50.5	51.3	53.0	55.2	56.5	57.0	57.0	58.7	59.4	61.4	dB	55	—■—
32.9	40.0	41.0	47.8	49.4	55.7	56.2	59.8	62.5	66.3	68.4	69.2	69.1	74.8	77.0	74.4	db	60	—+—

100	125	160	200	250	315	400	500	630	800	1000	1250	1600	2000	2500	3150	Hz	L'nTw	Key
58.4	59.7	59.0	57.3	54.7	54.1	54.0	54.8	54.5	51.8	49.3	43.9	40.9	38.4	34.6	29.4	dB	52	—■—
57.5	60.0	59.4	57.2	58.7	59.0	60.8	58.8	53.9	48.5	43.3	39.3	35.3	30.4	26.7	26.7	dB	54	—+—

The necessity to test compliance to regulations for Scottish flats results in much useful 'as built' data and has helped in the development of proven proprietary flooring systems.

Source: Heriot-Watt University/ A Proctor Developments Ltd

Timber floors

Floor finish

40 screed topping

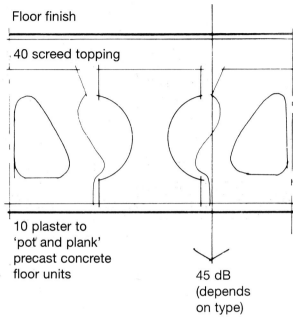

10 plaster to
'pot and plank'
precast concrete
floor units

45 dB
(depends
on type)

Floor finish

100 min.
concrete slab
(250 kg/m^2)

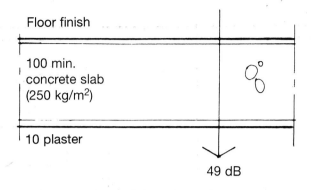

10 plaster

49 dB

Floor finish

100 min.
concrete
slab (250 kg/m^2)

Air gap
(min. 150)

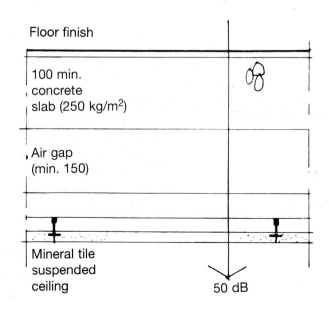

Mineral tile
suspended
ceiling

50 dB

Floor finish

150 min.
concrete slab
(365 kg/m^2)

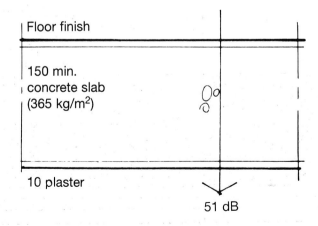

10 plaster

51 dB

Concrete floors

Standard details

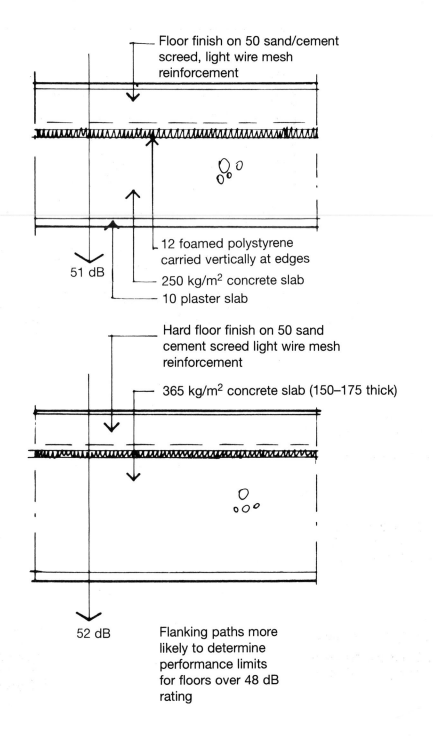

Floor finish on 50 sand/cement screed, light wire mesh reinforcement

12 foamed polystyrene carried vertically at edges

250 kg/m² concrete slab

10 plaster slab

51 dB

Hard floor finish on 50 sand cement screed light wire mesh reinforcement

365 kg/m² concrete slab (150–175 thick)

52 dB

Flanking paths more likely to determine performance limits for floors over 48 dB rating

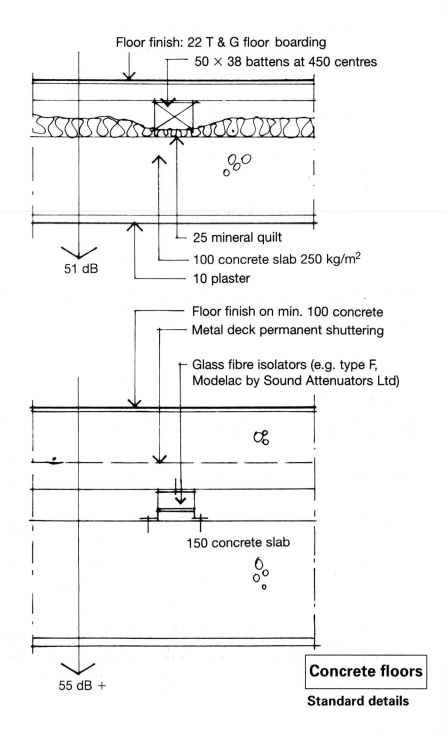

Floor finish: 22 T & G floor boarding

50 × 38 battens at 450 centres

25 mineral quilt

100 concrete slab 250 kg/m²

10 plaster

51 dB

Floor finish on min. 100 concrete

Metal deck permanent shuttering

Glass fibre isolators (e.g. type F, Modelac by Sound Attenuators Ltd)

150 concrete slab

55 dB +

Concrete floors

Standard details

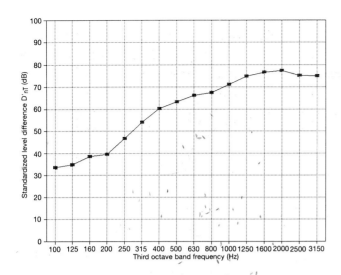

100	125	160	200	250	315	400	500	630	800	1000	1250	1600	2000	2500	3150	Hz	$D_{nT,w}$
33.6	34.8	38.5	39.5	46.7	54.0	60.2	63.3	66.2	67.5	71.1	74.8	76.5	77.4	75.1	75.0	dB	58

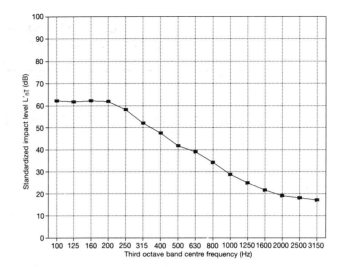

100	125	160	200	250	315	400	500	630	800	1000	1250	1600	2000	2500	3150	Hz	$L'_{nT,w}$
62.1	61.7	62.2	61.8	58.1	52.0	47.4	41.7	39.0	34.2	28.7	24.9	21.6	19.0	18.0	17.0	dB	53

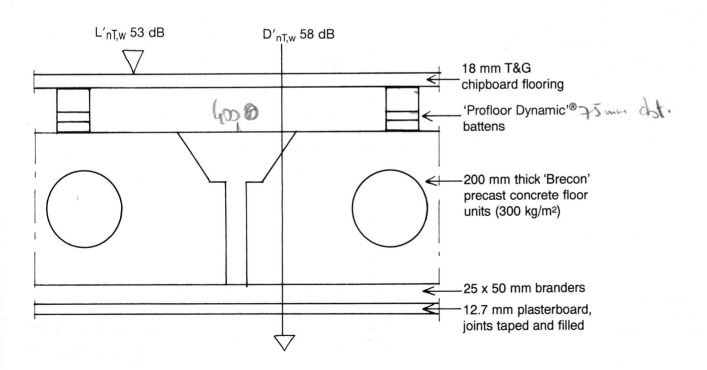

$L'_{nT,w}$ 53 dB

$D'_{nT,w}$ 58 dB

18 mm T&G chipboard flooring

'Profloor Dynamic'® 75 mm dpt. battens

200 mm thick 'Brecon' precast concrete floor units (300 kg/m²)

25 x 50 mm branders

12.7 mm plasterboard, joints taped and filled

Source: Heriot-Watt University/ A Proctor Developments Ltd

Concrete floors

79

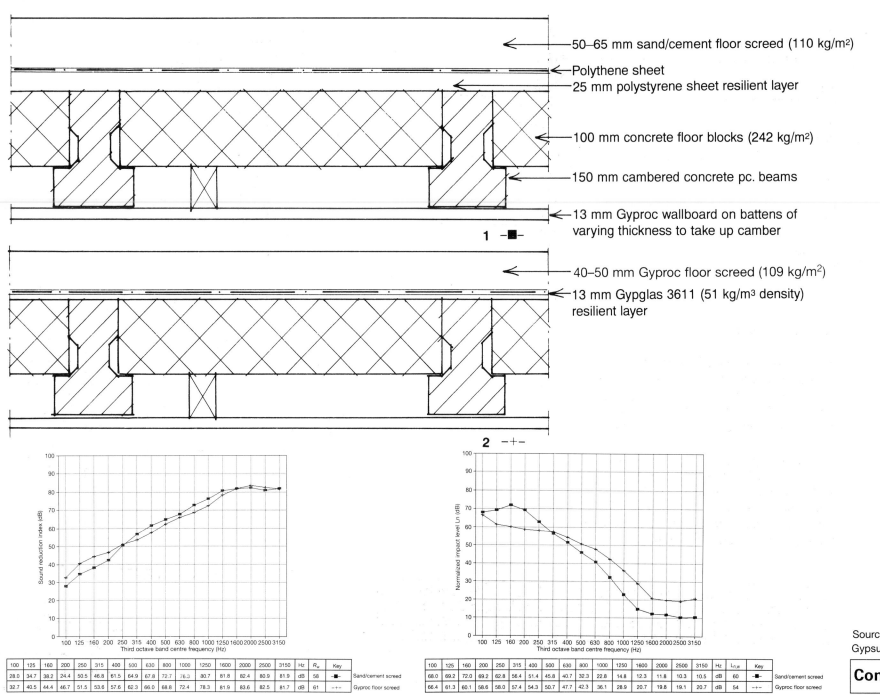

50–65 mm sand/cement floor screed (110 kg/m²)

Polythene sheet
25 mm polystyrene sheet resilient layer

100 mm concrete floor blocks (242 kg/m²)

150 mm cambered concrete pc. beams

13 mm Gyproc wallboard on battens of
varying thickness to take up camber

1 –■–

40–50 mm Gyproc floor screed (109 kg/m²)
13 mm Gypglas 3611 (51 kg/m³ density)
resilient layer

2 –+–

100	125	160	200	250	315	400	500	630	800	1000	1250	1600	2000	2500	3150	Hz	R_w	Key	
28.0	34.7	38.2	24.4	50.5	46.8	61.5	64.9	67.8	72.7	76.3	80.7	81.8	82.4	80.9	81.9	dB	58	–■–	Sand/cement screed
32.7	40.5	44.4	46.7	51.5	53.6	57.6	62.3	66.0	68.8	72.4	78.3	81.9	83.6	82.5	81.7	dB	61	–+–	Gyproc floor screed

100	125	160	200	250	315	400	500	630	800	1000	1250	1600	2000	2500	3150	Hz	$L_{n,w}$	Key	
68.0	69.2	72.0	69.2	62.8	56.4	51.4	45.8	40.7	32.3	22.8	14.8	12.3	11.8	10.3	10.5	dB	60	–■–	Sand/cement screed
66.4	61.3	60.1	58.6	58.0	57.4	54.3	50.7	47.7	42.3	36.1	28.9	20.7	19.8	19.1	20.7	dB	54	–+–	Gyproc floor screed

Source: British
Gypsum Ltd

Concrete floors

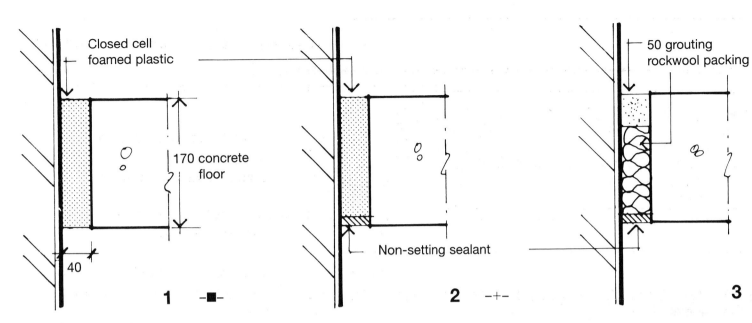

1 —■— **2** —+— **3** —×—

Closed cell foamed plastic

170 concrete floor

40

Non-setting sealant

50 grouting rockwool packing

Vertical sections

Sound level difference between two rooms caused by a 2-metre slot in one side of a floor (laboratory test). Good sealing of gaps necessary for speech frequency privacy, sealing less critical at low frequencies.

A small storey-height crack 0.2 mm wide in a wall 10 m^2 in area would result in a 7 dB loss in a 50 dB-rated wall, but 1 dB only reduction of insulation in a 35 dB partition: lack of cracks or gaps is particularly important for substantial separating elements.

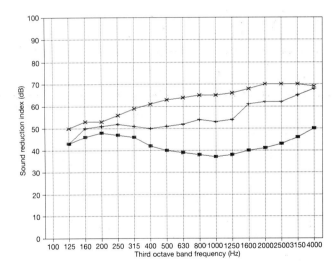

125	160	200	250	315	400	500	630	800	1000	1250	1600	2000	3150	3500	4000	Hz	Key	
43	46	48	47	46	42	40	39	38	37	38	40	41	43	46	50	dB	—■—	1
43	50	51	52	51	50	51	52	54	53	54	61	62	62	65	68	dB	—+—	2
50	53	53	56	59	61	63	64	65	65	66	68	70	70	70	69	dB	—×—	3

Source: Institut für Technische Physik Stuttgart

Concrete floors

81

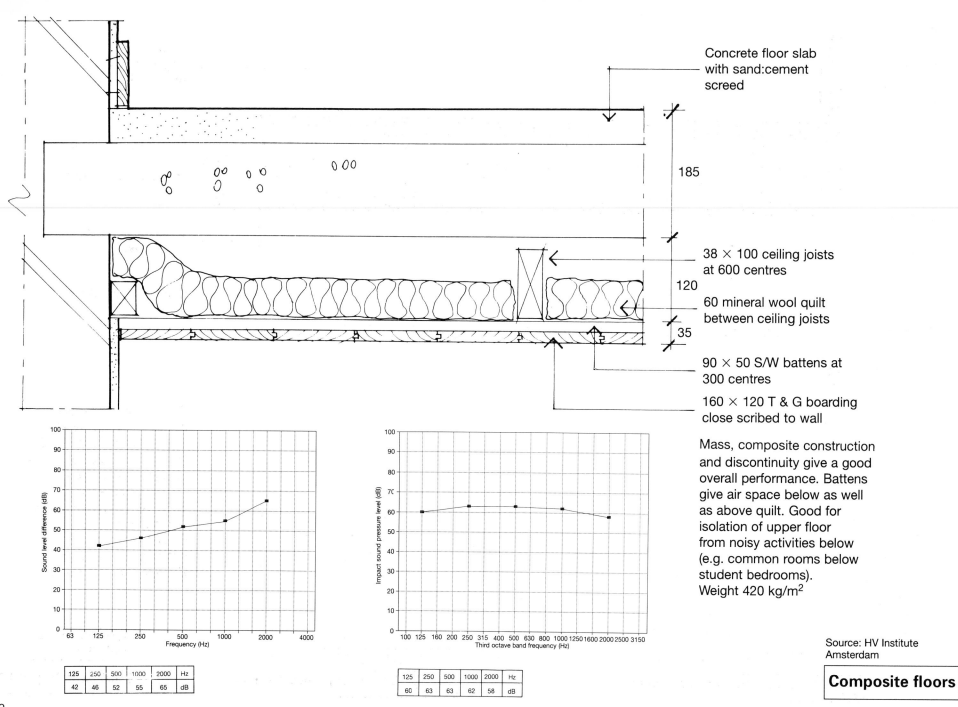

Concrete floor slab
with sand:cement
screed

185

38 × 100 ceiling joists
at 600 centres

120

60 mineral wool quilt
between ceiling joists

35

90 × 50 S/W battens at
300 centres

160 × 120 T & G boarding
close scribed to wall

Mass, composite construction
and discontinuity give a good
overall performance. Battens
give air space below as well
as above quilt. Good for
isolation of upper floor
from noisy activities below
(e.g. common rooms below
student bedrooms).
Weight 420 kg/m²

Source: HV Institute
Amsterdam

Composite floors

125	250	500	1000	2000	Hz
42	46	52	55	65	dB

125	250	500	1000	2000	Hz
60	63	63	62	58	dB

82

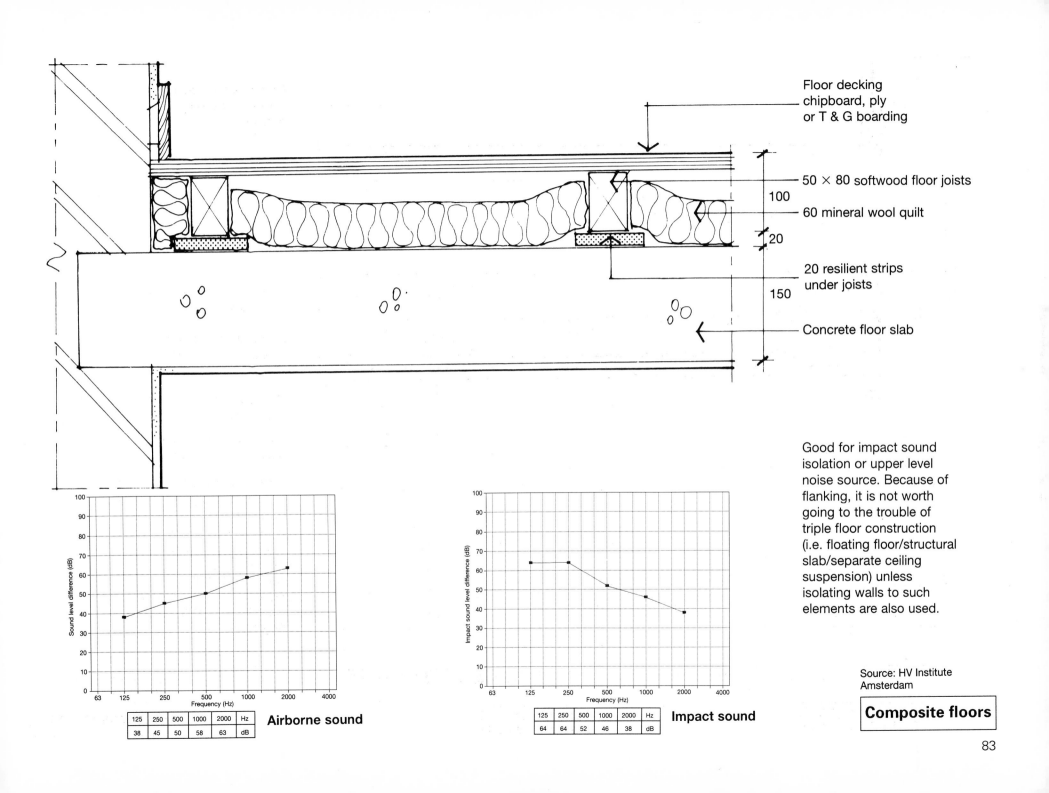

Floor decking
chipboard, ply
or T & G boarding

50 × 80 softwood floor joists

100

60 mineral wool quilt

20

20 resilient strips
under joists

150

Concrete floor slab

Good for impact sound
isolation or upper level
noise source. Because of
flanking, it is not worth
going to the trouble of
triple floor construction
(i.e. floating floor/structural
slab/separate ceiling
suspension) unless
isolating walls to such
elements are also used.

Source: HV Institute
Amsterdam

Airborne sound

125	250	500	1000	2000	Hz
38	45	50	58	63	dB

Impact sound

125	250	500	1000	2000	Hz
64	64	52	46	38	dB

Composite floors

83

Doors

SINGLE LEAF DOORS

Test R_w dB	Mass kg/m²	SRI (ave)	Dims m	63	125	250	500	1k	2k	4k	Notes
						SRI (dB) at OBCF (Hz)					
28	18	29	2.1 × 0.9 × 0.044		30	30	31	25	29	32	Flaxboard core + Schlegel 21 seals
32	27	32	2.1 × 0.9 × 0.044		32	33	30	29	34	38	Flaxboard core + Schlegel 21 seals
29	18.5	29	2.1 × 0.9 × 0.044		27	29	27	28	30	35	Solid core with Schlegel 21 seals
30	24	29	2.0 × 0.9 × 0.043		25	30	31	35	37	41	Chipboard core
36	34	33	2.0 × 0.9 × 0.043		26	29	32	35	39	42	Chipboard core + AAV seals
39	40	36	2.0 × 0.9 × 0.068		27	29	35	40	45	45	Chipboard core + AAV seals
31	28		2.1 × 0.7 × 0.054	25	26	30	28	29	33	39	Flaxboard core + 2 seals
36	63		2.1 × 0.7 × 0.064	26	32	36	35	34	37	40	Flaxboard + lead + 2 seals
42	100		2.1 × 0.7 × 0.068	26	35	38	41	41	41	49	Flaxboard + lead + 2 seals
46	43		2.1 × 1.0 × 0.104		32	39	44	45	44		All timber doors
44		40			25	35	42	46	48		
29	32		0.045 thick		22	27	32	25	28		Timber core
30	36		0.054 thick		21	25	25	30	32		Timber core
36	38		0.045 thick		25	28	32	34	39		Timber + aerated magnesium oxychloride
25	35		0.050 thick		20	22	19	31	39	47	
31	45		0.075 thick		17	29	26	30	34	38	
35	55		0.075 thick		23	34	32	35	37	36	
37	65		0.075 thick		17	34	33	37	40	42	
40	80		0.100 thick		35	38	39	39	41		
47	100		0.100 thick		36	39	43	47	54		
51	120		0.150 thick		35	41	47	52	57	59	
56	185		0.150 thick	34	40	47	50	58	65	68	

DOUBLE LEAF DOORS

Test R_w dB	Mass kg/m²	SRI (ave)	Dims m	63	125	250	500	1k	2k	4k	Notes
56	185	53	4.1 × 2.7 × 0.150	34	40	47	50	58	65	68	Double door, but test results for a single partition hung on head gear. Other doors available R_w 25-56
42	48	41		23	32	50	41	39	44	48	DnTw field test result. Double door but suspected single leaf under test.
		53	2.4 × 2.8 × 0.050	45	45	50	56	58	57	62	Double doorsets in lobby, separation 1.2 m, masonry walls (average of 3 BBC examples).

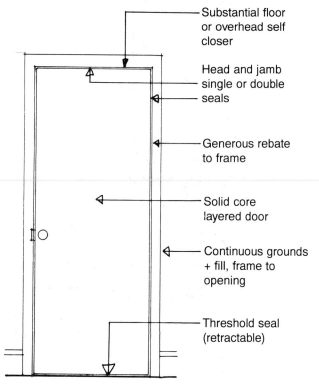

Labels on figure:
- Substantial floor or overhead self closer
- Head and jamb single or double seals
- Generous rebate to frame
- Solid core layered door
- Continuous grounds + fill, frame to opening
- Threshold seal (retractable)

Acoustic door desirable features

This table is a compilation of data from 10 manufacturers of acoustic doors. Claimed sound insulation properties for many manufacturers are exaggerated, for example '47 dB door' with R_w 39 dB. Typically doorset + surround wall in the laboratory standard aperture are tested which results in over-optimistic values. Octave band values quoted here have been corrected where necessary. There is significant variance of performance compared to surface mass, resulting from reliance on good rebates, edge and threshold seal systems.

Doors

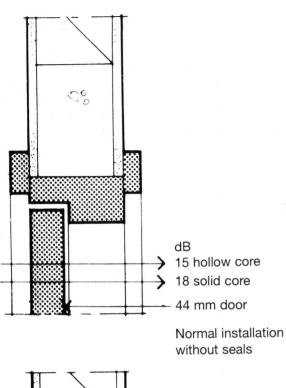

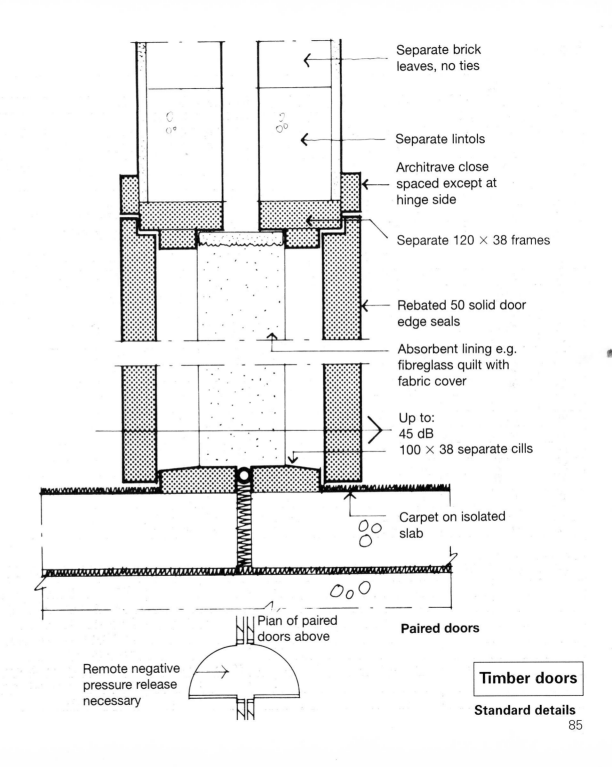

dB
15 hollow core
18 solid core
44 mm door

Normal installation
without seals

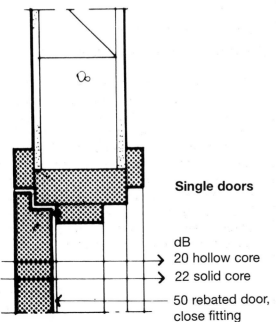

Single doors

dB
20 hollow core
22 solid core
50 rebated door,
close fitting

Separate brick
leaves, no ties

Separate lintols

Architrave close
spaced except at
hinge side

Separate 120 × 38 frames

Rebated 50 solid door
edge seals

Absorbent lining e.g.
fibreglass quilt with
fabric cover

Up to:
45 dB
100 × 38 separate cills

Carpet on isolated
slab

Paired doors

Plan of paired
doors above

Remote negative
pressure release
necessary

Timber doors

Standard details

85

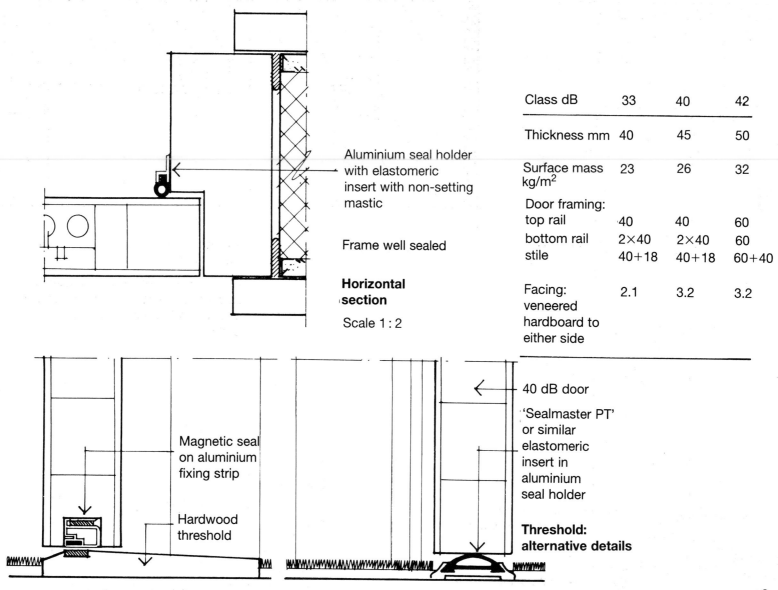

Aluminium seal holder with elastomeric insert with non-setting mastic

Frame well sealed

Horizontal section

Scale 1 : 2

Class dB	33	40	42
Thickness mm	40	45	50
Surface mass kg/m^2	23	26	32
Door framing:			
top rail	40	40	60
bottom rail	2×40	2×40	60
stile	40+18	40+18	60+40
Facing: veneered hardboard to either side	2.1	3.2	3.2

Magnetic seal on aluminium fixing strip

Hardwood threshold

40 dB door

'Sealmaster PT' or similar elastomeric insert in aluminium seal holder

Threshold: alternative details

Source:
Sound Acoustics Ltd

Timber doors

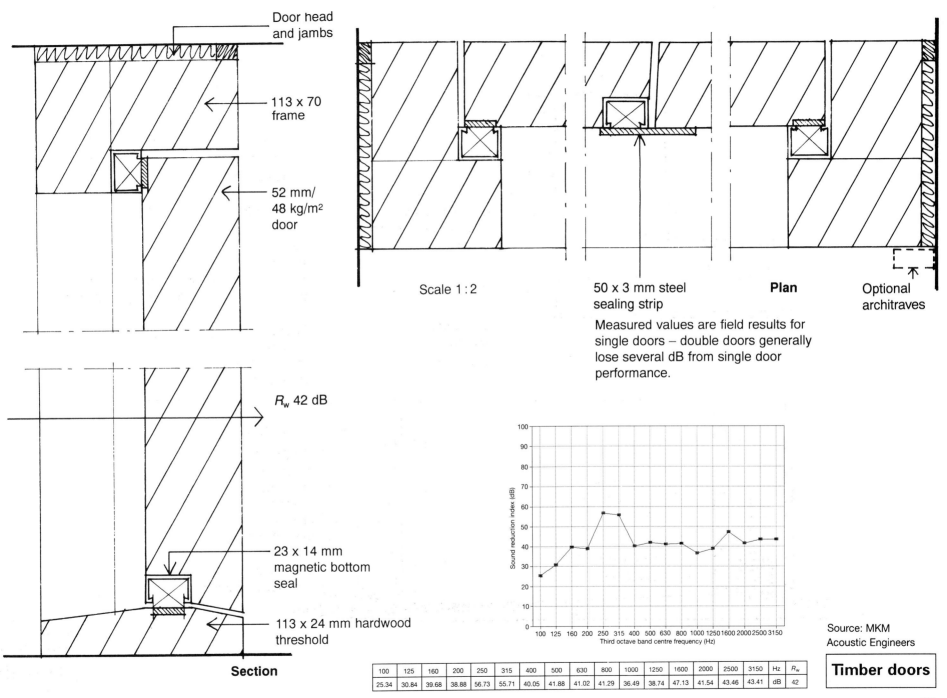

Door head
and jambs

113 x 70
frame

52 mm/
48 kg/m² door

Scale 1:2

50 x 3 mm steel
sealing strip

Plan

Optional
architraves

Measured values are field results for
single doors – double doors generally
lose several dB from single door
performance.

R_w 42 dB

23 x 14 mm
magnetic bottom
seal

113 x 24 mm hardwood
threshold

Section

Source: MKM
Acoustic Engineers

100	125	160	200	250	315	400	500	630	800	1000	1250	1600	2000	2500	3150	Hz	R_w
25.34	30.84	39.68	38.88	56.73	55.71	40.05	41.88	41.02	41.29	36.49	38.74	47.13	41.54	43.46	43.41	dB	42

Timber doors

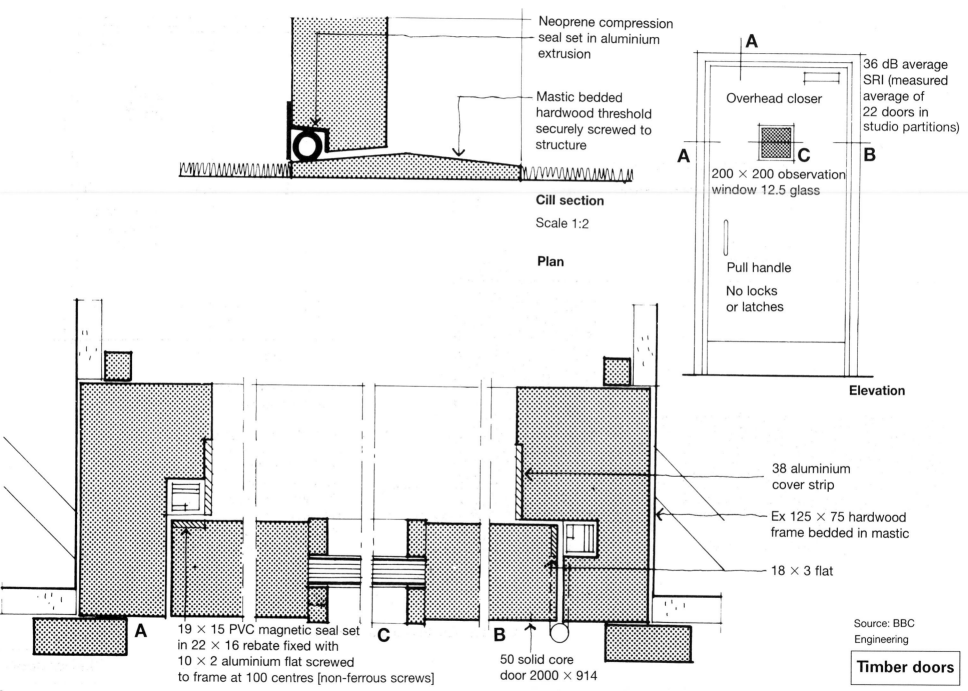

Neoprene compression seal set in aluminium extrusion

Mastic bedded hardwood threshold securely screwed to structure

Cill section

Scale 1:2

Plan

Overhead closer

36 dB average SRI (measured average of 22 doors in studio partitions)

200 × 200 observation window 12.5 glass

Pull handle

No locks or latches

Elevation

38 aluminium cover strip

Ex 125 × 75 hardwood frame bedded in mastic

18 × 3 flat

19 × 15 PVC magnetic seal set in 22 × 16 rebate fixed with 10 × 2 aluminium flat screwed to frame at 100 centres [non-ferrous screws]

50 solid core door 2000 × 914

Source: BBC Engineering

Timber doors

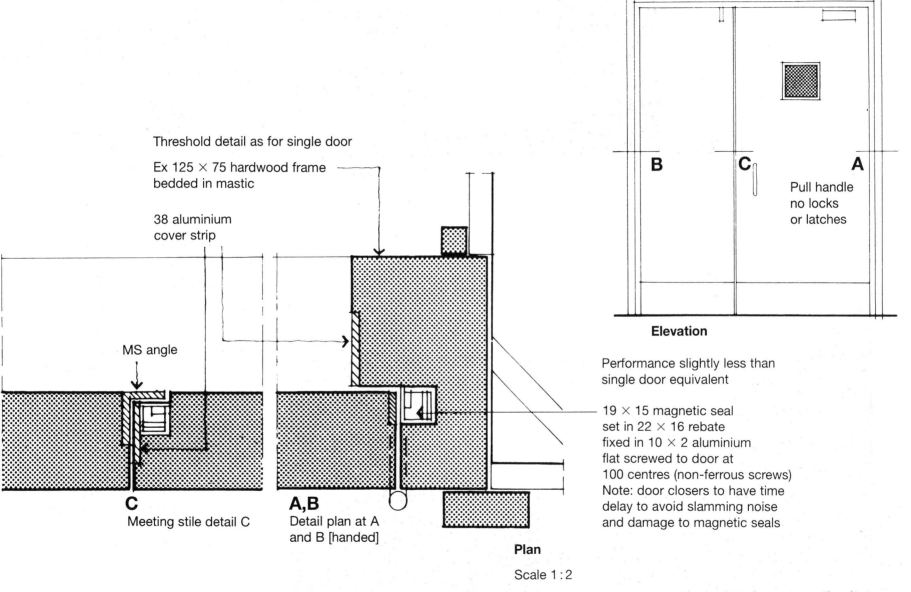

Threshold detail as for single door

Ex 125 × 75 hardwood frame
bedded in mastic

38 aluminium
cover strip

MS angle

C
Meeting stile detail C

A,B
Detail plan at A
and B [handed]

Elevation

Performance slightly less than
single door equivalent

19 × 15 magnetic seal
set in 22 × 16 rebate
fixed in 10 × 2 aluminium
flat screwed to door at
100 centres (non-ferrous screws)
Note: door closers to have time
delay to avoid slamming noise
and damage to magnetic seals

B   C   A

Pull handle
no locks
or latches

Plan

Scale 1 : 2

Acoustic double doors to studios

Source: BBC
Engineering

Timber doors

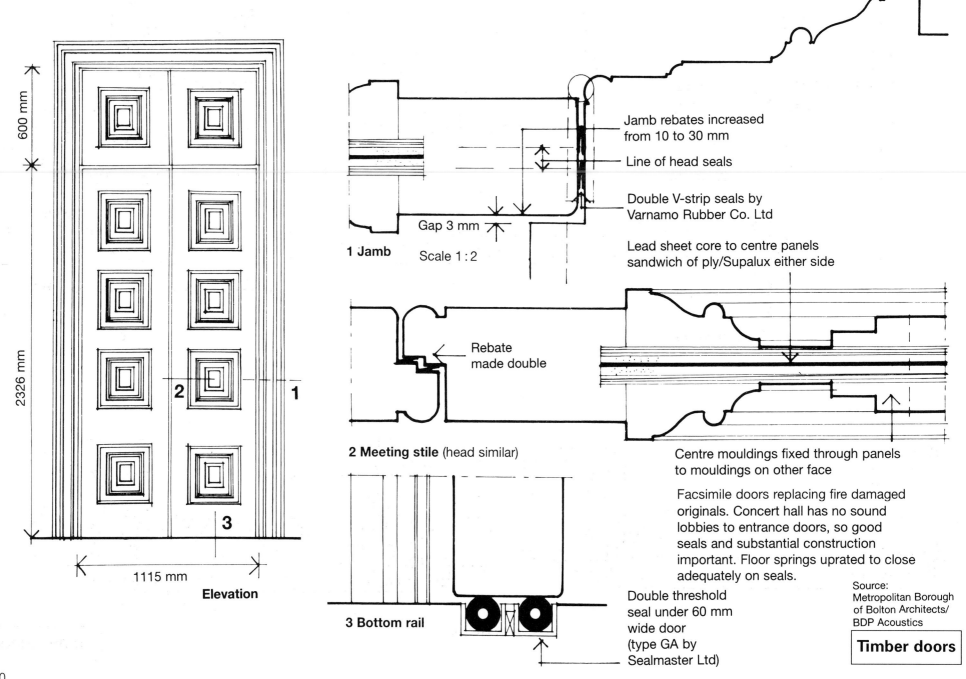

Elevation

600 mm

2326 mm

1115 mm

1 Jamb Scale 1:2

Gap 3 mm

Jamb rebates increased
from 10 to 30 mm

Line of head seals

Double V-strip seals by
Varnamo Rubber Co. Ltd

Lead sheet core to centre panels
sandwich of ply/Supalux either side

2 Meeting stile (head similar)

Rebate
made double

Centre mouldings fixed through panels
to mouldings on other face

Facsimile doors replacing fire damaged
originals. Concert hall has no sound
lobbies to entrance doors, so good
seals and substantial construction
important. Floor springs uprated to close
adequately on seals.

3 Bottom rail

Double threshold
seal under 60 mm
wide door
(type GA by
Sealmaster Ltd)

Source:
Metropolitan Borough
of Bolton Architects/
BDP Acoustics

Timber doors

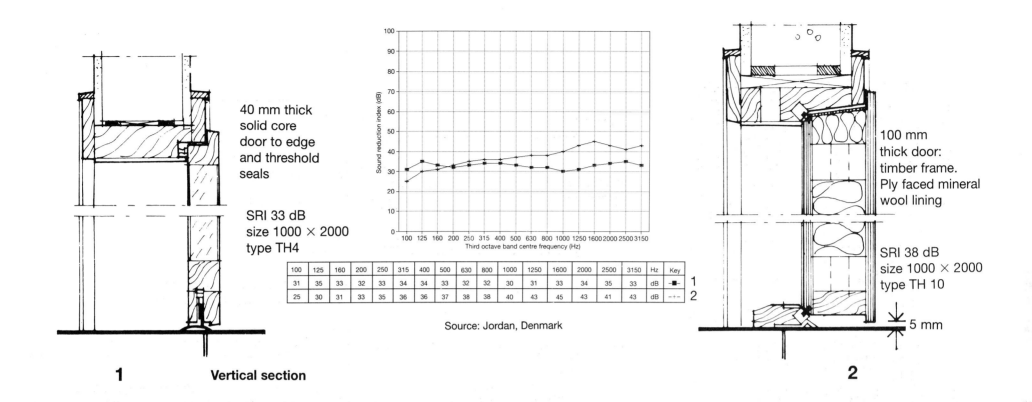

40 mm thick
solid core
door to edge
and threshold
seals

SRI 33 dB
size 1000 × 2000
type TH4

100 mm
thick door:
timber frame.
Ply faced mineral
wool lining

SRI 38 dB
size 1000 × 2000
type TH 10

5 mm

Source: Jordan, Denmark

100	125	160	200	250	315	400	500	630	800	1000	1250	1600	2000	2500	3150	Hz	Key	
31	35	33	32	33	34	34	33	32	32	30	31	33	34	35	33	dB	■	1
25	30	31	33	35	36	36	37	38	38	40	43	45	43	41	43	dB	+	2

1   **Vertical section**

2

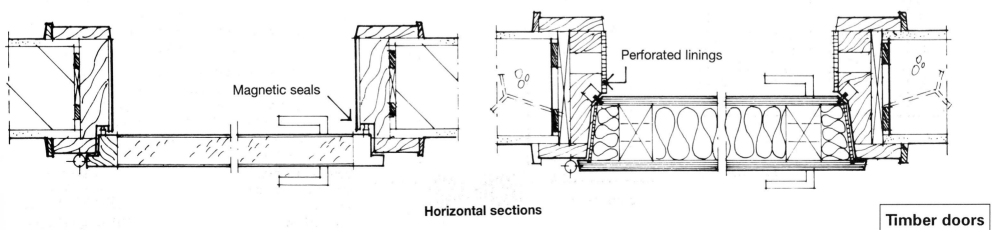

Magnetic seals

Perforated linings

Horizontal sections

Timber doors

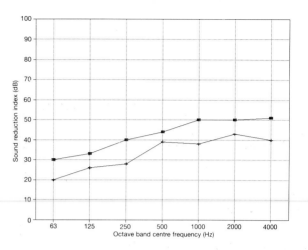

63	125	250	500	1000	2000	4000	Hz	Key	
30	33	40	44	50	50	51	dB	–■–	steel acoustic doors SRI. 44dB
20	26	28	39	38	43	40	dB	–+–	steel acoustic doors SRI. 37dB

Centre post removable

Max sizes: 1000 × 2000   2140 × 2000

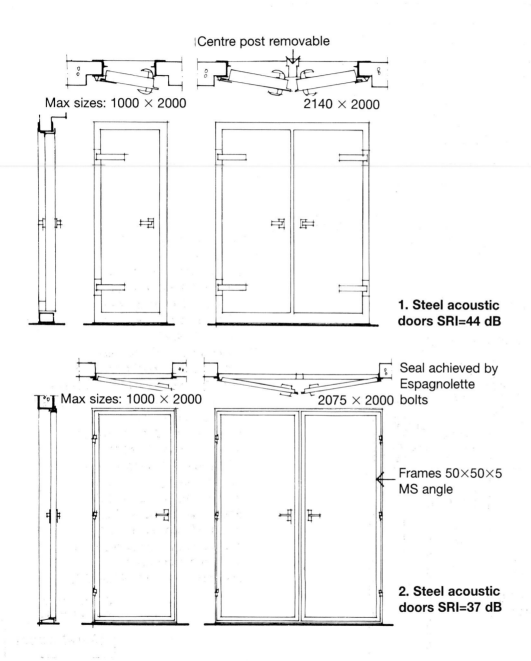

1. Steel acoustic doors SRI=44 dB

Max sizes: 1000 × 2000   2075 × 2000

Seal achieved by Espagnolette bolts

Frames 50×50×5 MS angle

2. Steel acoustic doors SRI=37 dB

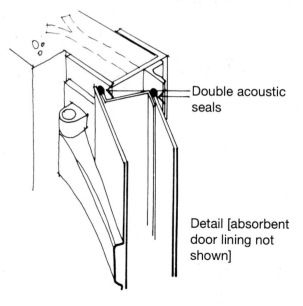

Double acoustic seals

Detail [absorbent door lining not shown]

Source:
Sound Attenuators Ltd

Metal doors

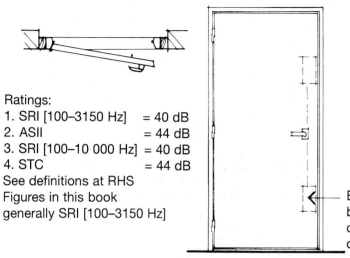

Ratings:
1. SRI [100–3150 Hz]   = 40 dB
2. ASII   = 44 dB
3. SRI [100–10 000 Hz] = 40 dB
4. STC   = 44 dB
See definitions at RHS
Figures in this book
generally SRI [100–3150 Hz]

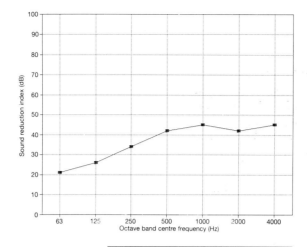

63	125	250	500	1000	2000	4000	Hz
21	26	34	42	45	42	45	dB

Espagnolette
bolts closing
door to
compression seals

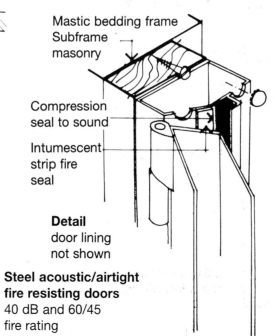

Mastic bedding frame
Subframe
masonry

Compression
seal to sound

Intumescent
strip fire
seal

Detail
door lining
not shown

**Steel acoustic/airtight
fire resisting doors**
40 dB and 60/45
fire rating

4 acoustic ratings are in
common use:
1. Sound Reduction Index
   (100–3150 Hz). Average of
   sound reduction indices in
   16 $\frac{1}{3}$ octave bands from
   100 to 3150 Hz.
2. Airborne Sound Insulation
   Index (ASII) measured sound
   reduction indices in 16 $\frac{1}{3}$ octave
   bands from 100–3150 Hz compared
   with reference values for
   airborne sound insulation, as
   specified in BS 5821:1980.
3. SRI (100–10 000 Hz) as in 1
   except average over 21 $\frac{1}{3}$
   octave bands 100–10 000 Hz.
4. Sound Transmission Class
   (STC). SR indices in 16 $\frac{1}{3}$
   octave bands compared with
   reference contours as
   specified in ASTM 3413–70 T.

Source: Sound
Attenuators Ltd

Metal doors

990 mm

2090 mm

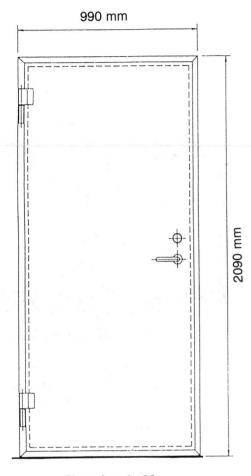

Elevation 1 : 20

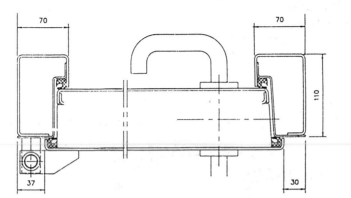

70   70

110

37   30

Horizontal section 1 : 5

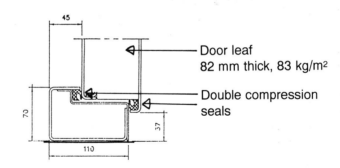

45

Door leaf
82 mm thick, 83 kg/m²

Double compression
seals

70   37

110

Threshold detail 1 : 5

100	125	160	200	250	315	400	500	630	800	1000	1250	1600	2000	2500	3150	Hz	R_w
35.8	39.8	42	42.9	39.6	42.1	42.8	44.1	47.2	48.3	48.8	48.6	49	51.4	52.4	51.7	dB	48

Source: Ecomax
Acoustics

Metal doors

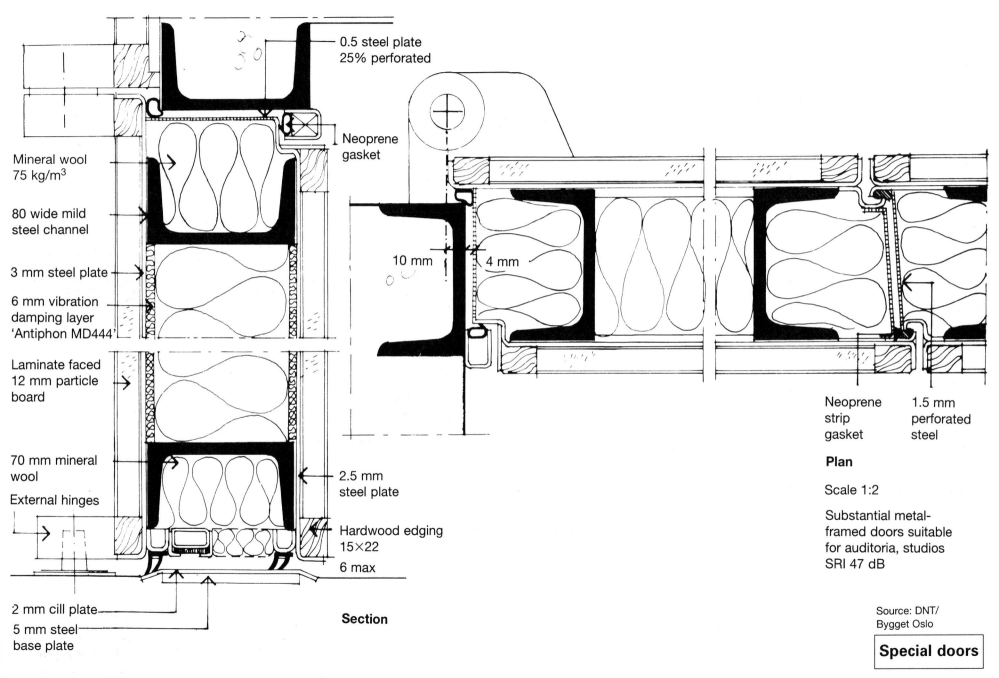

Mineral wool
75 kg/m³

80 wide mild
steel channel

3 mm steel plate

6 mm vibration
damping layer
'Antiphon MD444'

Laminate faced
12 mm particle
board

70 mm mineral
wool

External hinges

2 mm cill plate

5 mm steel
base plate

0.5 steel plate
25% perforated

Neoprene
gasket

2.5 mm
steel plate

Hardwood edging
15×22

6 max

Section

10 mm

4 mm

Neoprene
strip
gasket

1.5 mm
perforated
steel

Plan

Scale 1:2

Substantial metal-
framed doors suitable
for auditoria, studios
SRI 47 dB

Source: DNT/
Bygget Oslo

Special doors

95

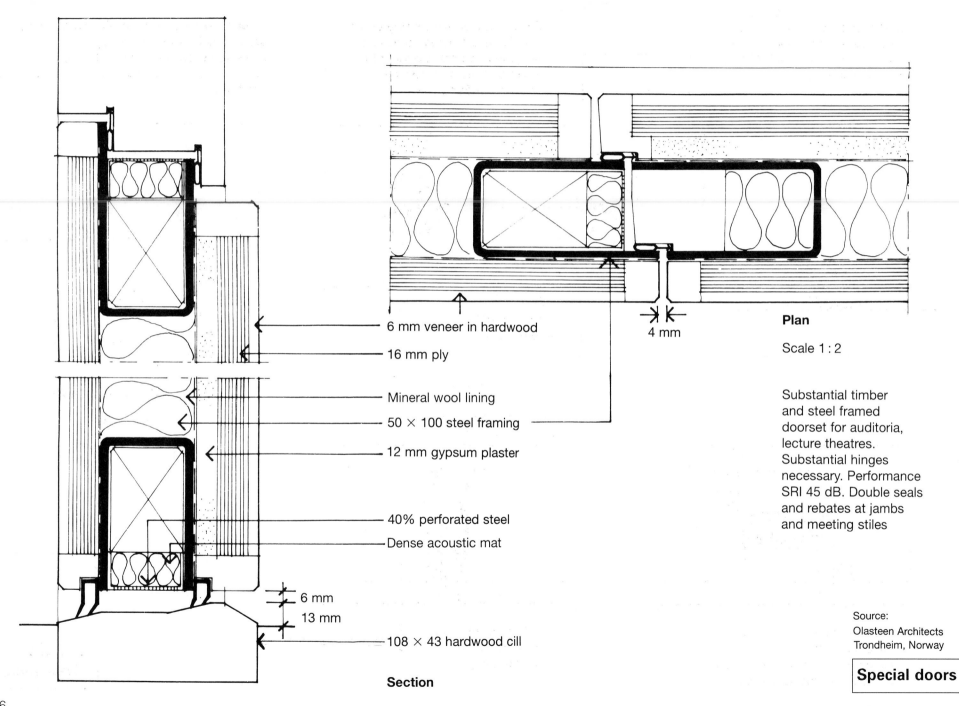

6 mm veneer in hardwood

16 mm ply

Mineral wool lining

50 × 100 steel framing

12 mm gypsum plaster

40% perforated steel

Dense acoustic mat

108 × 43 hardwood cill

4 mm

Plan

Scale 1 : 2

Substantial timber
and steel framed
doorset for auditoria,
lecture theatres.
Substantial hinges
necessary. Performance
SRI 45 dB. Double seals
and rebates at jambs
and meeting stiles

6 mm

13 mm

Section

Source:
Olasteen Architects
Trondheim, Norway

Special doors

Sealmaster PEFA type blade seal rebated into a sliding door, sliding against a PVC strip on the frame

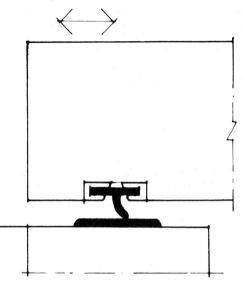

Sliding and two-way swing doors cannot have rebated frames and so good seals are important for anything more than nominal acoustic performance

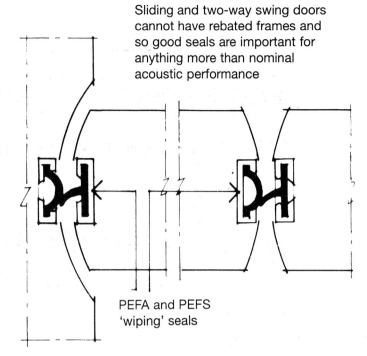

PEFA and PEFS 'wiping' seals

Source: Sealmaster Ltd

Advantageous over some 'O' compression seals in that only light closing pressure necessary: suitable for light doors and sliding sash windows.

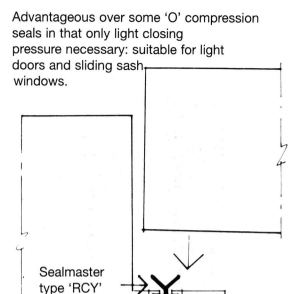

Sealmaster type 'RCY' elastomeric insert stop seal

Jamb plan details

Full scale

One-way swing door

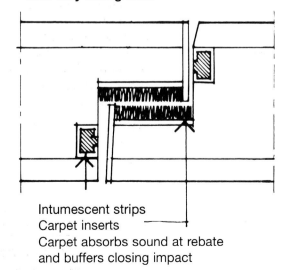

Intumescent strips
Carpet inserts
Carpet absorbs sound at rebate and buffers closing impact

Two-way swing door
Source: Arup Acoustics

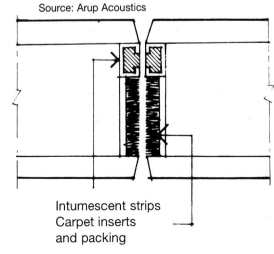

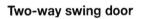

Intumescent strips
Carpet inserts
and packing

Door seals

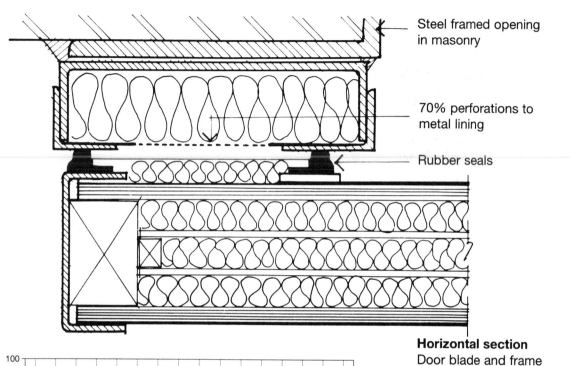

Steel framed opening
in masonry

70% perforations to
metal lining

Rubber seals

Door opening: 1340 × 2090 high
Operation: electrical – as door
closes, drops and moves 45° towards
frame to seal at sill and frame
Seals: rubber gaskets
Door: 90 mm thick, 18 mm
Rockwool core, 10 mm plywood
and 2 mm steel sheet either side

Good performance through
the frequency range. Used for
large-scale studio doors.
Very level floor across opening
needed

Horizontal section
Door blade and frame

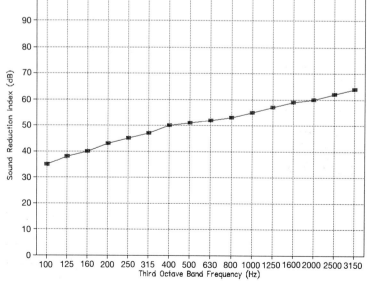

100	125	160	200	250	315	400	500	630	800	1000	1250	1600	2000	2500	3150	Hz
35	38	40	43	45	47	50	51	52	53	55	57	59	60	62	64	dB

Source:
Research Institute
for Environmental
Hygiene, Delft/Markus

Special doors

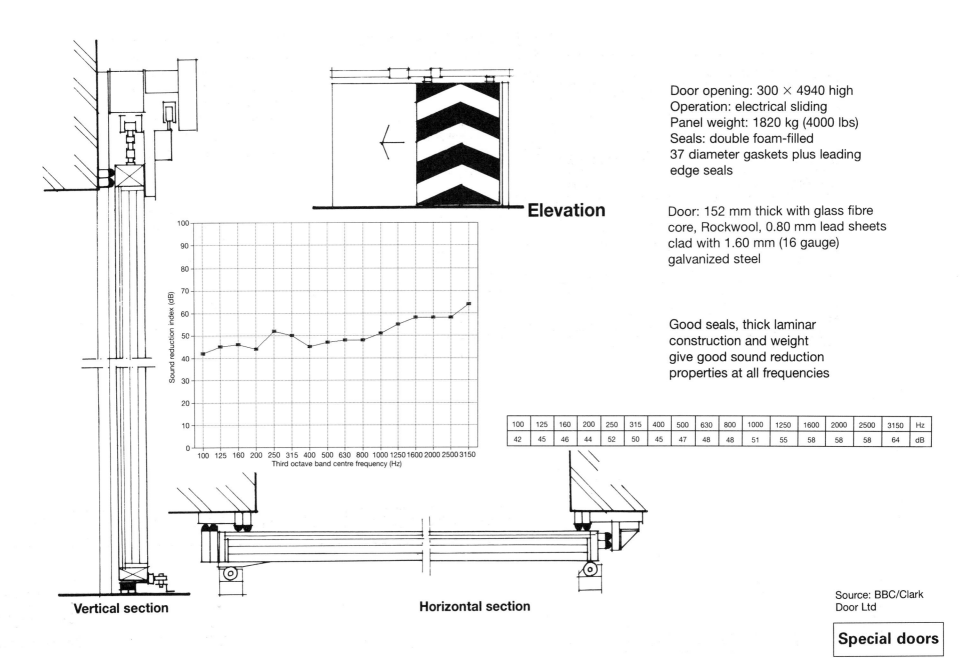

Elevation

Door opening: 300 × 4940 high
Operation: electrical sliding
Panel weight: 1820 kg (4000 lbs)
Seals: double foam-filled
37 diameter gaskets plus leading
edge seals

Door: 152 mm thick with glass fibre
core, Rockwool, 0.80 mm lead sheets
clad with 1.60 mm (16 gauge)
galvanized steel

Good seals, thick laminar
construction and weight
give good sound reduction
properties at all frequencies

100	125	160	200	250	315	400	500	630	800	1000	1250	1600	2000	2500	3150	Hz
42	45	46	44	52	50	45	47	48	48	51	55	58	58	58	64	dB

Vertical section

Horizontal section

Source: BBC/Clark
Door Ltd

Special doors

99

Windows

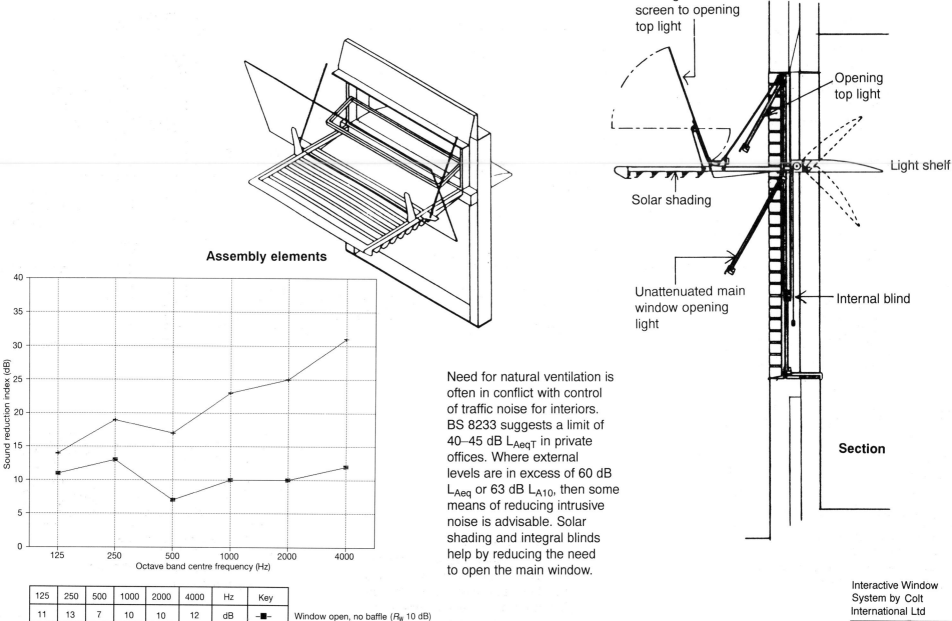

Assembly elements

Baffle glass screen to opening top light

Opening top light

Solar shading

Light shelf

Unattenuated main window opening light

Internal blind

Section

Need for natural ventilation is often in conflict with control of traffic noise for interiors. BS 8233 suggests a limit of 40–45 dB L_{AeqT} in private offices. Where external levels are in excess of 60 dB L_{Aeq} or 63 dB L_{A10}, then some means of reducing intrusive noise is advisable. Solar shading and integral blinds help by reducing the need to open the main window.

125	250	500	1000	2000	4000	Hz	Key	
11	13	7	10	10	12	dB	—■—	Window open, no baffle (R_W 10 dB)
14	19	17	23	25	31	dB	—+—	Window open, baffle, 15° (R_W 22 dB)

Interactive Window System by Colt International Ltd

Windows

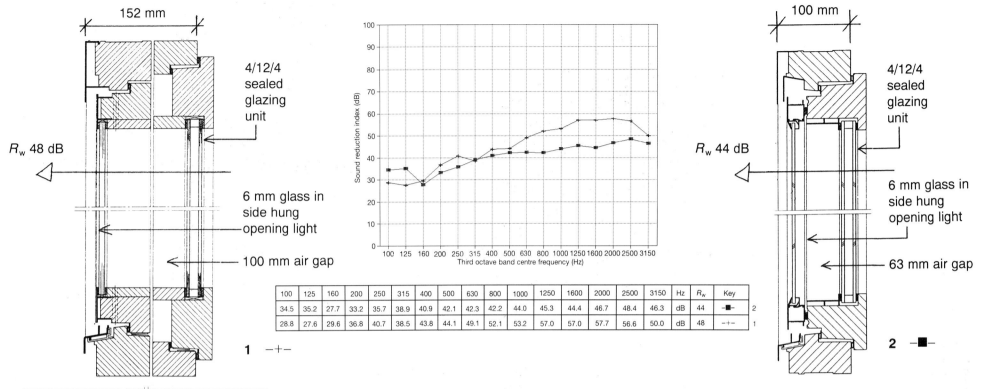

152 mm

4/12/4 sealed glazing unit

R_w 48 dB

6 mm glass in side hung opening light

100 mm air gap

1 —+—

100 mm

4/12/4 sealed glazing unit

R_w 44 dB

6 mm glass in side hung opening light

63 mm air gap

2 —■—

100	125	160	200	250	315	400	500	630	800	1000	1250	1600	2000	2500	3150	Hz	R_w	Key	
34.5	35.2	27.7	33.2	35.7	38.9	40.9	42.1	42.3	42.2	44.0	45.3	44.4	46.7	48.4	46.3	dB	44	—■—	2
28.8	27.6	29.6	36.8	40.7	38.5	43.8	44.1	49.1	52.1	53.2	57.0	57.0	57.7	56.6	50.0	dB	48	—+—	1

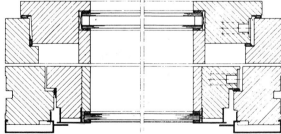

A 20 Special Performance Window by Sampson Windows Ltd

Dual frames 5 mm separated, plastic sealant between

Triple glazing

Some situations, e.g. hotel windows, call for the option to open, even if a hostile noise climate demands high 'window closed' performance. Blinds can be mounted in the cavity between.

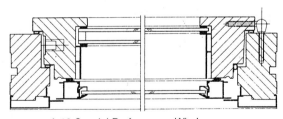

A 18 Special Performance Window by Sampson Windows Ltd

Single frame with side hung opening light

Windows

101

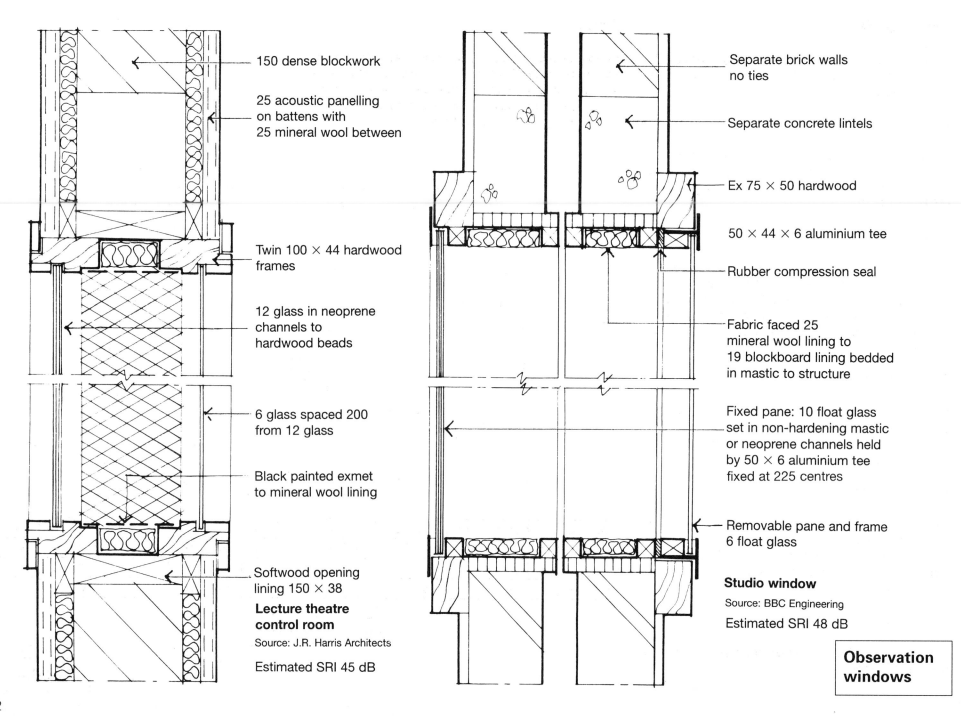

150 dense blockwork

25 acoustic panelling
on battens with
25 mineral wool between

Twin 100 × 44 hardwood
frames

12 glass in neoprene
channels to
hardwood beads

6 glass spaced 200
from 12 glass

Black painted exmet
to mineral wool lining

Softwood opening
lining 150 × 38

**Lecture theatre
control room**

Source: J.R. Harris Architects

Estimated SRI 45 dB

Separate brick walls
no ties

Separate concrete lintels

Ex 75 × 50 hardwood

50 × 44 × 6 aluminium tee

Rubber compression seal

Fabric faced 25
mineral wool lining to
19 blockboard lining bedded
in mastic to structure

Fixed pane: 10 float glass
set in non-hardening mastic
or neoprene channels held
by 50 × 6 aluminium tee
fixed at 225 centres

Removable pane and frame
6 float glass

Studio window

Source: BBC Engineering

Estimated SRI 48 dB

**Observation
windows**

Single glazing

Resonances interfere with performance depending on glass thickness (d). The weakest point is the critical frequency,

$$f_c = \frac{12\,000}{d} \text{ Hz}$$

Lamination improves sound insulation, PMMA better than PVB. Thick fire resistant/safety glass performs well, e.g. 'Pyrostop' 15 mm (36 kg/m²) 38 dB, 21 mm (48 kg/m²) 40 dB.

Double glazing

It may be seen that thermal double glazing is little better than single glass at half the weight. Resonance effects are suppressed if second pane differs by >30% in thickness. Cavity width is not a factor in the 6–20 mm usual range. Gas filling makes little difference.

Double frames

Between 50 and 150 mm air gap, there is a 10 dB uplift in insulation. Further improvement is marginal beyond 200 mm. Lining the reveals gives an improvement of 2–6 dB.

Window area

Doubling or halving window area relative to wall changes the composite insulation by 3 dB. Beside glass thickness, panel size may allow low-frequency resonance: resonant frequency,

$$f_r = \frac{60}{\sqrt{Md}} \text{ Hz}$$

where M is surface mass of glass panel and d is thickness in metres.

Frame

Hollow section types like uPVC and aluminium are adequate up to 38 dB R_w. Scandinavian split frame assemblies (for example wood/aluminium), developed for high thermal insulation, are good. Generous rebating of glass to frames helps.

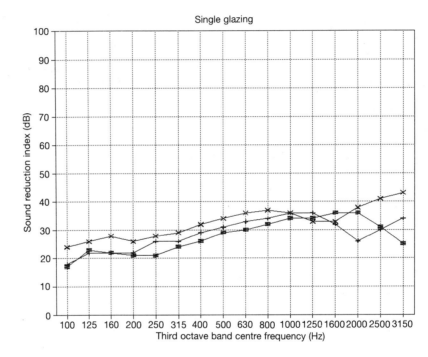

Single glazing

100	125	160	200	250	315	400	500	630	800	1000	1250	1600	2000	2500	3150	Hz	R_w	Key
17	23	22	21	21	24	26	29	30	32	34	34	36	36	31	25	dB	30	—■—
18	22	22	22	26	26	29	31	33	34	36	36	32	26	30	34	dB	32	—+—
24	26	28	26	28	29	32	34	36	37	36	33	33	38	41	43	dB	36	—×—

—■— 4 mm glass
—+— 6 mm glass
—×— 10 mm glass

Source:
Pilkington Glass

Windows

Double glazing units

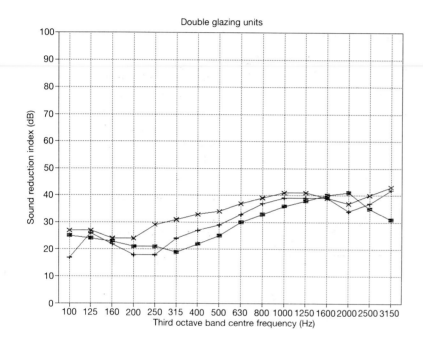

Sound reduction index (dB) vs Third octave band centre frequency (Hz)

100	125	160	200	250	315	400	500	630	800	1000	1250	1600	2000	2500	3150	Hz	R_w	Key
25	24	23	21	21	19	22	25	30	33	36	38	40	41	35	31	dB	31	–■–
17	26	22	18	18	24	27	29	33	37	39	39	39	34	37	42	dB	33	–+–
27	27	24	24	29	31	33	34	37	39	41	41	39	37	40	43	dB	38	–×–

–■– } 4/12/4   glass/cavity/glass
–+– } 6/12/6   (mm)
–×– } 10/12/6   sealed units

Double windows (Secondary sashes)

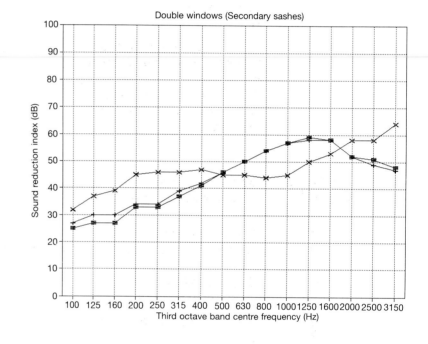

Sound reduction index (dB) vs Third octave band centre frequency (Hz)

100	125	160	200	250	315	400	500	630	800	1000	1250	1600	2000	2500	3150	Hz	R_w	Key
25	27	27	33	33	37	41	46	50	54	57	59	58	52	51	48	dB	46	–■–
27	30	30	34	34	39	42	46	50	54	57	58	58	52	49	47	dB	47	–+–
32	37	39	45	46	46	47	45	45	44	45	50	53	58	58	64	dB	49	–×–

–■– } 6/100/4   glass/cavity/glass
–+– } 6/150/4   (mm)
–×– } 10/200/6   in separate frames

Source: Pilkington Glass

Windows

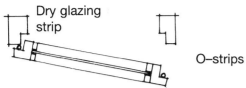

Dry glazing strip

O–strips

Inward opening light

Gap: test by closing door or window to plasticine. Combination of two strips may be necessary if door warped. Fixing by adhesive or stainless steel staples or brass tacks.

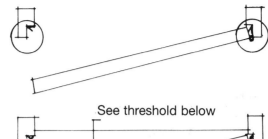

V-strips

See threshold below

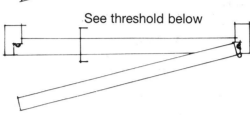

P-strips
Seals to sliding sash windows: a brush seal with central fin may be used ('Welvic' by Manton Insulations or similar)

D2-seal push fitted to frame-masonry edges

Dry glazing strip 8 × 4 up to 10 × 5 mm, to seal gaps 2–2.5 mm

O-strip in silicone rubber used for gaps 3–5 mm

V-strips used for door gaps 3–7 mm

P-strip, to suit gaps 3–5 mm

Resilient threshold 76 × 13
No restriction to wheel-chair traffic: useful in hospitals or schools

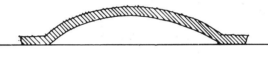

Joint seal sizes 13 × 8 (OD × ID) up to 35 × 28 to suit joints 5–35 mm

Acoustic seal strip 50 × 5

Sound seal for ceiling, wall or floor junction to partition sizes 35 × 10 up to 120 × 10

Triangle strip offers good seal for low closing force

Various types of edge seals

Source: the Varnamo Rubber Co (UK) Ltd

Windows and door seals

Buildings

Buildings and walls affect sound
levels locally, so locating rooms
and windows to more sheltered
elevations will give usefully
lower intrusive noise levels within.
Once line of sight from
a noise source is lost,
a significant reduction
(10 dB+) occurs.

Noise level at front   R1 = X
Noise level at sides   R2 = $X-6$ dB
                      R3 = $X-6$ dB
Noise level at rear   R4 = $X-10$ dB
Noise level at roof   R5 = $X-3$ dB
Noise level with no   R6 = $X-2.5$ dB
build-up resulting
from wall behind

Distance

The main factor affecting reduction
of noise level with distance is the
spread of energy, doubling distance
tends to cause a reduction of 6 dB.
Other factors affect the reduction
with distance: ground effects, temperature
wind, fog, snow and rain. For a linear noise
source like traffic, the reduction with
distance is much less – 3 dB/doubling.

Planting

Planting is of some
benefit for high
frequency attenuation
but otherwise of
limited use in
screening, say, traffic
noise compared
with mounding

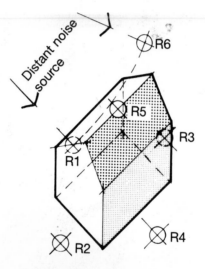

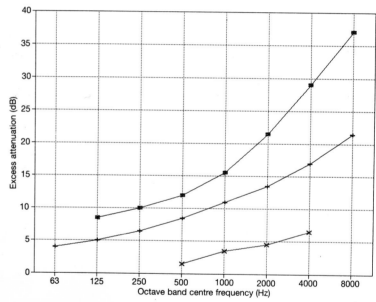

63	125	250	500	1000	2000	4000	8000	Hz	Key	
–	8.5	10	12	15.5	21.5	29	37	dB	–■–	Very dense pine forest (USSR)
4	5	6.5	8.5	11	13.5	17	21.5	dB	–+–	Average of all types of forest (USA)
–	–	–	1.5	3.5	4.5	6.5	–	dB	–×–	Bare trees

(Source: Beranek)

External noise

Barriers and Screens

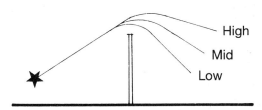

Varying diffraction over a barrier
at different frequencies

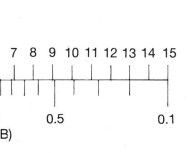

Difference in sound paths, $d = A + B - C$

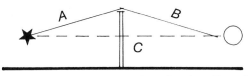

Difference in dB

0 1 2 3 4 5 6 7 8 9 10 11 12 13 14 15

3.0 2.5 2.0 1.5 1.0 0.5 0.1
Add to higher level (dB)

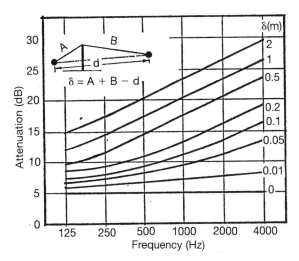

**Attenuation of a point sound
source by a very long screen**
(source: Parkin Humphreys & Cowell)

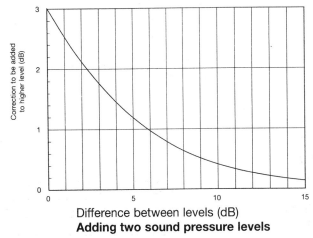

Difference between levels (dB)
Adding two sound pressure levels

Attenuation due to screens in open air
is related to how much further the
sound has to travel around the
screen. For attenuation due to a
finite screen length, carry out path
difference calculations in plan as
well as section and combine
attenuations. Weight of screen
material is immaterial, but needs
to be solid faced to noise side.

Combining sound levels, for example
in path difference calculations
above, can be carried out using
either of the figures at LHS.
For instance, a telephone bell
3 m away at 73 dB adds to the
background 70 dB in a typists'
pool to give a resultant sound
of 74.75 dB (i.e. 75)

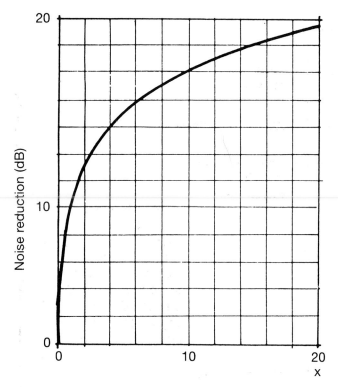

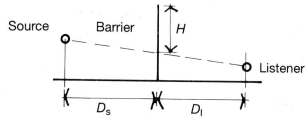

$X = H^2/\lambda D_s$ provided $D_l >> D_s$ and $D_s > H$
Height of barrier can be
determined if wavelength
of noise source and D_s are
known and required dB
reduction specified.

Enclosure with
one side open

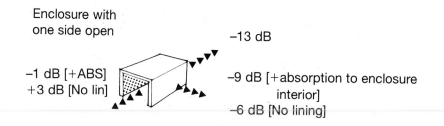

−13 dB

−1 dB [+ABS]
+3 dB [No lin]

−9 dB [+absorption to enclosure
interior]
−6 dB [No lining]

Open sided enclosure
and movable
screen

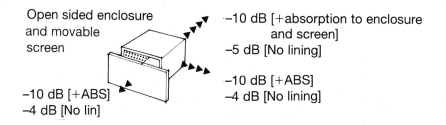

−10 dB [+absorption to enclosure
and screen]
−5 dB [No lining]

−10 dB [+ABS]
−4 dB [No lin]

−10 dB [+ABS]
−4 dB [No lining]

Tunnel

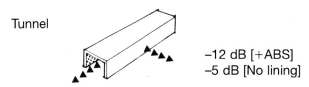

−12 dB [+ABS]
−5 dB [No lining]

−3 dB [+ABS]
+1 dB [No lin]

Effect on direct sound pressure
level frequency range 500–4 kHz
of some partial enclosures.

Source: Woods of Colchester.

(Note: indication only for points
in near field to enclosures.)

Noise barriers

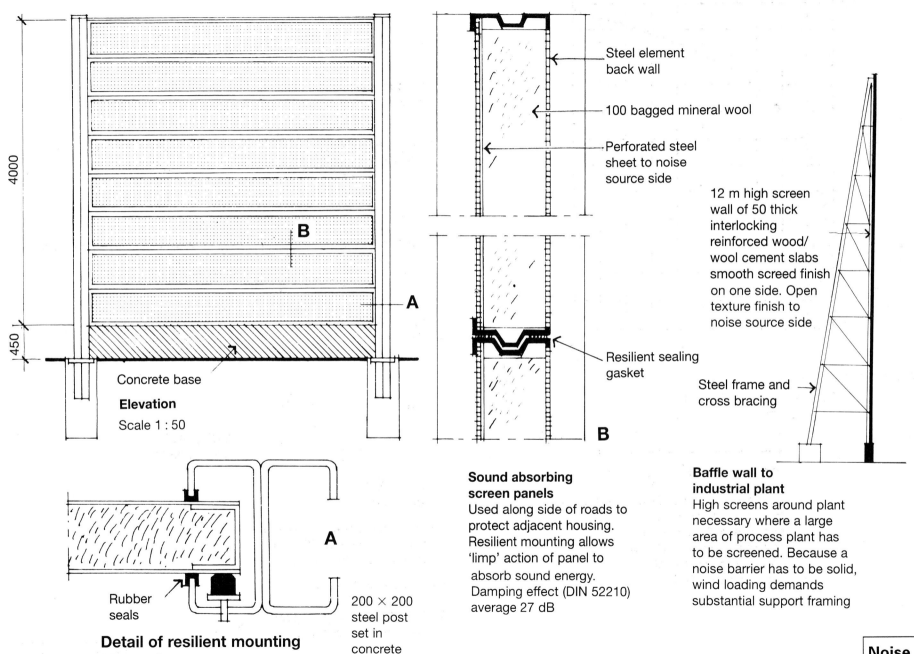

4000

450

Concrete base

Elevation

Scale 1 : 50

B

A

Detail of resilient mounting of panels

Rubber seals

A

200 × 200 steel post set in concrete

Steel element back wall

100 bagged mineral wool

Perforated steel sheet to noise source side

Resilient sealing gasket

B

Sound absorbing screen panels
Used along side of roads to protect adjacent housing. Resilient mounting allows 'limp' action of panel to absorb sound energy. Damping effect (DIN 52210) average 27 dB

12 m high screen wall of 50 thick interlocking reinforced wood/ wool cement slabs smooth screed finish on one side. Open texture finish to noise source side

Steel frame and cross bracing

Baffle wall to industrial plant
High screens around plant necessary where a large area of process plant has to be screened. Because a noise barrier has to be solid, wind loading demands substantial support framing

Noise barriers

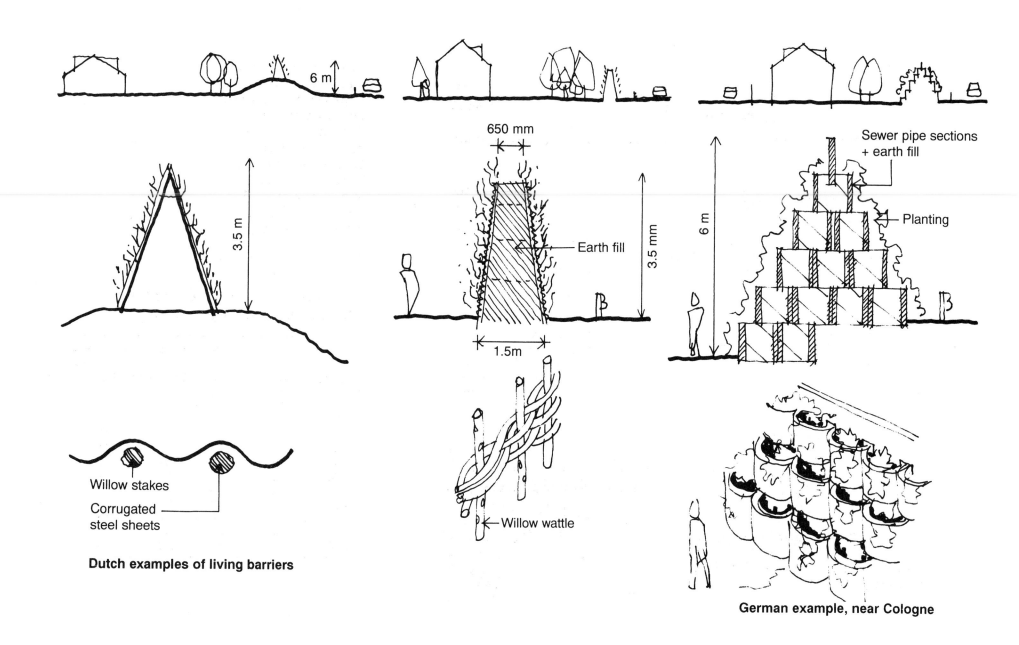

6 m

650 mm

3.5 m

Earth fill

3.5 mm

1.5m

Willow stakes

Corrugated
steel sheets

Dutch examples of living barriers

Willow wattle

6 m

Sewer pipe sections
+ earth fill

Planting

German example, near Cologne

Noise barriers

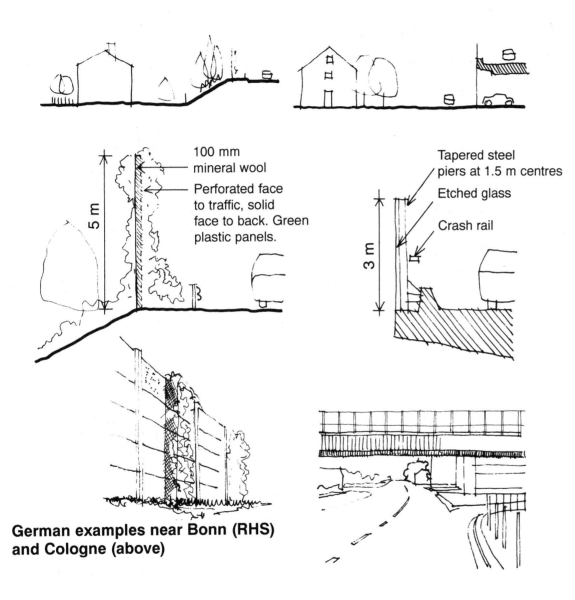

100 mm mineral wool

Perforated face to traffic, solid face to back. Green plastic panels.

5 m

Tapered steel piers at 1.5 m centres

Etched glass

Crash rail

3 m

German examples near Bonn (RHS) and Cologne (above)

Examples are taken from a report prepared for the Department of Transport by Travers Morgan. Screens can be used, or screen + bund, or bund alone. Bunds alone, however, need great width (e.g. 13 m width for 3 m height assuming 1 in 2 gradient either side).

Predicted noise levels using the various calculation methods

Distance from road (m)	Height of barrier (m)	12 hour Leq noise levels dB(A)		
		UK	Germany	France
20	0	75	74	77
50	0	70	70	73
250	0	60	59	62
20	2	74	74	78
50	2	66	68	72
250	2	58	57	57
20	4	66	67	68
50	4	61	61	63
250	4	54	52	51

Noise barriers

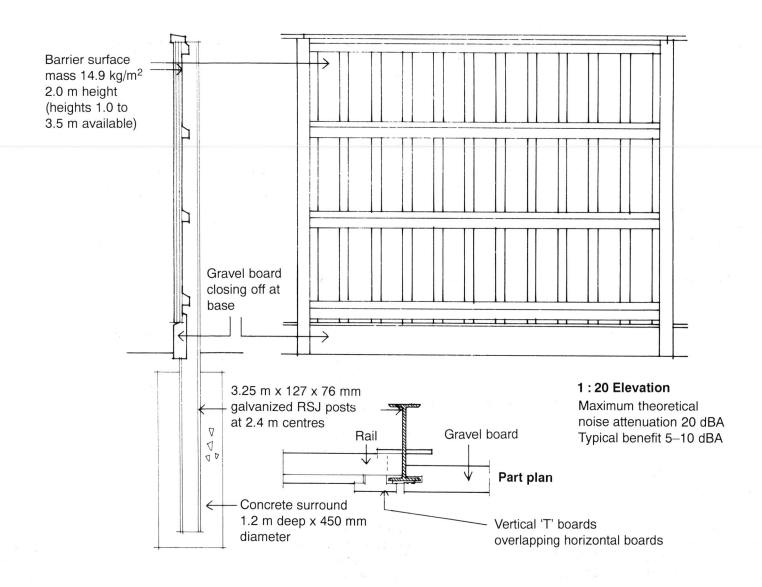

Barrier surface
mass 14.9 kg/m^2
2.0 m height
(heights 1.0 to
3.5 m available)

Gravel board
closing off at
base

3.25 m x 127 x 76 mm
galvanized RSJ posts
at 2.4 m centres

Rail

Gravel board

Concrete surround
1.2 m deep x 450 mm
diameter

Vertical 'T' boards
overlapping horizontal boards

1 : 20 Elevation
Maximum theoretical
noise attenuation 20 dBA
Typical benefit 5–10 dBA

Part plan

Source:
Berkshire Fencing
Special Projects Ltd.

Noise barriers

112

Impact Sound Insulation

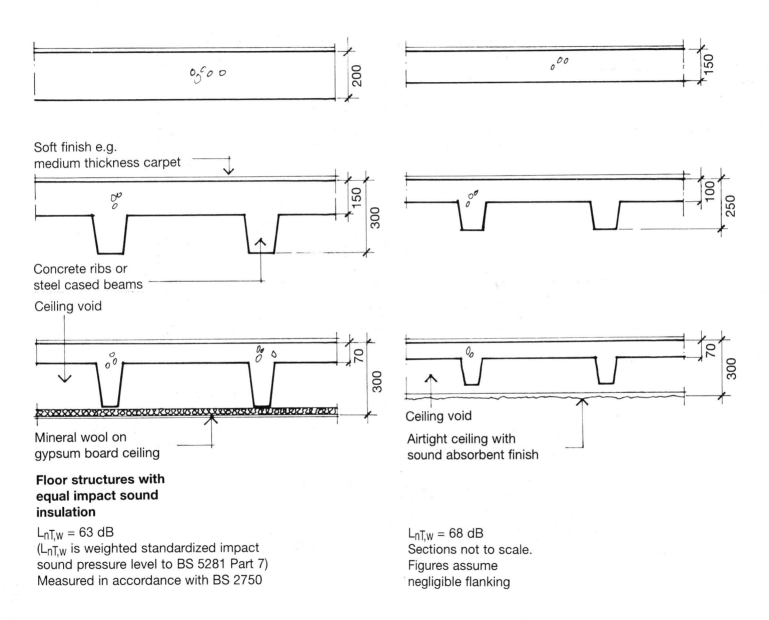

Soft finish e.g.
medium thickness carpet

Concrete ribs or
steel cased beams

Ceiling void

Mineral wool on
gypsum board ceiling

**Floor structures with
equal impact sound
insulation**

$L_{nT,w}$ = 63 dB
($L_{nT,w}$ is weighted standardized impact
sound pressure level to BS 5281 Part 7)
Measured in accordance with BS 2750

Ceiling void

Airtight ceiling with
sound absorbent finish

$L_{nT,w}$ = 68 dB
Sections not to scale.
Figures assume
negligible flanking

Source: Dr. Lang
Technologisches
Gewerbe Museum,
Vienna

Floors

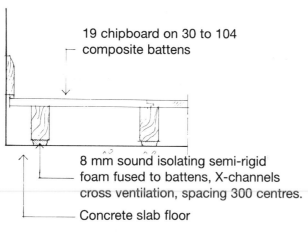

19 chipboard on 30 to 104 composite battens

8 mm sound isolating semi-rigid foam fused to battens, X-channels cross ventilation, spacing 300 centres.

Concrete slab floor

New construction:
Floating floor to achieve good impact sound insulation

Use in flats, maisonettes and open plan offices

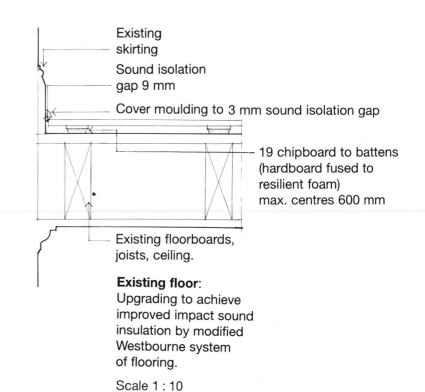

Existing skirting

Sound isolation gap 9 mm

Cover moulding to 3 mm sound isolation gap

19 chipboard to battens (hardboard fused to resilient foam) max. centres 600 mm

Existing floorboards, joists, ceiling.

Existing floor:
Upgrading to achieve improved impact sound insulation by modified Westbourne system of flooring.

Scale 1 : 10

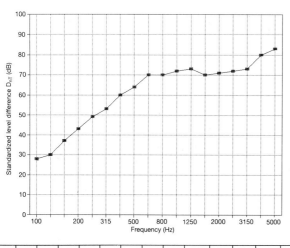

Airborne sound

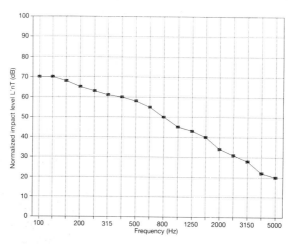

Impact sound

Source: Contiwood (Durabella) Ltd

100	125	160	200	250	315	400	500	630	800	1000	1250	1600	2000	2500	3150	4000	5000	Hz
28	30	37	43	49	53	60	64	70	70	72	73	70	71	72	73	80	83	dB

100	125	160	200	250	315	400	500	630	800	1000	1250	1600	2000	2500	3150	4000	5000	Hz
70	70	68	65	63	61	60	58	55	50	45	43	40	34	31	28	22	20	dB

Floor isolation

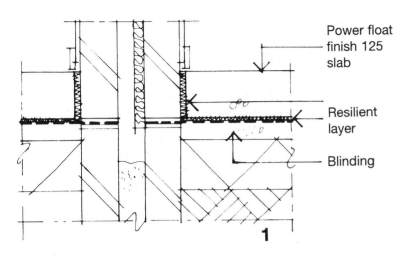

Power float finish 125 slab

Resilient layer

Blinding

1

Elastomeric layer over DPC

2

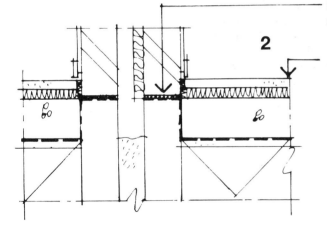

-■- Undamped concrete

-+- Concrete damped with Reduc mat

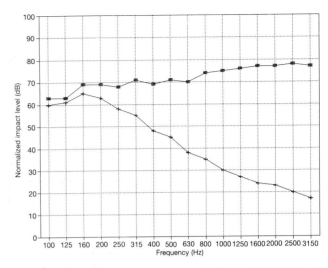

100	125	160	200	250	315	400	500	630	800	1000	1250	1600	2000	2500	3150	Hz
63	63	69	69	68	71	69	71	70	74	75	76	77	77	78	77	dB
60	61	65	63	58	55	48	45	38	35	30	27	24	23	20	17	dB

1 is poor compared with 3: resilient quilt is subject to extra compression load and water from concrete mix. Absorbent material in cavity cuts down tracking of noise across cavity.

1 – 4 show varying means of isolating floor slabs in adjacent rooms to prevent flanking (e.g. in music rooms, conference rooms) 4 is impractical to install

Proprietary built-up floor: 19 or 22 chipboard on expanded polystyrene to floor slab

Long fibreglass wool and mineral wool quilts have been suggested as the most proven materials (BRE 103). Fibreboard and hair felt have shown unsatisfactory compaction under continuous load. Material to be used to have following features:

A – density 15–25 kg/m³ min
B – thickness not less than 13 mm
C – board precompressed to half initial thickness with rapid recovery to 90% initial thickness. Thin materials are promising in performance: Reduc have a membrane only 1.5 mm thick. Other insulation panels e.g. TRT panels, consist of chipboard, hardboard or ply either side of a thin viscoelastic layer which has the property of a high degree of internal damping.

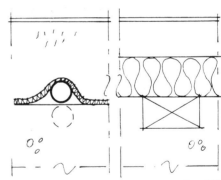

Conduit or pipe set under screed (not to exceed 25 in 50 screed)

Pockets under expanded polystyrene not exceeding 75 width

Floor isolation

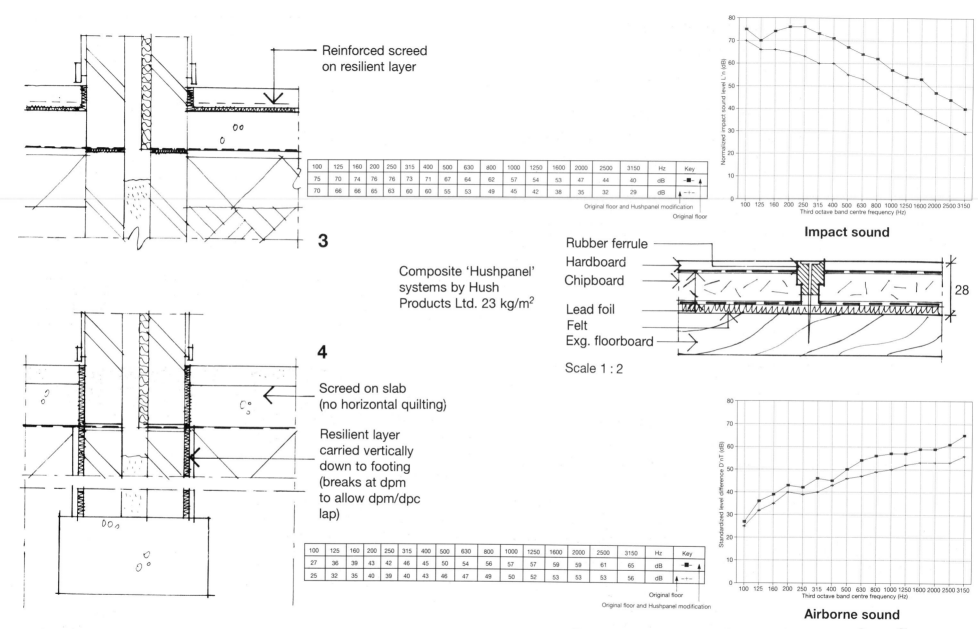

Reinforced screed on resilient layer

3

Composite 'Hushpanel' systems by Hush Products Ltd. 23 kg/m²

4

Screed on slab (no horizontal quilting)

Resilient layer carried vertically down to footing (breaks at dpm to allow dpm/dpc lap)

Rubber ferrule
Hardboard
Chipboard
Lead foil
Felt
Exg. floorboard

28

Scale 1 : 2

100	125	160	200	250	315	400	500	630	800	1000	1250	1600	2000	2500	3150	Hz	Key
75	70	74	76	76	73	71	67	64	62	57	54	53	47	44	40	dB	■
70	66	66	65	63	60	60	55	53	49	45	42	38	35	32	29	dB	+

Original floor and Hushpanel modification
Original floor

Impact sound

100	125	160	200	250	315	400	500	630	800	1000	1250	1600	2000	2500	3150	Hz	Key
27	36	39	43	42	46	45	50	54	56	57	57	59	59	61	65	dB	■
25	32	35	40	39	40	43	46	47	49	50	52	53	53	53	56	dB	+

Original floor
Original floor and Hushpanel modification

Airborne sound

Floors at Govanhill Glasgow uprated by added floor deck

Source: Glasgow College of Building

Floor isolation

116

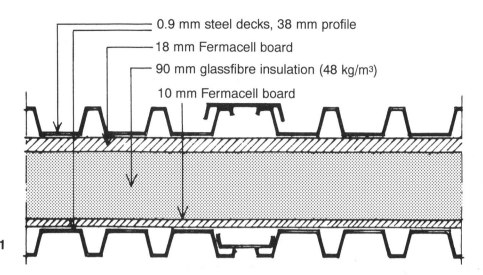

1
- 0.9 mm steel decks, 38 mm profile
- 18 mm Fermacell board
- 90 mm glassfibre insulation (48 kg/m³)
- 10 mm Fermacell board

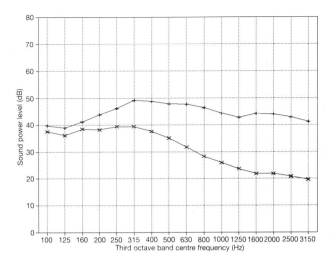

100	125	160	200	250	315	400	500	630	800	1000	1250	1600	2000	2500	3150	Hz	NC	Key	
39.8	39.0	41.2	43.7	46.2	49.2	48.8	47.8	47.7	46.5	44.4	42.7	44.3	44.0	42.8	41.1	dB	48	–+–	1
37.6	36.1	38.5	38.2	39.4	39.4	37.6	35.1	31.8	28.3	25.9	23.7	21.8	21.9	20.8	19.7	dB	32	–×–	2

3 mm aluminium tiles connected
to deck via 2 mm thick neoprene

2
- 0.9 mm steel decks, 38 mm profile
- Compressed 30 mm glassfibre quilt
- Wire mesh stretched over spacers grid
- 90 mm glassfibre insulation (48 kg/m³)
- 18 + 10 mm Fermacell boards

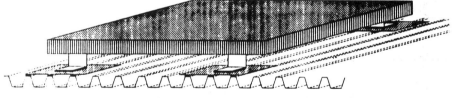

Rainfall simulation tests

Tests to look at impact noise generated in a
reverberation room under roof and gutter
detailed as 1, then 2, due to simulated
heavy rain (flowrate 333 mm/hr). Impact
area 1 m². Room volume 67 m³. Roof
area 29 m². NC is Noise Criterion level in
room.

Source:
Weatherwise Ltd/
University of Salford

Roofing

117

3 SOUND ABSORPTION/REFLECTION

Sound Absorption/Reflection

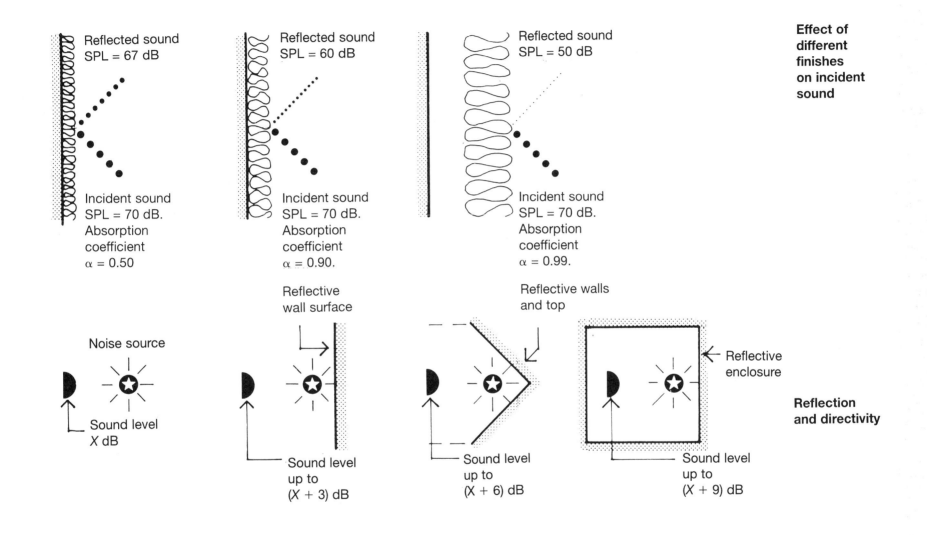

Reflected sound
SPL = 67 dB

Incident sound
SPL = 70 dB.
Absorption
coefficient
α = 0.50

Reflected sound
SPL = 60 dB

Incident sound
SPL = 70 dB.
Absorption
coefficient
α = 0.90.

Reflected sound
SPL = 50 dB

Incident sound
SPL = 70 dB.
Absorption
coefficient
α = 0.99.

**Effect of
different
finishes
on incident
sound**

Noise source

Sound level
X dB

Reflective
wall surface

Sound level
up to
(X + 3) dB

Reflective walls
and top

Sound level
up to
(X + 6) dB

Reflective
enclosure

Sound level
up to
(X + 9) dB

**Reflection
and directivity**

Sound absorption

**Amplification factor:
effect of enclosure**

1 Porous

2 Porous and air gap

3 Porous and perforated facing

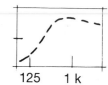

4 Fissured ceiling tile on solid backing

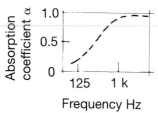

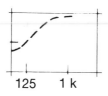

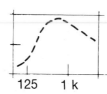

Absorption coefficient α

1.0
0.5
0

125   1 k

Frequency Hz

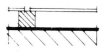

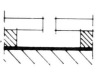

5 Thin membrane

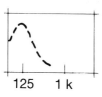

6 Resonator

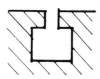

7 Cavity (Helmholtz) resonator

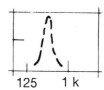

8 Reflector

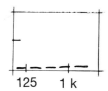

Absorption coefficient α

1.0
0.5
0

125   1 k

Frequency Hz

Performance of different wall or ceiling finishes

Sound absorption

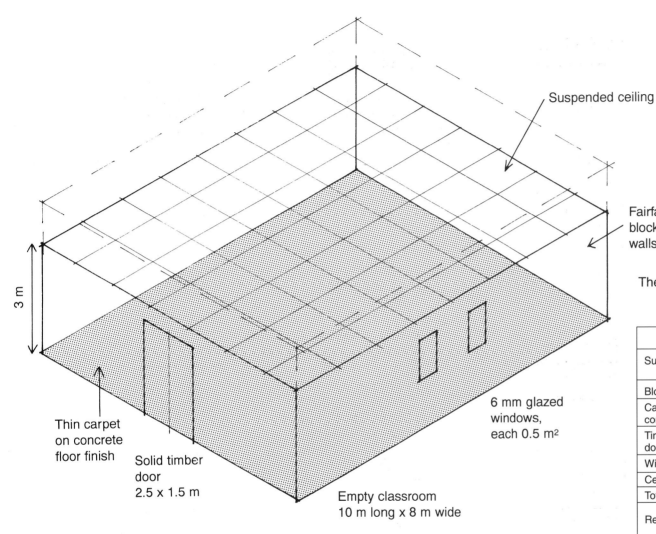

3 m

Suspended ceiling

Fairfaced
blockwork
walls

Thin carpet
on concrete
floor finish

Solid timber
door
2.5 x 1.5 m

6 mm glazed
windows,
each 0.5 m²

Empty classroom
10 m long x 8 m wide

Sample reverberation times
calculation
Absorption values based on coefficients
from Table 6.3 on page 194.

The reverberation time is calculated as follows:

Absorption $A = S \times \bar{\alpha}\ m^2$

Surface	Area (m²)	Octave band centre frequency (Hz)					
		125	250	200	1000	2000	4000
Blockwork	103.25	5.16	5.16	5.16	8.26	16.46	20.65
Carpet on concrete	80.00	2.40	7.20	16.00	43.20	56.00	57.60
Timber door	3.75	0.53	0.38	0.23	0.30	0.38	0.38
Windows	1.00	0.10	0.06	0.04	0.03	0.02	0.02
Ceiling	80	16.00	12.00	8.00	4.00	4.00	4.00
Total A		24.19	24.80	29.43	55.79	76.86	82.65
Reverberation time $T = \dfrac{0.161V}{A}$ s = (Sabine formula)		1.6	1.6	1.3	0.7	0.5	0.5

Room acoustics

Reflectors

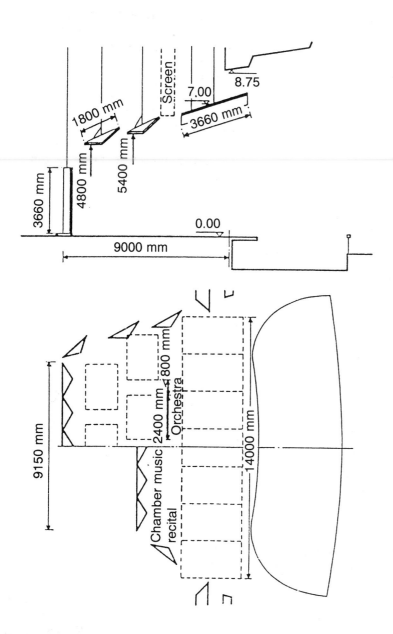

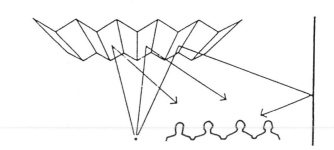

Reflectors as installed in Hangzhou Theatre, Beijing, to avoid recital sound loss into fly tower. Panel arrays are 'flown' hence removed for drama events.

Size: to be effective at longer wavelengths (i.e. lower frequencies) >0.5 m² per element
Proportion: length ≥4 x width
Materials: 'hard' e.g. wood, plexiglas or metal, mass >10 kg/m²
Height off platform: 7–10 m in full-sized concert hall
Purpose: • Improvement of balance between members of orchestra
 • support of weak sound source
 • blocking of echo or very late sound
 • improved diffusivity
 • improved level and clarity at rear seats.

Source: J. Han/Applied Acoustics

Overhead reflectors

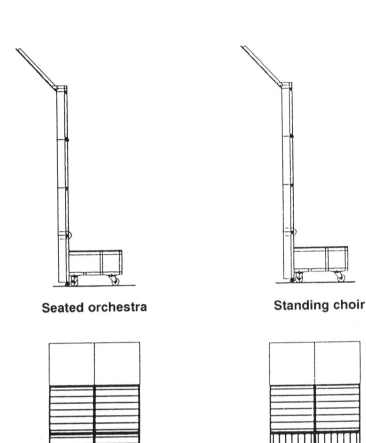

Seated orchestra

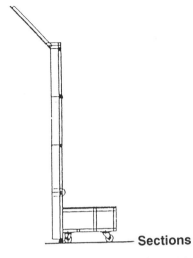

Standing choir

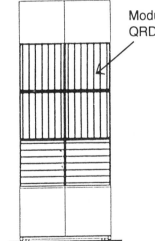

Choir on risers

Sections

Elevations 1:50

When musicians have to perform on open stages, side panel arrays help recreate the preferred 'bell' shape (side walls at about 18° on plan and modelled). The upper tilted panels are particularly important because cross reflection angles are less affected by glancing incidence across musicians. Musicians benefit by ease of maintaining ensemble, and listeners receive a blended, balanced sound with strong lateral energy.

Some proprietary 'portable vamps' are shown, complete with modular diffuser faces.

Modular 610 x 610 mm QRD diffuser panels

Rindel suggests that to be useful the excess path length should be $a_1+a_2-a_0<27$ m where a_0 = direct sound path between source and receiver, a_1 and a_2 the incident and reflected sound paths.

Source: RPG Europe Ltd

Reflector panels

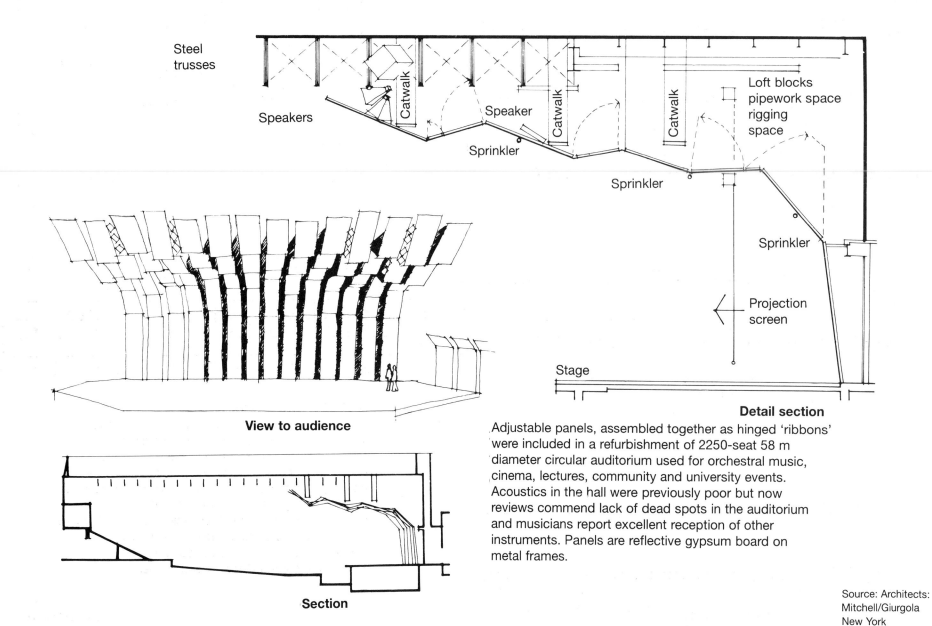

Steel trusses

Speakers

Catwalk

Speaker

Catwalk

Sprinkler

Catwalk

Loft blocks
pipework space
rigging
space

Sprinkler

Sprinkler

Projection
screen

Stage

Detail section

View to audience

Section

Adjustable panels, assembled together as hinged 'ribbons' were included in a refurbishment of 2250-seat 58 m diameter circular auditorium used for orchestral music, cinema, lectures, community and university events. Acoustics in the hall were previously poor but now reviews commend lack of dead spots in the auditorium and musicians report excellent reception of other instruments. Panels are reflective gypsum board on metal frames.

Source: Architects:
Mitchell/Giurgola
New York

Stage canopy

Ceilings

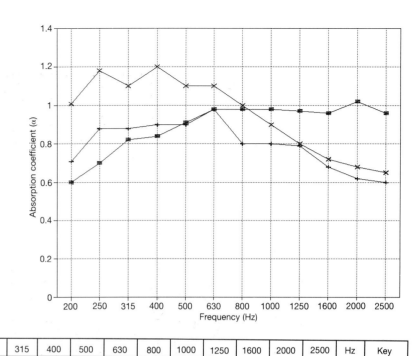

200

Mineral wool boards
Plain TRP 200 decking

750

−■− 1

−×− 2

Soft insulation
TRP with perforated ribs
and downstands

−+− 3

Built-up felt roof
on hard insulation
TRP with perforated ribs

Scale 1:10

200	250	315	400	500	630	800	1000	1250	1600	2000	2500	Hz	Key	
0.6	0.7	0.82	0.84	0.91	0.98	0.98	0.98	0.97	0.96	1.02	0.96	α	−■−	1
1.01	1.18	1.1	1.2	1.1	1.1	1.0	0.9	0.8	0.72	0.68	0.65	α	−×−	2
0.71	0.88	0.88	0.9	0.9	0.89	0.8	0.8	0.79	0.68	0.62	0.6	α	−+−	3

Structural steel decking

Steel decking can be problematic when exposed
internally in industrial or even office buildings.
This form of roofing has deep ribs which diffuse
reflected sound at the higher [speech] frequencies,
and a good proportion of perforations located on part
of the decking not critical for strength.
In assessing perforated steel deck roofs, check gauge
of steel and thickness of membrane immediately
above the perforations – both can affect α.
17% of the current Plannja deck is open.

Source: Plannja

Roofs

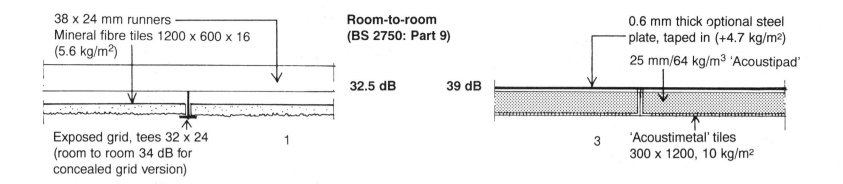

38 x 24 mm runners
Mineral fibre tiles 1200 x 600 x 16
(5.6 kg/m²)

**Room-to-room
(BS 2750: Part 9)**

0.6 mm thick optional steel
plate, taped in (+4.7 kg/m²)

25 mm/64 kg/m³ 'Acoustipad'

32.5 dB   **39 dB**

Exposed grid, tees 32 x 24
(room to room 34 dB for
concealed grid version)   1

3   'Acoustimetal' tiles
300 x 1200, 10 kg/m²

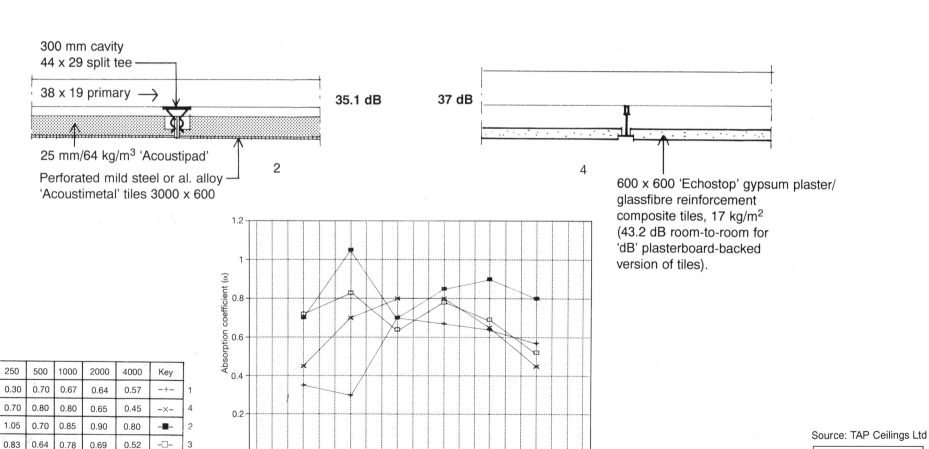

300 mm cavity
44 x 29 split tee

38 x 19 primary →

35.1 dB   **37 dB**

25 mm/64 kg/m³ 'Acoustipad'
Perforated mild steel or al. alloy
'Acoustimetal' tiles 3000 x 600   2

4

600 x 600 'Echostop' gypsum plaster/
glassfibre reinforcement
composite tiles, 17 kg/m²
(43.2 dB room-to-room for
'dB' plasterboard-backed
version of tiles).

125	250	500	1000	2000	4000	Key	
0.35	0.30	0.70	0.67	0.64	0.57	−+−	1
0.45	0.70	0.80	0.80	0.65	0.45	−×−	4
0.70	1.05	0.70	0.85	0.90	0.80	−■−	2
0.72	0.83	0.64	0.78	0.69	0.52	−□−	3

Source: TAP Ceilings Ltd

Ceilings

Ceiling void 370

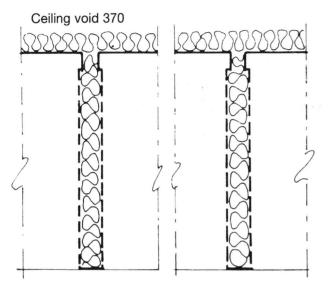

Proprietary 'Dampa' baffles of perforated
aluminium on 600 × 600 module
packed with 25 mineral wool
packed in polythene foil. 22% perforations.

0.22   0.27   0.61   0.71   0.71   0.80

Ceiling void

Perforated 'Dampa' trays with
25 mineral wool pads
on polythene foil.
600 × 600 module in aluminium
or steel

0.68   0.66   0.57   0.58   0.52   0.62

Absorption figures relate to octave band
frequencies (Hz):

125   250   500   1 k   2 k   4 k

Ceiling void 125

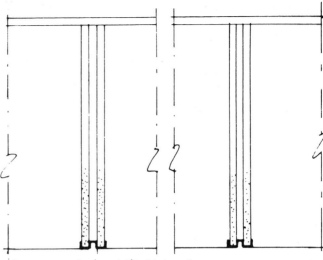

Armstrong fissured 15 thick twin
panels of mineral wool

0.10   0.30   0.55   1.35   1.15   0.90

Ceiling void

'Roclaine' metal panels
5% perforated with 20
glass fibre faced in
black fibre felt

0.13   0.27   0.55   0.79   0.90   1.00

Ceilings

Standard details

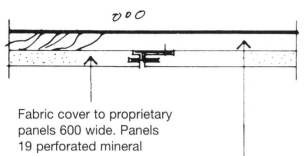

Fabric cover to proprietary
panels 600 wide. Panels
19 perforated mineral
fibreboard by Armstrong.
50 × 25 battens on masonry

0.22 0.58 0.56 0.72 0.76 0.81

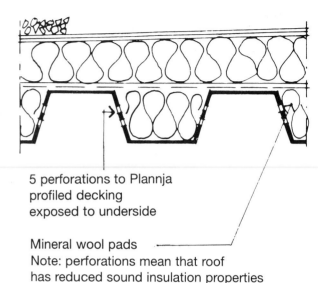

5 perforations to Plannja
profiled decking
exposed to underside

Mineral wool pads
Note: perforations mean that roof
has reduced sound insulation properties

0.20 0.50 0.80 0.85 0.60 0.50

50 × 25 battens

25 air gap

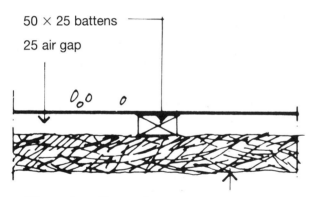

50 woodwool/cement
building slabs (prescreeded 'Woodcemaire')

0.30 0.40 0.50 0.85 0.50 0.65

0.15 0.20 0.55 0.75 0.65 0.85 (no air gap)

Absorption figures relate to octave band
frequencies (Hz):
125 250 500 1 k 2 k 4 k

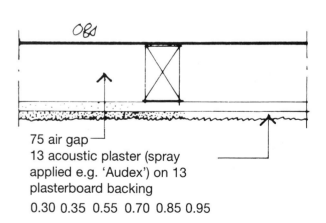

75 air gap
13 acoustic plaster (spray
applied e.g. 'Audex') on 13
plasterboard backing

0.30 0.35 0.55 0.70 0.85 0.95

Ceilings finishes

Standard details

128

Solid soffit

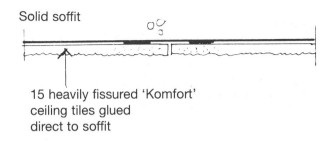

15 heavily fissured 'Komfort'
ceiling tiles glued
direct to soffit

0.09 0.30 0.82 0.95 0.76 0.61

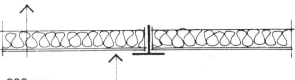

200 mm
ceiling void
25 lightweight lay-in
glass fibre suspended
ceiling tiles. Matt
white coat finish to
underside (type: Roclaine Diapaison 'P')

0.33 0.84 0.84 0.88 0.89 0.92

40 fibreglass tiles over 400 void
0.70 0.75 0.65 0.75 0.60 0.35

300 void

15 heavily fissured
concealed grid plaster 'Gyptone'
ceiling tiles. Metal
suspension system

0.30 0.35 0.40 0.55 0.80 0.70

Absorption figures relate to octave band
frequencies (Hz):

125 250 500 1 k 2 k 4 k

300 ceiling void

15 fissured-finish Armstrong 'Ceramguard'
kiln-fired mineral
fibre tiles (for use
in corrosive or humid
situation, e.g. swimming pools)

0.25 0.25 0.45 0.70 0.80 1.10

Ceilings

Standard details

Parallel pattern

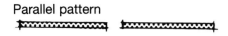

0.28   0.58   0.96   0.91 0.86   0.81
(one piece per square metre)

Cross pattern

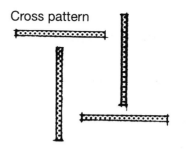

0.34   0.59   0.91   0.92 0.93   0.81
(one piece per square metre)

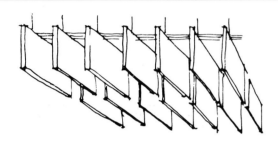

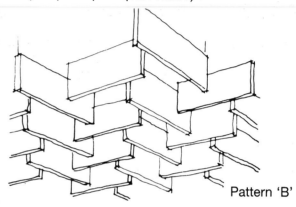

Pattern 'B'

This form of acoustical control is useful for industrial buildings, workshops, aircraft hangers where there is little inherent absorbent material

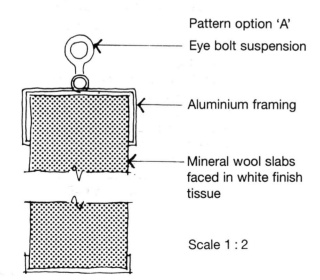

Pattern option 'A'

Eye bolt suspension

Aluminium framing

Mineral wool slabs faced in white finish tissue

Scale 1 : 2

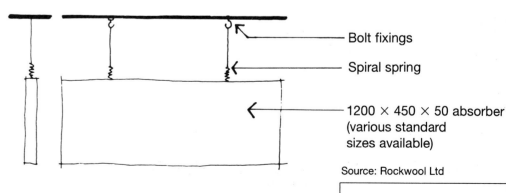

Bolt fixings

Spiral spring

1200 × 450 × 50 absorber (various standard sizes available)

Source: Rockwool Ltd

Overhead sound absorbers

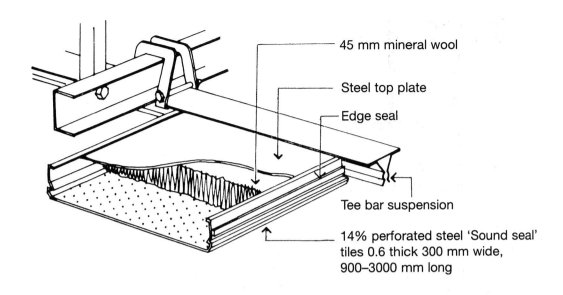

45 mm mineral wool

Steel top plate

Edge seal

Tee bar suspension

14% perforated steel 'Sound seal' tiles 0.6 thick 300 mm wide, 900–3000 mm long

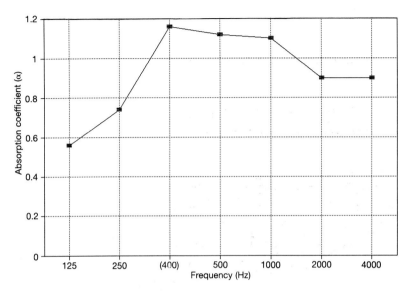

125	250	(400)	500	1000	2000	4000	Hz
0.56	0.74	1.16	1.12	1.10	0.9	0.9	α

Metal tiles
Metal top plates to tiles ensure good sound insulation, which is normally a weakness of acoustically absorbing ceilings. Weight: 14.5 kg/m² Room-to-room (BS 2750) average normalized sound level difference 40 dB

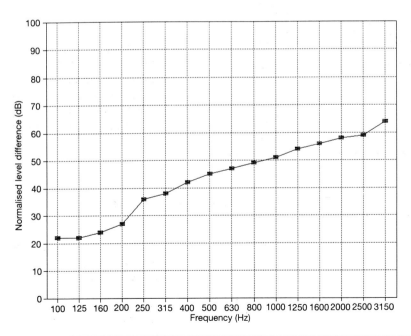

100	125	160	200	250	315	400	500	630	800	1000	1250	1600	2000	2500	3150	Hz
22	22	24	27	36	38	42	45	47	49	51	54	56	58	59	64	dB

Source: Burgess
Steel Ceilings

Ceilings

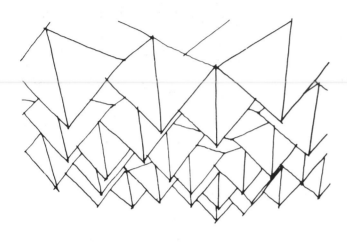

Special metal ceiling units
600 × 600 × 0.6 thick pyramids
forming a sound diffusing
ceiling

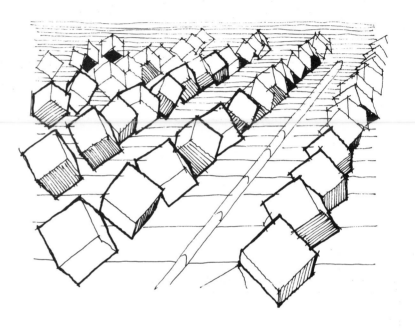

Cube sound absorbers
in a Porsche factory,
Stuttgart

Ceilings

Special profiles

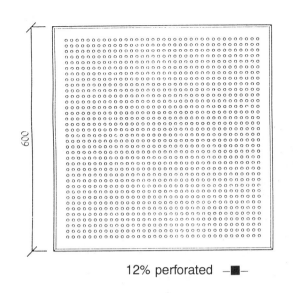

600

12% perforated —■—

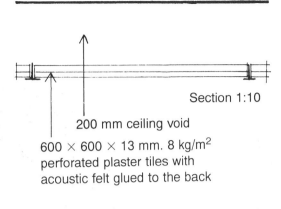

Section 1:10

200 mm ceiling void

600 × 600 × 13 mm. 8 kg/m² perforated plaster tiles with acoustic felt glued to the back

Tile patterns 1:10   —×—
15% slotted

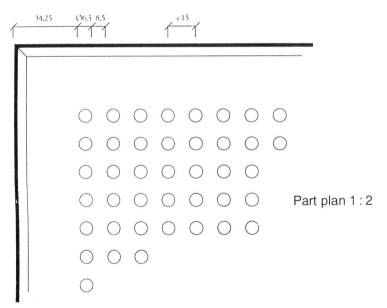

Part plan 1 : 2

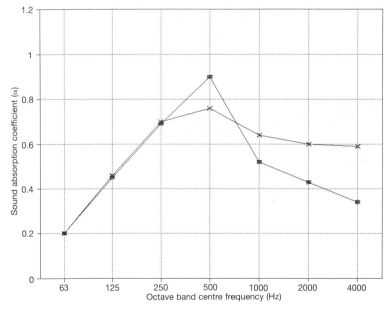

63	125	250	500	1000	2000	4000	Hz	Key	
0.20	0.45	0.69	0.9	0.52	0.43	0.34	α	—■—	12% perforated
0.20	0.46	0.70	0.76	0.64	0.60	0.59	α	—×—	15% slotted

Source: Gyproc,
Sweden

Ceilings

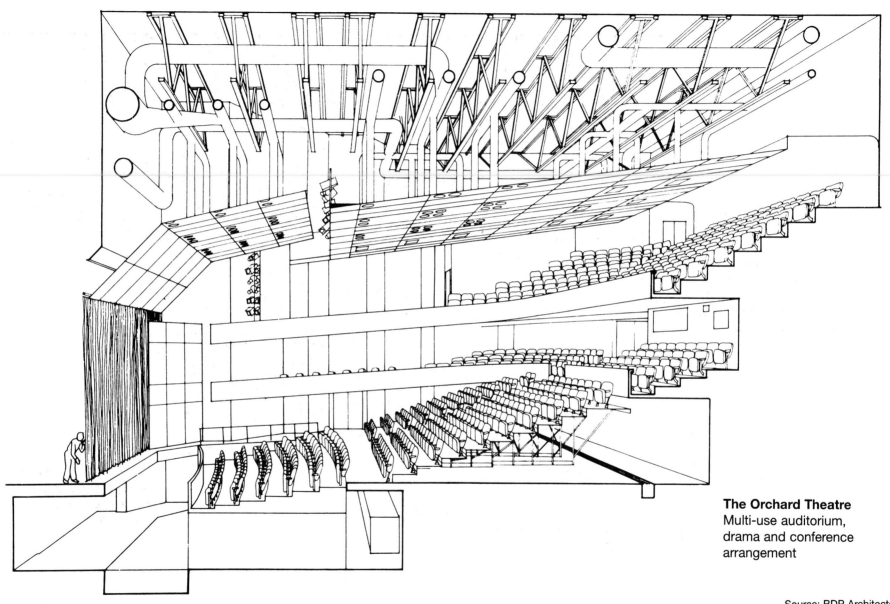

The Orchard Theatre
Multi-use auditorium,
drama and conference
arrangement

Source: BDP Architects/
Theatre Projects

Adjustable ceiling

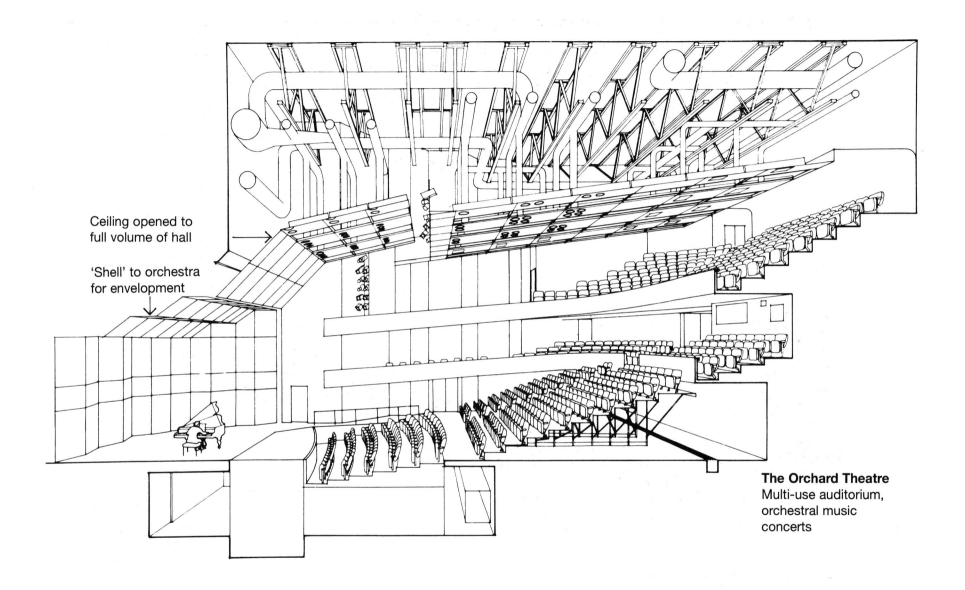

Ceiling opened to
full volume of hall

'Shell' to orchestra
for envelopment

The Orchard Theatre
Multi-use auditorium,
orchestral music
concerts

Source: BDP Architects/
Theatre Projects

Adjustable ceiling

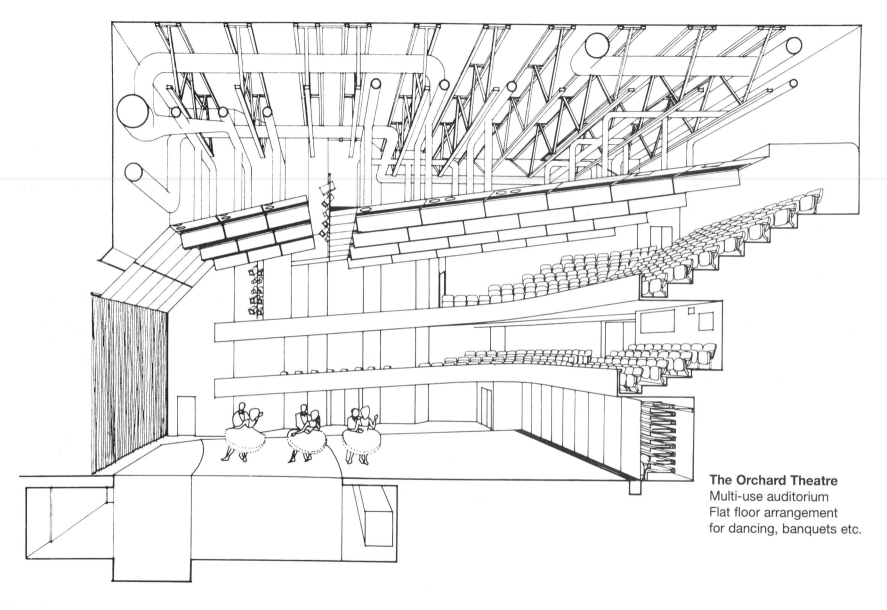

The Orchard Theatre
Multi-use auditorium
Flat floor arrangement
for dancing, banquets etc.

Source: BDP Architects/
Theatre Projects

Adjustable ceiling

RHS and T-sections
hung from main
roof trusses

'Idenden' insulation hanger
with one self-locking washer
either side of mineral wool

12 ply
32 × 100 SW frames
50 mineral wool
152 × 102 MS T-section

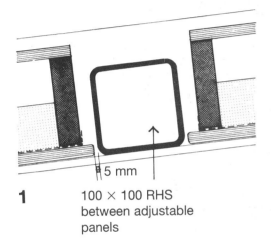

5 mm

1

100 × 100 RHS
between adjustable
panels

2

Lids attached to frames
with cranked hinges
staggered to minimize gap

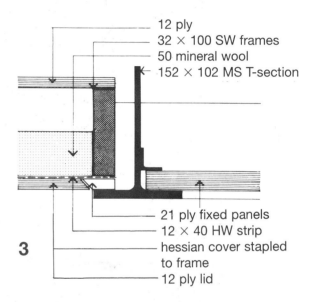

3

21 ply fixed panels
12 × 40 HW strip
hessian cover stapled
to frame
12 ply lid

The Orchard Theatre
Multi-use auditorium,
detail section of ceiling

**Devices to adjust the layout and
acoustics: flat floor for dancing,
banquets and exhibitions.**

Source: BDP Architects/
Theatre Projects

Adjustable ceiling

137

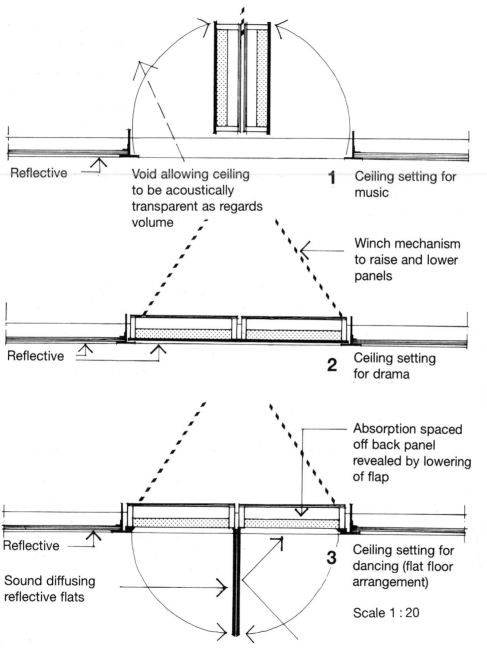

The design RT from model studies is 1.50 seconds at mid-frequencies for music, 1.30 seconds for flat floor and 1.00 second for drama

Reflective

Void allowing ceiling to be acoustically transparent as regards volume

1 Ceiling setting for music

Winch mechanism to raise and lower panels

Overhead early reflections (under 50 ms) are useful for reinforcing loudness and intelligibility of speech. Low-frequency membrane absorbers are incorporated elsewhere to prevent reverberant masking of high-frequency speech sounds.

Reflective

2 Ceiling setting for drama

Absorption spaced off back panel revealed by lowering of flap

Absorption and diffusion offset removal of seating below.

Reflective

3 Ceiling setting for dancing (flat floor arrangement)

Sound diffusing reflective flats

Scale 1 : 20

The Orchard Theatre
Multi-use auditorium, moving ceiling

Source: BDP Architects/ Theatre Projects

Adjustable ceiling

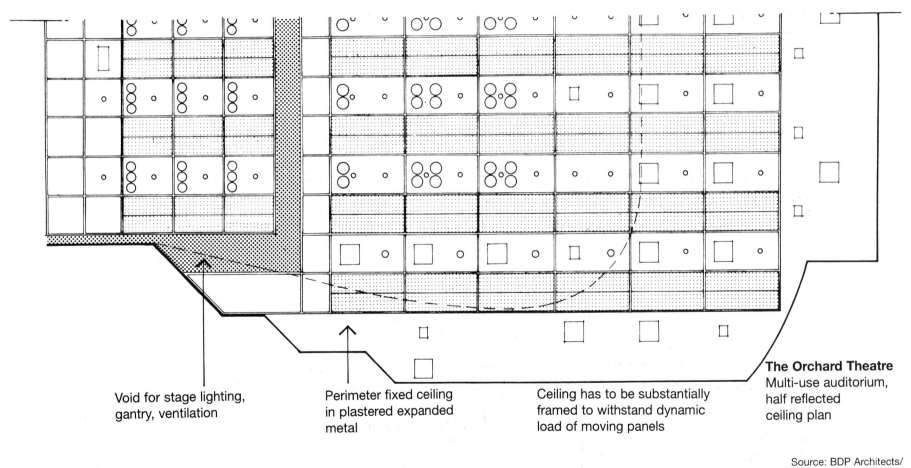

Panels which hinge upwards or downwards.
Fire detection, lighting and ventilation co-ordinated to fixed panels. Paired panels 1215 × 2400 opening area 50% of main ceiling. Main air grilles 584 × 584

Void for stage lighting, gantry, ventilation

Perimeter fixed ceiling in plastered expanded metal

Ceiling has to be substantially framed to withstand dynamic load of moving panels

The Orchard Theatre
Multi-use auditorium, half reflected ceiling plan

Source: BDP Architects/ Theatre Projects

Adjustable ceiling

Wall Finishes

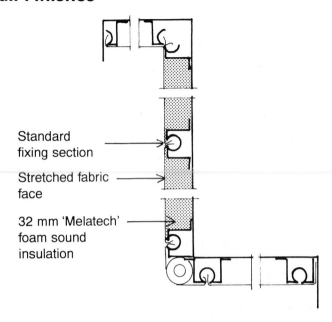

Standard
fixing section →

Stretched fabric
face →

32 mm 'Melatech'
foam sound
insulation →

Horizontal section 1 : 5

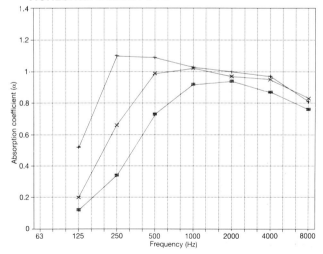

125	250	500	1000	2000	4000	8000	Hz	Key	
0.12	0.34	0.73	0.92	0.94	0.87	0.76	α	—■—	30 mm Quilt
0.20	0.66	0.99	1.02	0.97	0.95	0.83	α	—×—	50 mm
0.52	1.10	1.09	1.03	1.00	0.97	0.81	α	—+—	100 mm

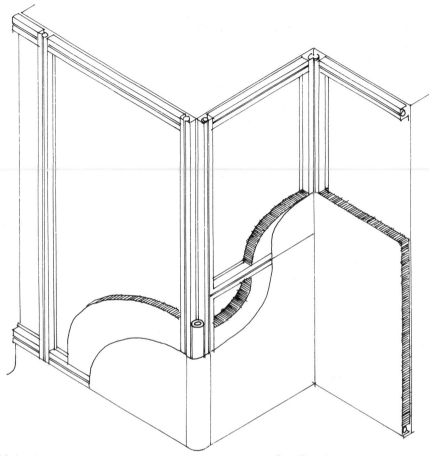

Application

Melamine open-cell foam
has certain advantages
over mineral wool and
glass fibre: no migration of
strands of material into
into the air, and light
weight

System: 'Soundcheck' by Bridgeplex Ltd.

Acoustic wall cladding

140

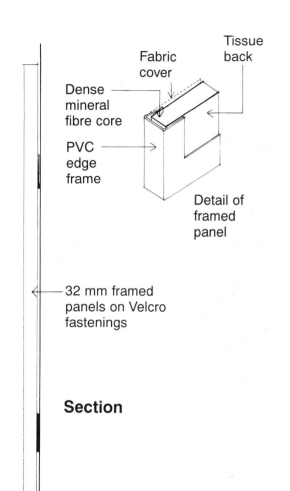

Fabric cover

Tissue back

Dense mineral fibre core

PVC edge frame

Detail of framed panel

32 mm framed panels on Velcro fastenings

Section

Base support

Wall-mounted framed panels

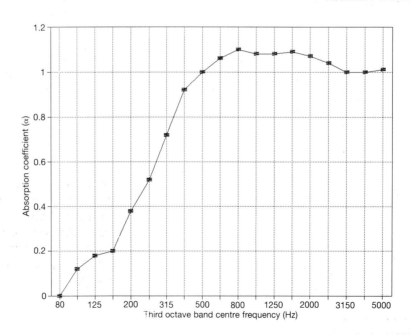

Panels mounted on workstation screens

System by 'Soundsorba' Acoustic Products

Absorption coefficient (α)

1.2

1

0.8

0.6

0.4

0.2

0

80   125   200   315   500   800   1250   2000   3150   5000

Third octave band centre frequency (Hz)

80	100	125	160	200	250	315	400	500	630	800	1000	1250	1600	2000	2500	3150	4000	5000	Hz
0	0.12	0.18	0.2	0.38	0.52	0.72	0.92	1.0	1.06	1.1	1.08	1.08	1.09	1.07	1.04	1.00	1.00	1.01	α

Acoustic wall panels

141

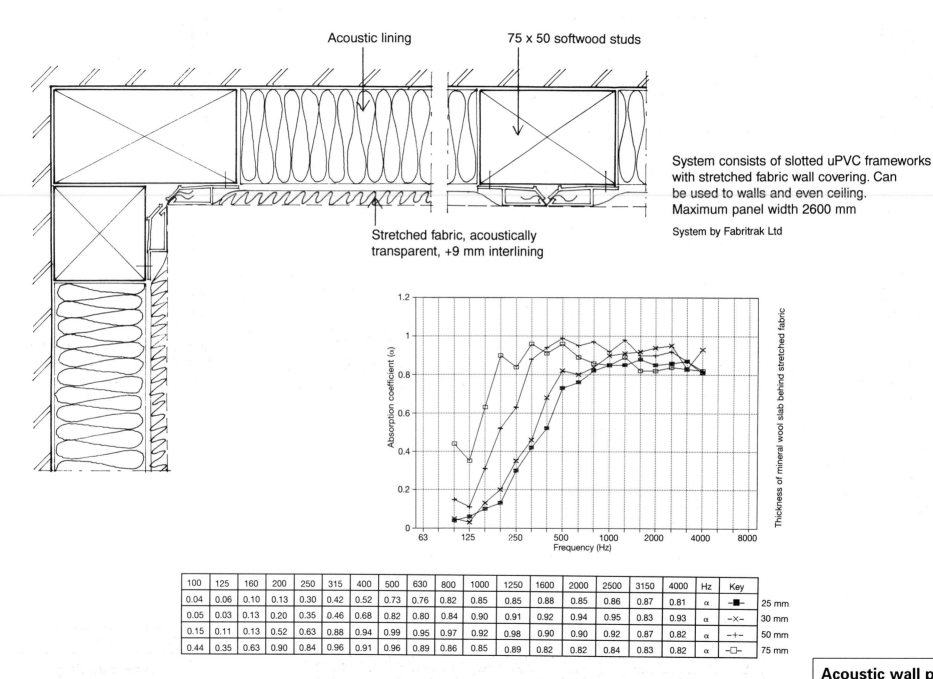

Acoustic lining

75 x 50 softwood studs

System consists of slotted uPVC frameworks with stretched fabric wall covering. Can be used to walls and even ceiling. Maximum panel width 2600 mm

System by Fabritrak Ltd

Stretched fabric, acoustically transparent, +9 mm interlining

Thickness of mineral wool slab behind stretched fabric

100	125	160	200	250	315	400	500	630	800	1000	1250	1600	2000	2500	3150	4000	Hz	Key	
0.04	0.06	0.10	0.13	0.30	0.42	0.52	0.73	0.76	0.82	0.85	0.85	0.88	0.85	0.86	0.87	0.81	α	–■–	25 mm
0.05	0.03	0.13	0.20	0.35	0.46	0.68	0.82	0.80	0.84	0.90	0.91	0.92	0.94	0.95	0.83	0.93	α	–×–	30 mm
0.15	0.11	0.13	0.52	0.63	0.88	0.94	0.99	0.95	0.97	0.92	0.98	0.90	0.90	0.92	0.87	0.82	α	–+–	50 mm
0.44	0.35	0.63	0.90	0.84	0.96	0.91	0.96	0.89	0.86	0.85	0.89	0.82	0.82	0.84	0.83	0.82	α	–□–	75 mm

Acoustic wall panels

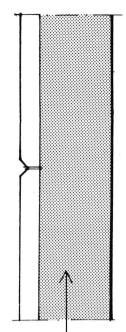
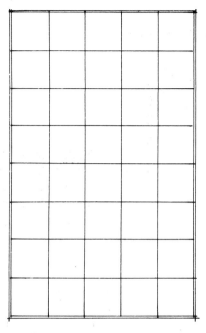

29 mm/ 40 kg/m² 'Coustone' tiles laid on spacers to 100 mm/ 60 kg/m³ mineral wool, to solid substrate

'Coustone' is a resin-bonded flint material which is hardwearing but can be used for both good sound absorption and sound insulation properties.

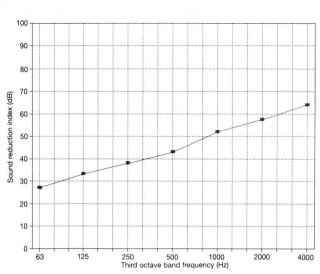

40 tiles, 500 x 500 mm. As arranged in sound absorption tests, edged with 18 mm thick timber boards

63	125	250	500	1000	2000	4000	Hz
27.2	33.4	38.1	43.2	52.1	57.6	64.1	dB

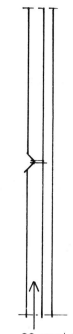

29 mm/ 40 kg/m² 'Coustone' tiles backed by 12 mm Carlite plaster. Arrangement for sound absorption tests.

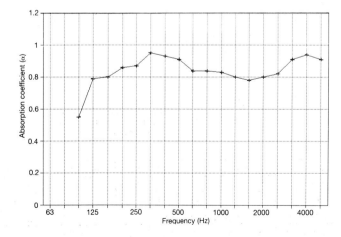

100	125	160	200	250	315	400	500	630	800	1000	1250	1600	2000	2500	3150	4000	5000
0.55	0.79	0.80	0.86	0.87	0.95	0.93	0.91	0.84	0.84	0.83	0.80	0.78	0.80	0.82	0.91	0.94	0.91

Source: Sound Absorption Ltd/ University of Salford

Wall cladding

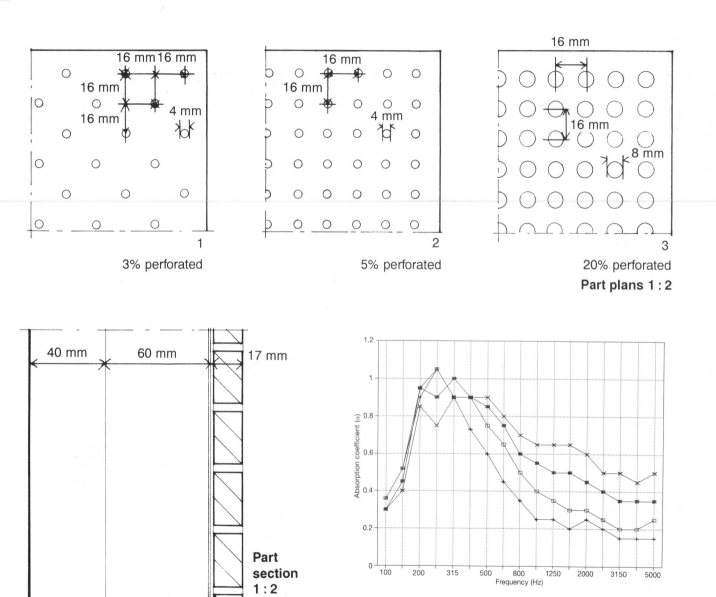

3% perforated

5% perforated

20% perforated

Part plans 1 : 2

Part section 1 : 2

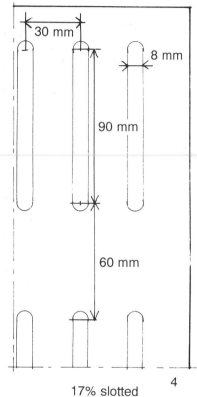

17% slotted

MDF boards faced in wood grain with different perforation patterns

Source: Société Industrielle Ober/ CEBTP

100	125	200	250	315	400	500	630	800	1000	1250	1600	2000	2500	3150	4000	5000	Hz	Key	
0.30	0.45	0.95	0.90	1.00	0.90	0.85	0.75	0.60	0.55	0.50	0.50	0.45	0.40	0.35	0.35	0.35	α	—■—	4
0.30	0.40	0.85	0.75	0.90	0.90	0.90	0.80	0.70	0.65	0.65	0.65	0.60	0.50	0.50	0.45	0.50	α	—×—	3
0.36	0.52	0.90	1.05	0.90	0.73	0.60	0.45	0.35	0.25	0.25	0.20	0.25	0.20	0.15	0.15	0.15	α	—+—	1
0.36	0.52	0.95	1.05	0.90	0.90	0.75	0.65	0.50	0.40	0.35	0.30	0.30	0.25	0.20	0.20	0.25	α	—□—	2

Wall cladding

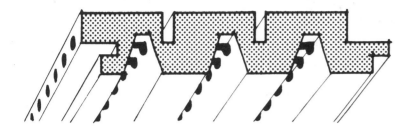

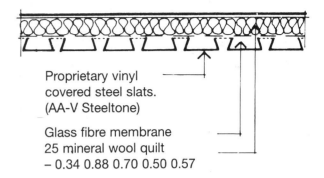

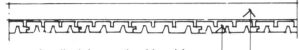

Applied Acoustics Venables
Profiled proprietary
hardwood panels
pattern perforated
as sketch

50 × 50 battens to ceiling (or wall)
0.1 0.35 0.80 0.40 0.25 0.35

Proprietary vinyl
covered steel slats.
(AA-V Steeltone)

Glass fibre membrane
25 mineral wool quilt
– 0.34 0.88 0.70 0.50 0.57

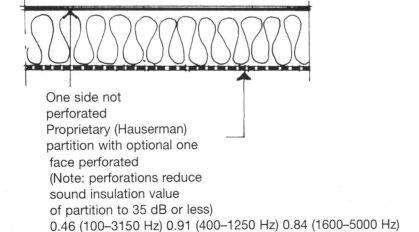

One side not
perforated
Proprietary (Hauserman)
partition with optional one
face perforated
(Note: perforations reduce
sound insulation value
of partition to 35 dB or less)
0.46 (100–3150 Hz) 0.91 (400–1250 Hz) 0.84 (1600–5000 Hz)

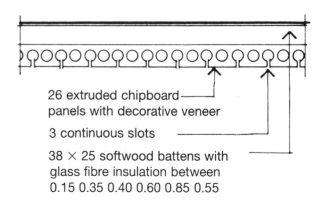

26 extruded chipboard
panels with decorative veneer

3 continuous slots

38 × 25 softwood battens with
glass fibre insulation between
0.15 0.35 0.40 0.60 0.85 0.55

Walls

Standard details

145

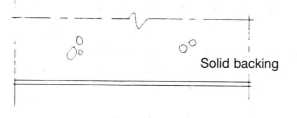

Solid backing

Medium weave
of curtains hung
in deep folds

Plan

Room elevation
Areas of curtains distributed
around are more effective
in terms of sound absorption
and give more even sound quality
than if concentrated in one area

1 Too loose a weave density
and material is acoustically
transparent

2 Medium weave gives much better
absorption than 1 or 3. Test by
trying to blow through material.
It should be possible to blow
through the fabric but with some
resistance: fabric has optimum
flow resistance to sound

3 Too tight a weave and the material
is only slightly sound absorptive

Best use of curtain is as in plan.
With medium weave free standing
divider curtains are less effective.
Curtains are a simple method of
providing an adaptable amount of
absorption, e.g. in music practice
rooms.
Curtain lining also improves sound
absorption.

100	125	160	200	250	315	400	500	630	800	1000	1250	1600	2000	2500	3150	4000	5000	Hz	Key
0.17	0.16	0.12	0.23	0.30	0.44	0.56	0.64	0.71	0.68	0.59	0.56	0.61	0.62	0.61	0.63	0.68	0.69	α	–+–	Curtain spaced 190 mm from solid wall
0.05	0.02	0.02	0.08	0.10	0.12	0.21	0.27	0.34	0.43	0.52	0.66	0.71	0.79	0.78	0.75	0.69	0.69	α	–■–	Curtain flush against wall

Source:
University of
Salford

Curtains

146

⅓OBCF. (Hz) Thickness	Key	100	125	160	200	250	315	400	500	630	800	1000	1250	1600	2000	2500	3150	4000	5000
25 mm	1	0.10	0.04	0.12	0.13	0.22	0.30	0.45	0.54	0.64	0.72	0.74	0.81	0.84	0.88	0.91	0.92	0.92	0.95
	2	0.13	0.12	0.18	0.22	0.28	0.32	0.46	0.55	0.63	0.61	0.71	0.68	0.72	0.74	0.79	0.82	0.83	0.90
	3	0.09	0.11	0.21	0.23	0.32	0.34	0.51	0.56	0.61	0.65	0.77	0.76	0.80	0.89	0.85	0.90	0.91	0.93
40 mm	4	0.10	0.15	0.20	0.30	0.40	0.60	0.70	0.80	0.95	0.90	1	1	1	0.95	0.95	0.85	0.90	1
	5	0.10	0.15	0.20	0.35	0.45	0.60	0.70	0.95	1	1	1	1	1	1	0.95	0.95	1	0.95
50 mm	1	0.15	0.12	0.28	0.34	0.54	0.80	0.92	0.97	0.99	1	1	1	1	0.99	0.99	0.99	1	0.99
	2	0.18	0.17	0.31	0.48	0.45	0.55	0.76	0.80	0.88	0.86	0.89	0.92	0.96	0.97	0.95	0.99	0.94	0.91
	3	0.20	0.27	0.39	0.46	0.54	0.68	0.95	0.94	0.89	1	1	1	1	0.96	1	1	0.99	0.99
	4	0.15	0.20	0.30	0.40	0.55	0.80	0.95	1	1	1	1	1	1	1	1	1	1	1
	5	0.25	0.30	0.55	0.65	0.80	1	1	1	1	1	1	1	1	1	1	1	1	1
75 mm	2	0.29	0.30	0.57	0.64	0.69	0.76	1	0.94	1	0.93	1	0.98	0.98	1	0.99	1	1	1
	3	0.28	0.28	0.56	0.73	0.79	0.98	1	1	1	1	1	1	1	1	1	1	1	0.97
	4	0.30	0.37	0.42	0.76	0.85	0.93	1	1	1	1	1	1	1	1	1	1	1	1
	5	0.24	0.43	0.48	0.88	0.97	1	1	1	1	1	1	1	1	1	1	1	1	1
100 mm	1	0.26	0.20	0.47	0.63	0.84	1	1	1	1	1	1	1	1	1	1	1	0.97	0.92
	2	0.38	0.43	0.80	0.81	0.86	1	1	1	1	1	1	1	1	1	1	1	1	1
	3	0.40	0.46	0.80	0.94	1	1	1	1	1	1	1	1	1	1	1	1	1	0.97
	4	0.53	0.53	0.73	1	0.92	1	1	1	1	1	1	1	1	1	1	1	1	1

Sound absorption values for mineral wool and glass fibre are very similar for the same thickness and similar densities.

At lower densities, glass fibre holds together better in quilt form whereas at higher densities there is greater choice in panels or batts of mineral wool.

Fibre migration is of concern for either material or tissue facing, in the case of attenuator linings held in by perforated metal.

Recent elastic foams are also acceptable regarding acoustic and fire properties, without loose strands.

Any decorative facings should be acoustically transparent. It may be seen that there is little benefit at speech frequencies for absorption thickness exceeding 50 mm.

Source: University of Salford/The Noise Control Centre

Key
1 11 kg/m³ Melatech foam (melamine-based elastic foam)
2 16 kg/m³ Gypglas 1605 (Glass fibre quilt)
3 24 kg/m³ Gypglas 2405
4 33 kg/m³ Gypglas 3205
5 48 kg/m³ Gypglas 4805

Measured absorption coefficients exceeding 1.0 rounded to 1.

Sound absorptive lining

Absorption coefficients from a variety of tests

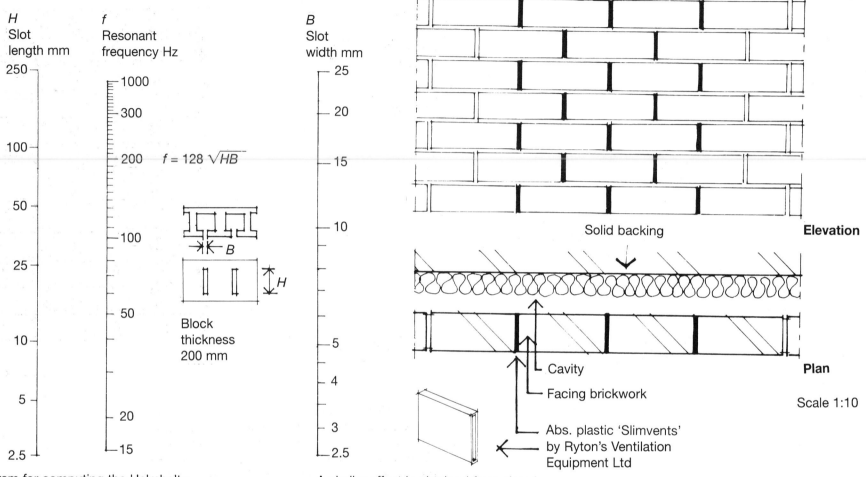

H
Slot
length mm

250

100

50

25

10

5

2.5

f
Resonant
frequency Hz

1000

300

200

100

50

20

15

$$f = 128 \sqrt{HB}$$

Block
thickness
200 mm

B
Slot
width mm

25

20

15

10

5

4

3

2.5

Solid backing

Elevation

Cavity

Facing brickwork

Abs. plastic 'Slimvents'
by Ryton's Ventilation
Equipment Ltd

Plan

Scale 1:10

Nomogram for computing the Helmholtz
frequency for slotted hollow concrete
block. (Source: Herrick Laboratories,
Purdue University Indiana US)
Absorption coefficients for slotted 200
block filled with incombustible fibrous
material (125 to 4000 Hz):
0.72   0.55   0.42   0.34   0.35   0.34

A similar effect is obtained from slots in
brickwork with cavity behind (Note: leaf
ineffective for sound reduction between
spaces). To assess absorption characteristics
laboratory tests are required for the brick,
spacing and slot pattern proposed. Application:
selective absorption at low frequencies.

**Sound
absorptive walling**

'Acoustic Bricks' by Blockleys Ltd., Telford
Type: BA1

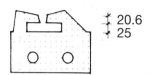

20.6
25

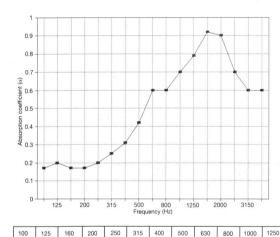

Absorption coefficient
of standard fairfaced
brickwork

100	125	160	200	250	315	400	500	630	800	1000	1250	1600	2000	2500	3150	4000	Hz
0.17	0.2	0.17	0.17	0.2	0.25	0.31	0.42	0.6	0.6	0.7	0.79	0.92	0.9	0.7	0.6	0.6	α

BA2

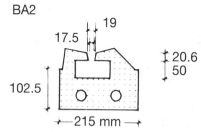

19
17.5
20.6
50
102.5
← 215 mm →

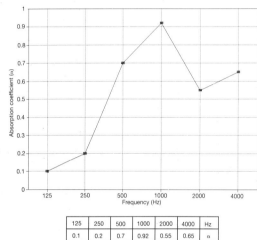

125	250	500	1000	2000	4000	Hz
0.1	0.2	0.7	0.92	0.55	0.65	α

BA3

8.7   9.5

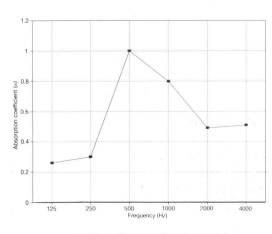

125	250	500	1000	2000	4000	Hz
0.26	0.3	1.0	0.8	0.49	0.51	α

Special design bricks may be considered to 'soften'
the sound quality of a space where hard finishes
are required. A mix of the three types will achieve
good sound absorption in the range 500–2000 Hz.
Angled faces help diffuse incident sound. More costly
than slots between standard bricks, but advantageous
in that wall retains some sound insulation value.

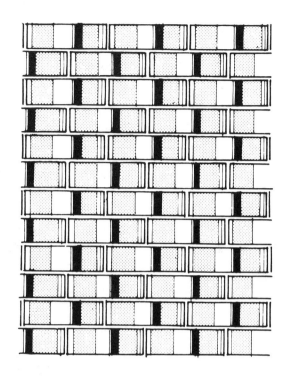

Elevation

Scale 1:10

**Sound
absorptive walling**

149

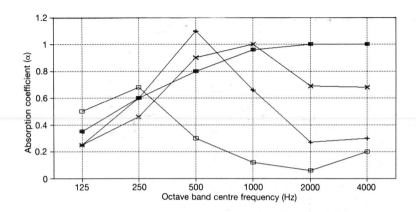

125	250	500	1000	2000	4000	Hz	Key	
0.35	0.6	0.8	0.96	1.0	1.0	α	–■–	1
0.25	0.46	0.9	1.0	0.69	0.68	α	–×–	2
0.25	0.6	1.1	0.66	0.27	0.30	α	–+–	3
0.5	0.68	0.3	0.12	0.06	0.20	α	–□–	4

Wall panels can be designed to provide absorption over a narrow range of frequencies by adjusting the gap between planks. The principle of the slit resonator is the same as for a Helmholtz resonator, resonant frequency being dependent on slit width depth and cross-sectional area of the space behind the slits formed by the planks.

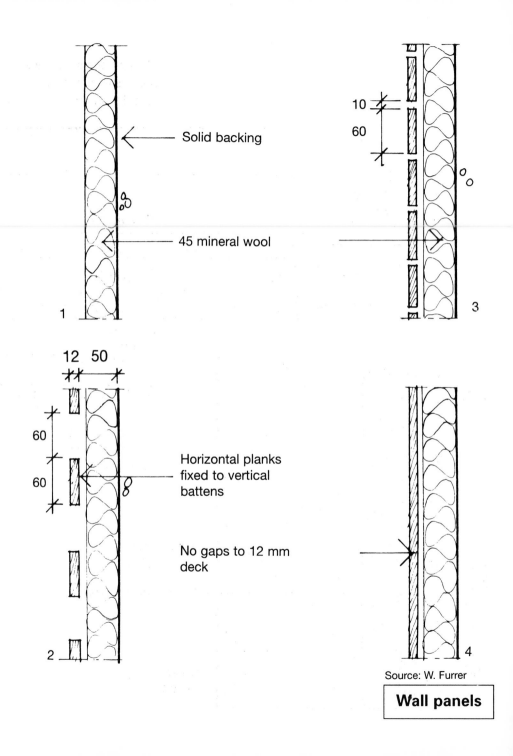

Source: W. Furrer

Wall panels

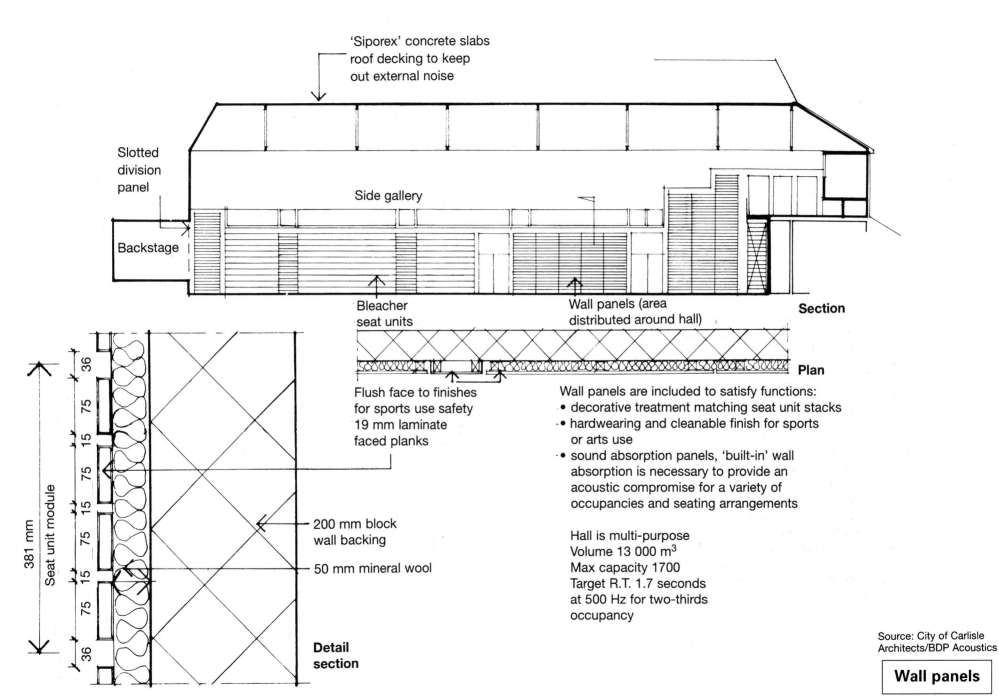

'Siporex' concrete slabs roof decking to keep out external noise

Slotted division panel

Side gallery

Backstage

Bleacher seat units

Wall panels (area distributed around hall)

Section

Plan

Flush face to finishes for sports use safety 19 mm laminate faced planks

36

75

15

75

15

75

15

75

15

75

36

381 mm

Seat unit module

200 mm block wall backing

50 mm mineral wool

Detail section

Wall panels are included to satisfy functions:
- decorative treatment matching seat unit stacks
- hardwearing and cleanable finish for sports or arts use
- sound absorption panels, 'built-in' wall absorption is necessary to provide an acoustic compromise for a variety of occupancies and seating arrangements

Hall is multi-purpose
Volume 13 000 m^3
Max capacity 1700
Target R.T. 1.7 seconds
at 500 Hz for two-thirds
occupancy

Source: City of Carlisle Architects/BDP Acoustics

Wall panels

151

Installations, Furnishings

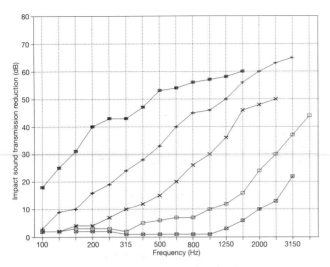

100	125	160	200	250	315	400	500	630	800	1000	1250	1600	2000	2500	3150	4000	Hz	Key	
18	23	31	40	43	43	47	53	54	56	57	58	60	–	–	–	–	dB	–■–	Thick carpet + underlay
3	9	10	16	19	24	28	33	40	45	46	50	56	60	63	65	–	dB	–+–	Thick carpet
2	2	4	4	7	10	12	15	20	26	30	36	46	48	50	–	–	dB	–×–	Contract carpet
2	2	3	3	3	2	5	6	7	7	10	12	16	24	30	37	44	dB	–□–	Backed vinyl sheet
–	–	2	2	2	1	1	1	1	1	1	1	3	6	10	13	22	–	dB	–⊠–	Linoleum

125	250	500	1000	2000	4000	Hz	Key	
0.03	0.3	0.58	0.9	0.92	0.85	α	–■–	Thick carpet + underlay
0.02	0.1	0.18	0.32	0.55	0.85	α	–×–	Thick carpet
0.01	0.04	0.39	0.42	0.43	0.41	α	–+–	Thin carpet + bonded underlay
0.01	0.01	0.02	0.1	0.43	0.77	α	–□–	Corded contract carpet

Carpet

Carpet is useful for both impact sound reduction [footfall and to floor below] and for sound absorption. Values are shown in appendix but for thin carpet on solid backing [typical office for lease] values are low for low and mid frequencies. Carpet is sometimes used as a hardwearing wall finish, for example in cinemas. Carpets on thin wall panels give a broader frequency performance.

Vinyl sheet

Cushioned vinyl sheet only 3 mm thick (Polytread or sim.) on a concrete slab can give impact sound transmission performance, exceeding Grade I Building Regulations. This is a useful material for hospitals, schools and old people's homes where carpet cannot be used.

Finishes [BRS103 definition]

Soft: cushioned vinyl sheet. Thin carpet with underlay. Thick carpet with or without underlay, cork tiles over 8 mm tiles.

Source: SRL/
Tretford Carpets

Floor finishes

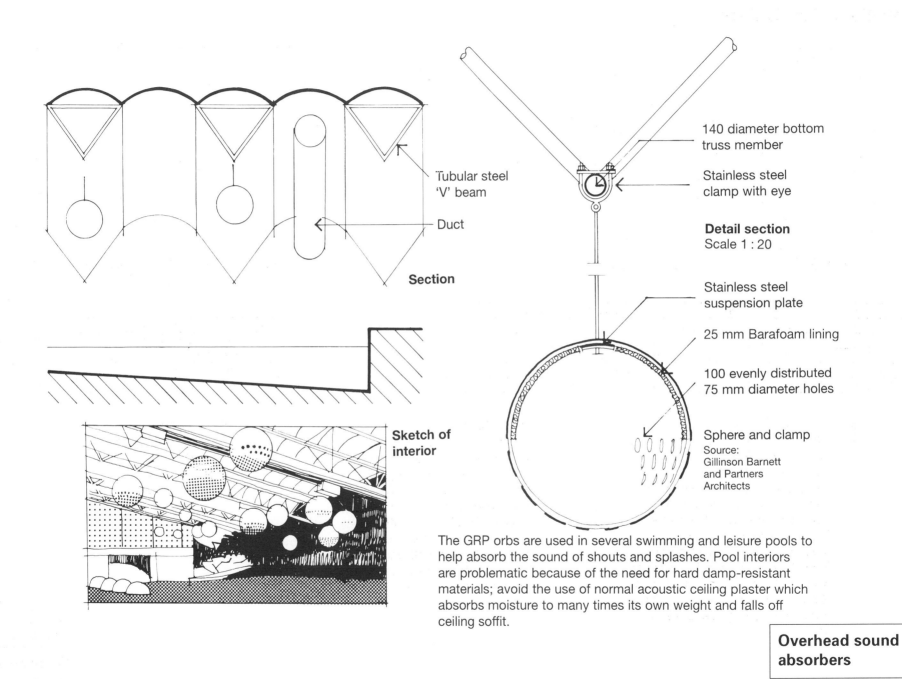

Section

Tubular steel 'V' beam

Duct

Sketch of interior

140 diameter bottom truss member

Stainless steel clamp with eye

Detail section
Scale 1 : 20

Stainless steel suspension plate

25 mm Barafoam lining

100 evenly distributed 75 mm diameter holes

Sphere and clamp
Source:
Gillinson Barnett and Partners Architects

The GRP orbs are used in several swimming and leisure pools to help absorb the sound of shouts and splashes. Pool interiors are problematic because of the need for hard damp-resistant materials; avoid the use of normal acoustic ceiling plaster which absorbs moisture to many times its own weight and falls off ceiling soffit.

Overhead sound absorbers

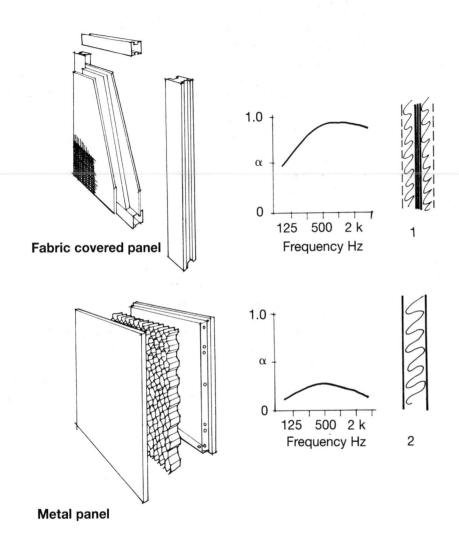

Fabric covered panel

α

1.0

0

125 500 2 k
Frequency Hz

1

Metal panel

α

1.0

0

125 500 2 k
Frequency Hz

2

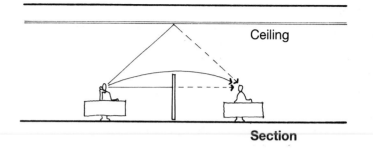

Ceiling

Section

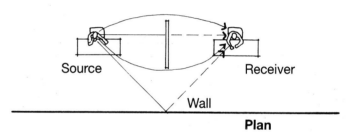

Source

Receiver

Wall

Plan

For a reasonable spacing of occupants, e.g. 12–14 m²/person sound attenuation between workplaces only 20–25 dBA max, empirical formula to check adequate privacy: background noise (dBA)+ sound attenuation ⩾75. By this criterion many offices have an ambient level too low and masking sound may be considered.

In choosing partition systems or divider panels, look for sandwich of absorption-solid core-absorption if a good absorption rating (over 0.6) is required. Both example 1 and 2 above are effective as screens. Good absorption at 1–2 kHz important to mask speech.

Open-plan offices

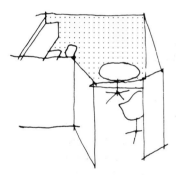

Enclose noisy activities, use screens extending to floor.

L-shaped workspaces afford privacy

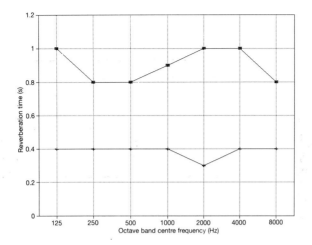

125	250	500	1000	2000	4000	8000	Hz	Key
1.0	0.8	0.8	0.9	1.0	1.0	0.8	s	–■–
0.4	0.4	0.4	0.4	0.3	0.4	0.4	s	–+–

Measured reverberation times in open-plan offices 12 m wide with columns on 4 m grid, ceiling height 3 m. Suspended ceiling of mineral tiles. Carpet tiles floor finish. Measurements in empty office (–■–) and with occupied workstations, filled shelves, and loose chairs (–+–) (Source: BDP)

Selection of work angles allows variety, inward face for privacy.

Design guide

1. Design in a space over 11 metres wide.
2. Plan 12 m²/person including circulation.
3. Zone office machines apart and screen.
4. Develop 'arena' orientation layouts.
5. Contain background sound level within range 40–50 dBA.
6. Develop good screen layouts, avoid 'spokes' and 'cubicles'.
7. Locate acoustic panels around sound sources to be controlled: within 1200 mm.
8. Designate one-third of panels to be acoustic rather than hard surface.
9. Choose high (2100) panels where workers stand or circulate.
10. Choose a high-absorption ceiling.
11. Choose a thick carpet on a dense underlay.
12. Consider whether masking background sound may be necessary.
13. Minimize noise from impulse or intermittent source – telephones, typewriters, computers.
14. Check for speech privacy: good if a listener 5 metres from a person reading at normal conversational level can only understand 10% of speech (standard speech articulation test). Increase absorptive screens if necessary.
15. Check reverberation times: general office desired mid-frequency 0.70 seconds. Executive offices 0.5 sec, open plan 0.45 sec.

Source: Herman Miller Research Corporation

Open-plan offices

155

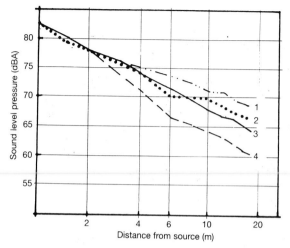

1

Sound level pressure (dBA) vs Distance from source (m)

1. Open gangway, untreated factory
2. Across benches, untreated factory
3. Open gangway, absorbent-lined factory
4. Across machines, absorbent_lined machines

Source: P. Wilson
Lucas Industrial Noise Centre

Factory type	Decay rate: dB/doubling distance
Hard empty	–3
Hard with scatter elements	–4
Absorbent lined empty	–4
Absorbent lined with scatter elements	–5

2

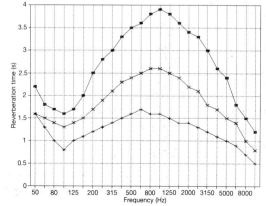

3

Factory 45 × 43 × 43 m
hard finishes

Source: M. Hodgson
University of Cambridge

Design guide

1. Where employees exposed to ≥ 8 hr leq. of 85 dB (A), noise reduction measures to be taken as far as reasonably practicable. Ear defenders to be worn.
EC proposal for Council Directive (18 October 1982): daily exposure must not exceed 85 dB (A) but to take account of feasibility, 5 years were allowed for implementation.

2. Classical description of sound in enclosures (e.g. Sabine) not applicable. Tendency for absence of constant reverberant sound level outside direct sound field of sources. This means absorbent treatments do not necessarily produce marked sound level reductions if remote.

3. Lack of reverberant sound field means zoning of noisy from quiet processes and local screening are effective measures.

4. Overhead suspended absorbers coupled with local screening are often the best form of incorporating sound absorption.

5. Operator experience of noise is not improved by treatment in factory space – no variation in decay rate > 2 m (1.).

6. For decay rate from an omnidirectional source in a factory space, guide lines (2.) may be considered.

7. Machinery and plant themselves provide significant scatter and absorption (3.).

50	63	80	100	125	160	200	250	315	400	500	630	800	1000	1250	1600	2000	2500	3150	4000	5000	6300	8000	10,000	Hz	Key	
2.2	1.8	1.7	1.6	1.7	2.0	2.5	2.8	3.0	3.3	3.5	3.6	3.8	3.9	3.8	3.6	3.4	3.3	3.0	2.6	2.4	1.8	1.5	1.2	s	–■–	No machines
1.6	1.5	1.4	1.3	1.4	1.5	1.7	1.9	2.1	2.3	2.4	2.5	2.6	2.6	2.5	2.4	2.2	2.1	1.8	1.7	1.5	1.4	1.0	0.8	s	–×–	25 machines
1.6	1.3	1.0	0.8	1.0	1.1	1.2	1.3	1.4	1.5	1.6	1.7	1.6	1.6	1.5	1.4	1.4	1.3	1.2	1.1	1.0	0.9	0.7	0.5	s	–+–	50 machines

Absorption of machines within a factory interior.

Industrial buildings

156

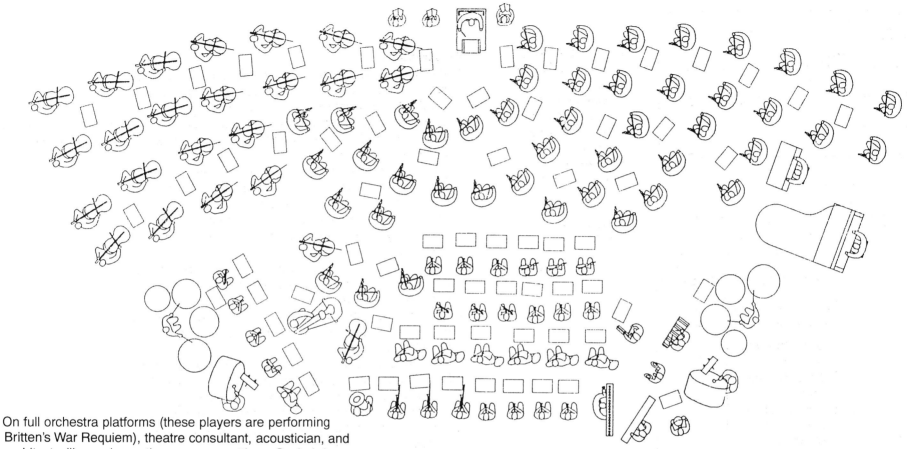

On full orchestra platforms (these players are performing Britten's War Requiem), theatre consultant, acoustician, and architect will examine optimum venue settings. Scaled-down ensembles could be planned using these musician templates with allowances:

1.25 m² upper string and wind instruments
5 m² cello and larger wind instruments
1.8 m² double bass
10 m² timpani
20 m² other percussion
0.5 m² each choir member

100 mm/rise should be used in elevating rear sections, riser widths being 1.25 m for upper strings and woodwind, 1.4 m for brass and cellos, 0.8 m for choir rows. A platform size of 190 m² will hold a 100-piece orchestra, <17 m width and 11 m depth. Side wall optimum angles (diffusing/modelling profile) 16°–17° on plan.

Choral soloists

Strings	Bassoons
Timpani	English horn
Percussion	Oboes
(organ)	Flutes
Pianoforte	Harp
Tuba	Clarinets
Trombones	Double bassoon
Trumpets	(chorus)
Horns	

Scale 1:100

Orchestra layout

Seats: front row ASL10 portable/stacking chair
Second row: ASL10 retractable folding chair
Third row: ASL10 fixed chair
Fourth row: ASL10 fixed chair (high back)
Riser heights 265 mm, tiers 850 mm wide
except rear tier, 915 mm
Absorption tests in the laboratory (BS 3638) demand
an area of at least 10 m² and edge barriers, to avoid
edge absorption. This test of four rows of six seats
reflects the typical mix of seats in a hall, including
stepped platforms. Because of their significant surface
area, seat characteristics are a key influence on
auditorium acoustics.

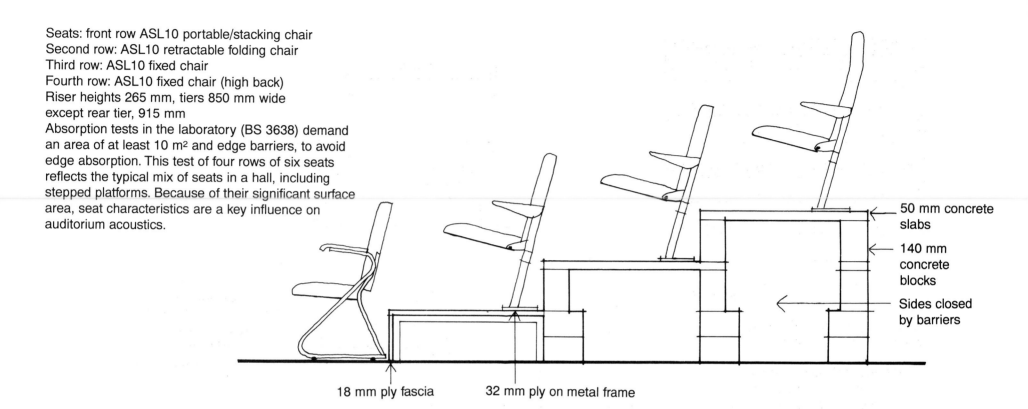

50 mm concrete slabs

140 mm concrete blocks

Sides closed by barriers

18 mm ply fascia

32 mm ply on metal frame

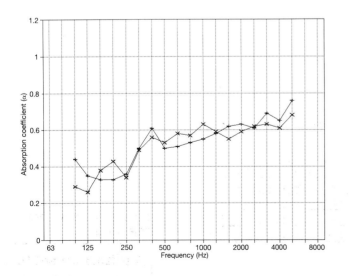

100	125	160	200	250	315	400	500	630	800	1000	1250	1600	2000	2500	3150	4000	5000	Hz	Key	
0.44	0.35	0.33	0.33	0.36	0.50	0.61	0.50	0.51	0.53	0.55	0.58	0.62	0.63	0.61	0.69	0.65	0.76	α	−+−	1
0.29	0.26	0.38	0.43	0.34	0.49	0.56	0.53	0.58	0.57	0.63	0.59	0.55	0.59	0.62	0.63	0.61	0.68	α	−×−	2

1 Unoccupied seats on tiers
2 Occupied seats on tiers

Source: Auditoria Services Ltd/
University of Salford

Auditorium seating

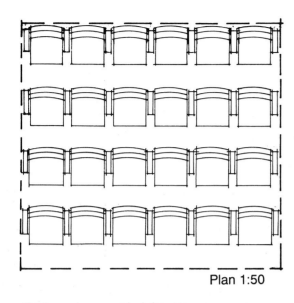

Plan 1:50

Test arrangement in laboratory
3.4 m wide x 3.2 m long

These tests of 'spare' seats from
a major concert hall were used
in a research programme looking
at the effects of edge barriers,
occupying seats and corner-room
placement. For technique, see
'Measuring Auditorium Seat
Absorption', *Journal of Acoustical
Society of America*, August 1994,
96 (2), pp. 879-888.

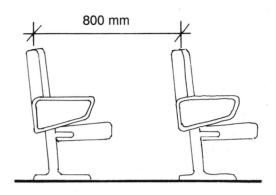

800 mm

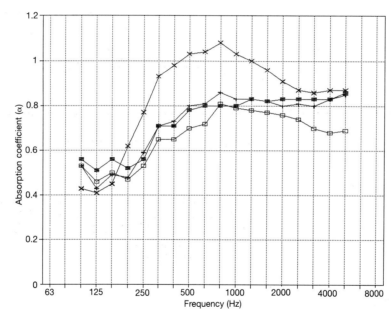

1 Occupied concert hall seats
  in corner, with barriers

2 Unoccupied seats in laboratory
  room centre, with barriers

3 Unoccupied seats in room
  centre, no barriers

4 Unoccupied seats in corner,
  with barriers

100	125	160	200	250	315	400	500	630	800	1000	1250	1600	2000	2500	3150	4000	5000	Hz	Key	
0.56	0.51	0.56	0.52	0.56	0.71	0.71	0.78	0.80	0.80	0.80	0.83	0.82	0.83	0.83	0.83	0.83	0.86	dB	—■—	1
0.53	0.43	0.49	0.48	0.59	0.71	0.73	0.80	0.81	0.86	0.83	0.83	0.82	0.80	0.81	0.80	0.83	0.85	dB	—+—	2
0.43	0.41	0.45	0.62	0.77	0.93	0.98	1.03	1.04	1.08	1.03	1.00	0.96	0.91	0.87	0.86	0.87	0.87	dB	—×—	3
0.53	0.46	0.50	0.47	0.53	0.65	0.65	0.70	0.72	0.81	0.79	0.78	0.77	0.76	0.74	0.70	0.68	0.69	dB	—□—	4

Source: University of Salford/
BDP Acoustics

Auditorium seating

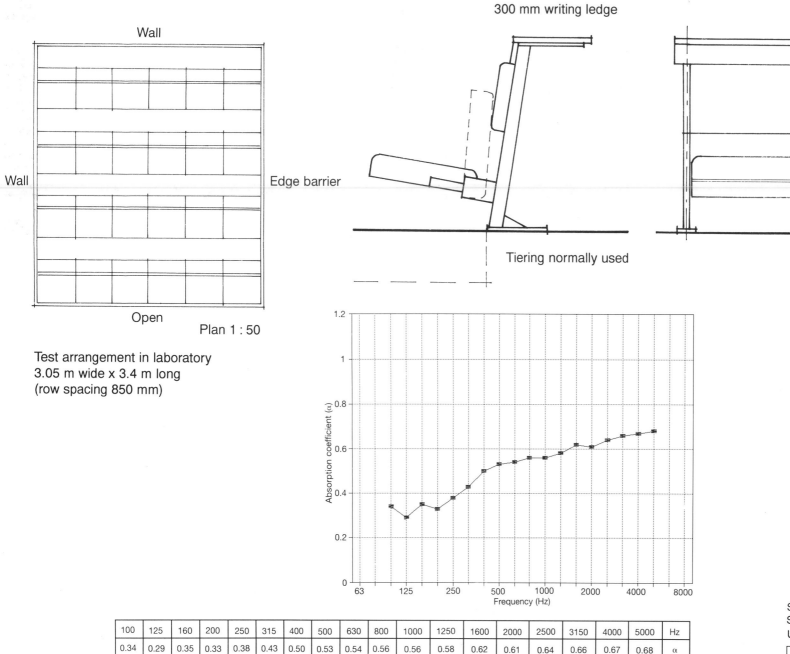

Wall

Wall

Open

Edge barrier

Plan 1 : 50

Test arrangement in laboratory
3.05 m wide x 3.4 m long
(row spacing 850 mm)

300 mm writing ledge

Tiering normally used

100	125	160	200	250	315	400	500	630	800	1000	1250	1600	2000	2500	3150	4000	5000	Hz
0.34	0.29	0.35	0.33	0.38	0.43	0.50	0.53	0.54	0.56	0.56	0.58	0.62	0.61	0.64	0.66	0.67	0.68	α

Source: Hussey Seating
Systems (Europe)) Ltd/
University of Salford

Lecture theatre seating

4 SERVICES

Criteria

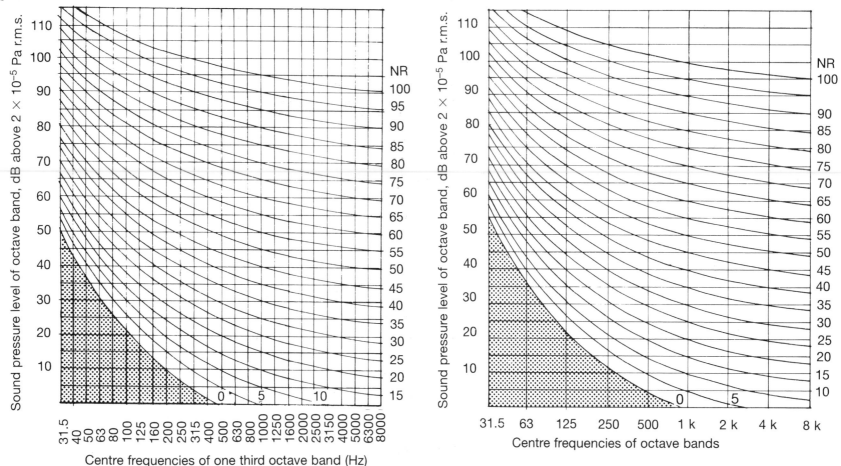

Centre frequencies of one third octave band (Hz)

Centre frequencies of octave bands

Noise rating curves

It is convenient to specify the level of a particular noise by equal loudness contours which recognize that the subjective response by the ear is to find low-frequency noise less noticeable than high frequency for the same sound power level. The contours above are noise rating (NR) curves, another form is PNC curves which are very similar at most frequencies. Curves can be used to monitor that the ambient sound level in a space is not at an unsuitably high level due to external, ventilation, machinery or adjacent room noises. The maximum band level of the noise spectral distribution determines its NR curve rating. Sound insulation values can be used to check sound penetrating at each frequency band.

Noise measurement

162

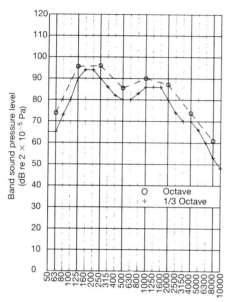

1/3 Octave band centre frequency (Hz)

Comparison of the same
noise measured: octave
and one-third octave
spectra.

Noise analysis in a canteen

Care should be taken that figures used are for
octave band analysis as one-third octave
band requires use of the above set of NR curves.
Because of the reduced band-width component
individual levels are 4.8 dB/octave down and
the one-third octave NR curves allow for this
when one-third octave band levels are added
together. A higher figure results as the level
over the whole frequency range.

Recommended noise ratings

For ambient noise control to suit use	NR
Studios spaces for recording or broadcast	15
Concert halls	15–20
Theatres, multi-purpose halls, conference rooms, court rooms	25
Hospital wards, hotel bedrooms, libraries	25–30
Classrooms, meeting rooms for small groups, executive offices, homes	30
Restaurants, open plan and general offices	35
Cafeterias, circulation	40
Kitchens, toilets and workshops, computer rooms	45
Car parks, shopping malls, bus, rail or airport concourses	50
Office (print rooms)	55
Workshops, industrial process	65

Desirable dB (A) criteria 5–10 above
recommended NR level, depending on noise spectrum

Noise measurement

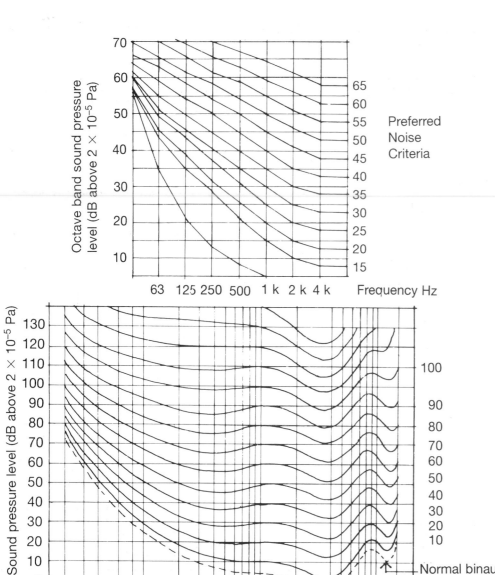

Reference curves

NR curves tend to be used in Europe, whereas in the USA the 1971 Preferred Noise Criteria (PNC) curves have replaced the earlier Noise Criterion (NC) curves. They have, however, not received universal acceptance. Comparison with the Equal Loudness Contours shows the intention of either set of curves to reflect the different sensitivity of the ear at different parts of the frequency range.

Criteria values (in dB)

Criterion value	Criterion	OBCF (Hz)								
		31.5	63	125	250	500	1 k	2 k	4 k	8 k
15	NR	66	47	35	26	19	15	12	9	7
	PNC	58	43	35	28	21	15	10	8	8
20	NR	69	51	39	31	24	20	17	14	13
	PNC	59	46	39	32	26	20	15	13	13
25	NR	72	55	44	35	29	25	22	20	18
	PNC	60	49	43	37	31	25	20	18	18
30	NR	76	59	48	40	34	30	27	25	23
	PNC	61	52	46	41	35	30	25	23	23
35	NR	79	63	52	45	39	35	32	30	28
	PNC	62	55	50	45	40	35	30	28	28
40	NR	83	67	57	49	44	40	37	35	33
	PNC	64	59	54	50	45	40	36	33	33
45	NR	86	71	61	54	49	45	42	40	38
	PNC	67	63	58	54	50	45	41	38	38

Noise measurement

In the absence of international standards in general use for measuring services noise, the Association of Noise Consultants (ANC) have brought out guidelines. These notes are an extract only. 'Steady' noise is that free of audible fluctuations in level or frequency content.

'Minimum', 'maximum' or 'peak' levels should not be used. Specific noise levels and residual (background in absence of specific) noise levels should be taken, with plant at normal duty, then 'off'.

Measure at the noisiest normally occupied room position, or on a grid across a large room. Microphone height 1.2–1.5 m, and more than 1.5 m from noise source, or 1 m from reflecting surfaces.

Measuring equipment should be types 0, 1 or 2 in BS 5969, octave filter sets BS 2475, calibrators IEC, Class 0 or 1.

Confidence limits of readings

Sound level meter type	Instrumentation confidence limit (+/–)
Type 0	
31.5–63 Hz	1.0 dB
125 Hz–2 kHz	0.7 dB
4 kHz*	1.2 dB
8 kHz*	2.2 dB
Type 1	
31.5–63 Hz	1.5 dB
125 Hz–2 kHz	1.0 dB
4 kHz*	1.5 dB
8 kHz*	2.5 dB
Type 2	
31.5–63 Hz	1.8 dB
125 Hz–2 kHz	1.3 dB
4 kHz*	3.3 dB
8 kHz*	8.3 dB

*The figures at 4 kHz and 8 kHz apply to non-reverberant conditions and cases where the measurement position is close to a dominant noise source. These will therefore apply in most cases. In reverberant conditions away from dominant noise sources, the limits for the range 125 Hz to 2 kHz apply.

It has been assumed that a Class 1 calibrator will be used. If a Class 0 calibrator is used, 0.1 dB should be deducted from the figures in the table.

The figures in this table have been developed with due regard to figures set out in BS 5969, and are in accordance with the general experience of ANC members. In particular, the table assumes that in non-diffuse fields, the microphone is to be pointed towards the dominant noise source or within an angle of +/– 30 degrees, and that a free-field microphone is used to comply with BS 5969.

Measuring building services noise pressure levels

Type of noise	Continuous	Intermittent
Steady	$L_{90,T}$[1]. T not less than 10 seconds.	As for continuous steady noise – measure both with plant on (or high) and off (or low) [2].
Non-steady	$L_{eq,30s}$[3] and	As for continuous non-steady noise – measure both with with plant on (or high) and off (or low)[2].
	Highest $L_{eq,1s}$ over a 30 s period[4]	
	Where the noise cycles over a period of more than 30 s, measure both when the noise is at the highest and lowest points of the cycle [5].	
Impulsive	As for non-steady, continuous noise.	As for non-steady, intermittent noise[2].

[1] Minimum slow SPL may be used as a general indication of levels but in the event of dispute $L_{90,T}$ is preferred. It should be noted that if another parameter L_n is measured and the resulting levels are below those specified, where n<90, the L_{90} must also be below the specified levels (e.g. $L_{90}<L_{10}$). It may also be assumed that the L_{eq} level is above the L_{90} level for any source likely to be measured.
[2] Where levels are not specified for masking noise, it will normally be sufficient to measure only in the 'on' or 'high' condition.

[3] For L_{eq} and L_n measurements, the sound level meter should be set to F time weighting.

[4] An approximation to the highest $L_{eq,1s}$ may be achieved by measuring $L_{1,100s}$ or maximum slow SPL but the latter is not the preferred method as this quantity is not standardized and may vary between different meters. In the event of a dispute, therefore, the use of $L_{eq,1s}$ is preferred.

[5] Consultants may also find it instructive to measure and record $L_{90,30s}$ as this may lead to an objective method of assessing the steadiness of noise.

Measurements to check compliance with criteria

Type of noise	Continuous	Intermittent
Steady	Measured $L_{90,10s}$ not to exceed specified level.	Highest measured $L_{90,10s}$ not to exceed specified level.
Non-steady	$L_{eq,30s}$ not to exceed specified level. Highest value of $L_{eq,1s}$ not to exceed specified level by more than 2 dB in any octave band. [1]	As for continuous non-steady noise.
Impulsive	As for non-steady, continuous noise but 5[2] (NR, NC, dB(A), etc.) to be deducted from specified level.	As for non-steady, intermittent noise but 5[2] (NR, NC, dB(A), etc.) to be deducted from specified level.
Tonal	If in addition to its other attributes the noise is tonal, 5[2] units (NR, NC, dB(A), etc.) to be deducted from the specified level. (Where the noise is both tonal and impulsive, the overall correction is 10 units.)	

[1] Where the specified levels are only in terms of dB(A), the highest value of $L_{eq,1s}$ is not to exceed the specified criterion by more than 2 dB(A).

[2] This is consistent with corrections proposed in CIBSE Guide A1.

Measuring services noise

Ducts and Pipes

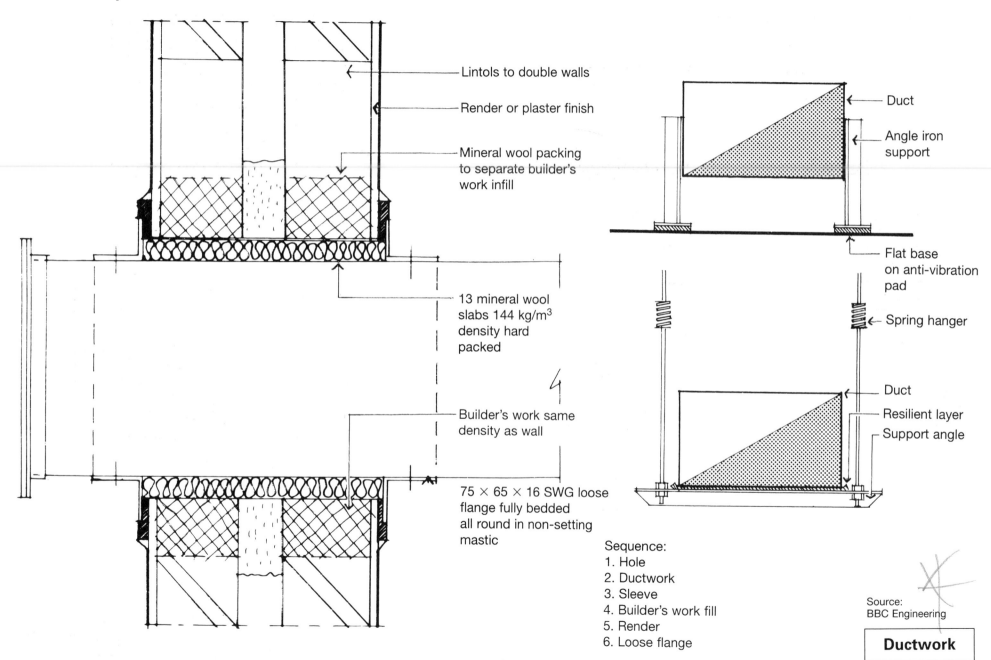

Lintols to double walls

Render or plaster finish

Mineral wool packing to separate builder's work infill

13 mineral wool slabs 144 kg/m³ density hard packed

Builder's work same density as wall

75 × 65 × 16 SWG loose flange fully bedded all round in non-setting mastic

Duct

Angle iron support

Flat base on anti-vibration pad

Spring hanger

Duct

Resilient layer

Support angle

Sequence:
1. Hole
2. Ductwork
3. Sleeve
4. Builder's work fill
5. Render
6. Loose flange

Source:
BBC Engineering

Ductwork

Round versus rectangular ducts

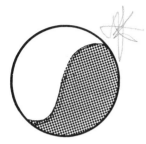 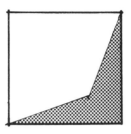 

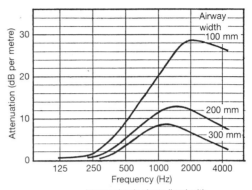

Attenuation in ducts lined with
25 mm mineral wool

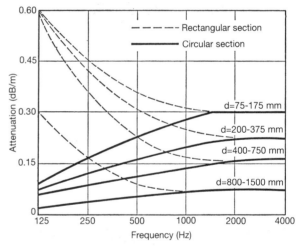

Attenuation in unlined ducts of
minimum width d.

Circular ducts are
inherently rigid and of
minimum perimeter
for sectional area:
noise is contained
within rather than
transmitted through
duct to space. Use of
circular ductwork
may therefore be
preferable for
exposed installations.
Circular attenuators
tend to be less efficient:
often transformation pieces
from circular ductwork to
rectangular silencers are
used in practice.

Rectangular ducts
have less rigid walls
and noise within excites
the flat metal sections.
This gives useful low
frequency attenuation
along ducts. There is also
a larger internal area
for lining with mineral
wool: use of square or
rectangular ductwork is
best for installations mounted
in ceilings. Supplying or
extracting air at a low noise
level, inherent attenuation
may allow economy of
attenuators along ducts. Lining
ducts is particularly effective
for small ducts and for higher
frequencies.

Ductwork

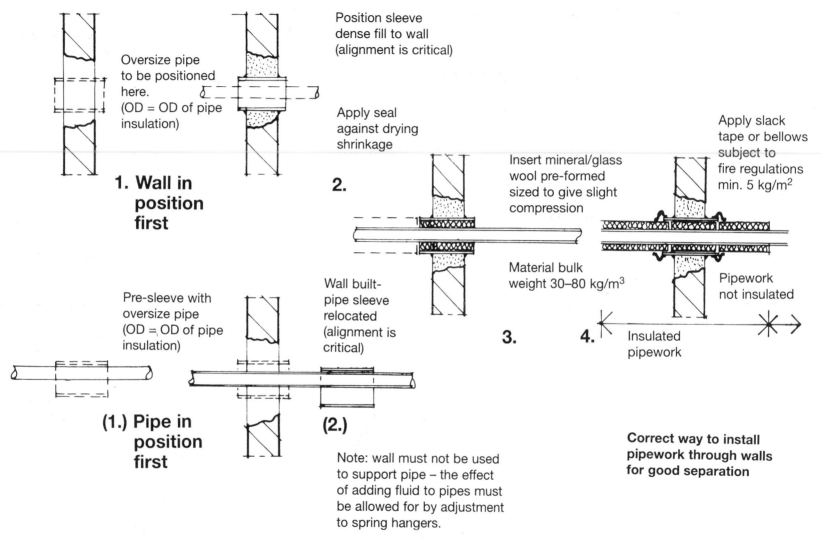

Oversize pipe to be positioned here. (OD = OD of pipe insulation)

1. Wall in position first

Position sleeve dense fill to wall (alignment is critical)

Apply seal against drying shrinkage

2.

Pre-sleeve with oversize pipe (OD = OD of pipe insulation)

(1.) Pipe in position first

Wall built-pipe sleeve relocated (alignment is critical)

(2.)

Note: wall must not be used to support pipe – the effect of adding fluid to pipes must be allowed for by adjustment to spring hangers.

Insert mineral/glass wool pre-formed sized to give slight compression

Material bulk weight 30–80 kg/m^3

3.

Apply slack tape or bellows subject to fire regulations min. 5 kg/m^2

Pipework not insulated

4. Insulated pipework

Correct way to install pipework through walls for good separation

Source: Arup Acoustics

Pipe penetrations

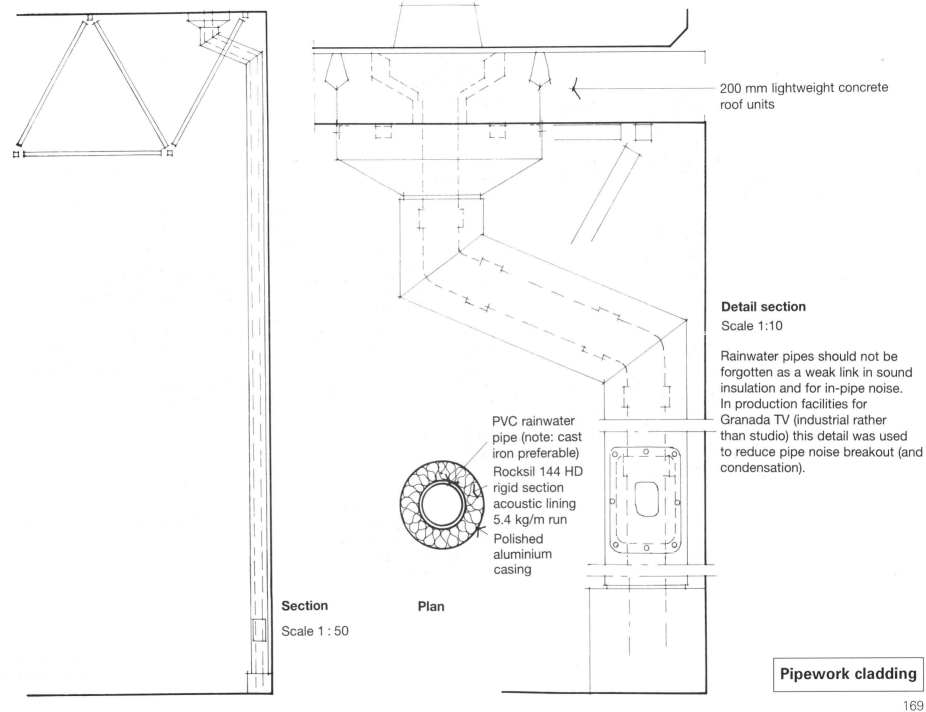

200 mm lightweight concrete roof units

Detail section

Scale 1:10

Rainwater pipes should not be forgotten as a weak link in sound insulation and for in-pipe noise. In production facilities for Granada TV (industrial rather than studio) this detail was used to reduce pipe noise breakout (and condensation).

PVC rainwater pipe (note: cast iron preferable)

Rocksil 144 HD rigid section acoustic lining 5.4 kg/m run

Polished aluminium casing

Section

Scale 1 : 50

Plan

Pipework cladding

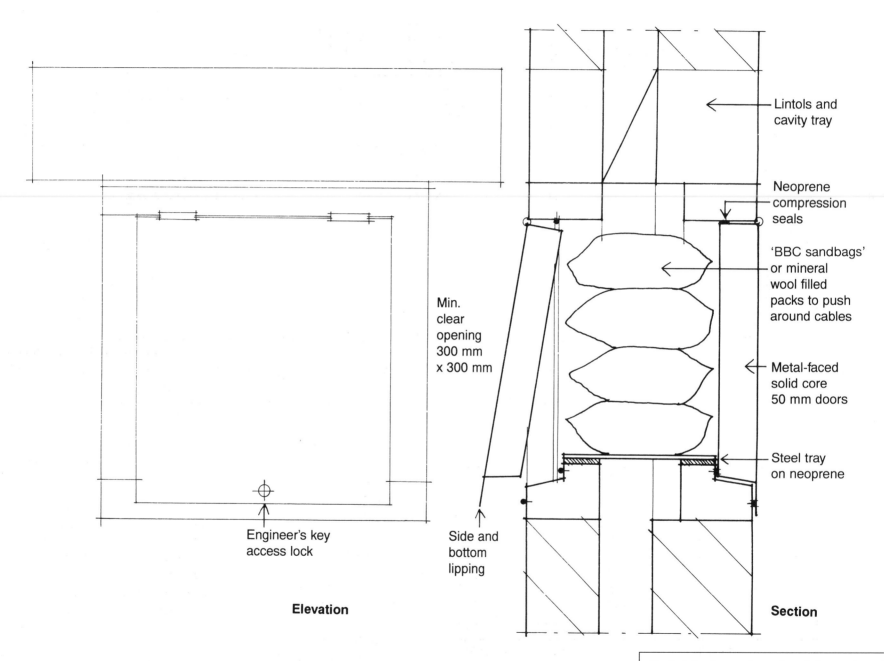

Min.
clear
opening
300 mm
x 300 mm

Lintols and
cavity tray

Neoprene
compression
seals

'BBC sandbags'
or mineral
wool filled
packs to push
around cables

Metal-faced
solid core
50 mm doors

Steel tray
on neoprene

Engineer's key
access lock

Side and
bottom
lipping

Elevation

Section

Outside broadcast cable entry doors

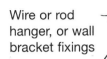

Wire or rod hanger, or wall bracket fixings

Resilient 'clip strip' e.g. by 'Tico' alternatively group pipes on a resiliently mounted carrier.

Resilent clamp block e.g. 'Tico'.

Resilient pipe mountings

Avoid noise transmitted along pipes being regenerated via structure and thermal movement 'clicking' at pipe fixings.

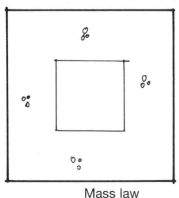

Mass law

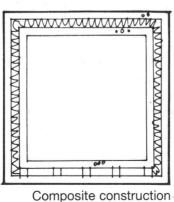

Composite construction

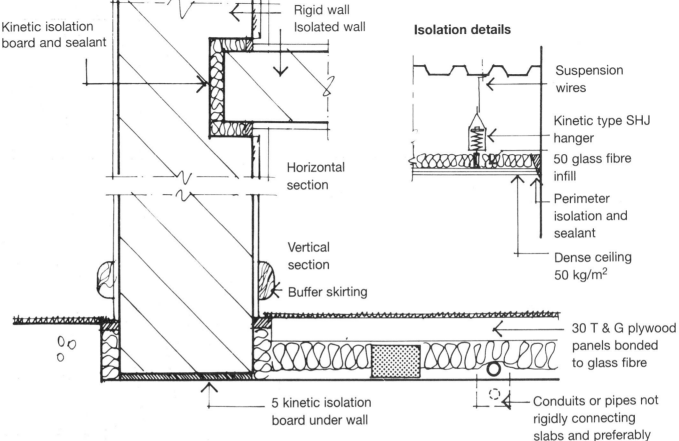

Kinetic isolation board and sealant

Rigid wall
Isolated wall

Isolation details

Horizontal section

Suspension wires

Kinetic type SHJ hanger

50 glass fibre infill

Perimeter isolation and sealant

Dense ceiling 50 kg/m²

Vertical section

Buffer skirting

30 T & G plywood panels bonded to glass fibre

5 kinetic isolation board under wall

Conduits or pipes not rigidly connecting slabs and preferably set in main slab

Isolation system

Enables greater sound reduction to be achieved than 3× mass. Each doubling of mass only achieves an extra 5 dB on SRI value.
Enclosures with equivalent SRI (Sound Reduction Index dB)

Note: lightweight composite construction suitable in, e.g., offices to prevent transmission of speech (higher frequencies) but heavy composite construction required to screen low frequencies, e.g. plant noise.

Source: Sound Attenuators Ltd

Noise isolation

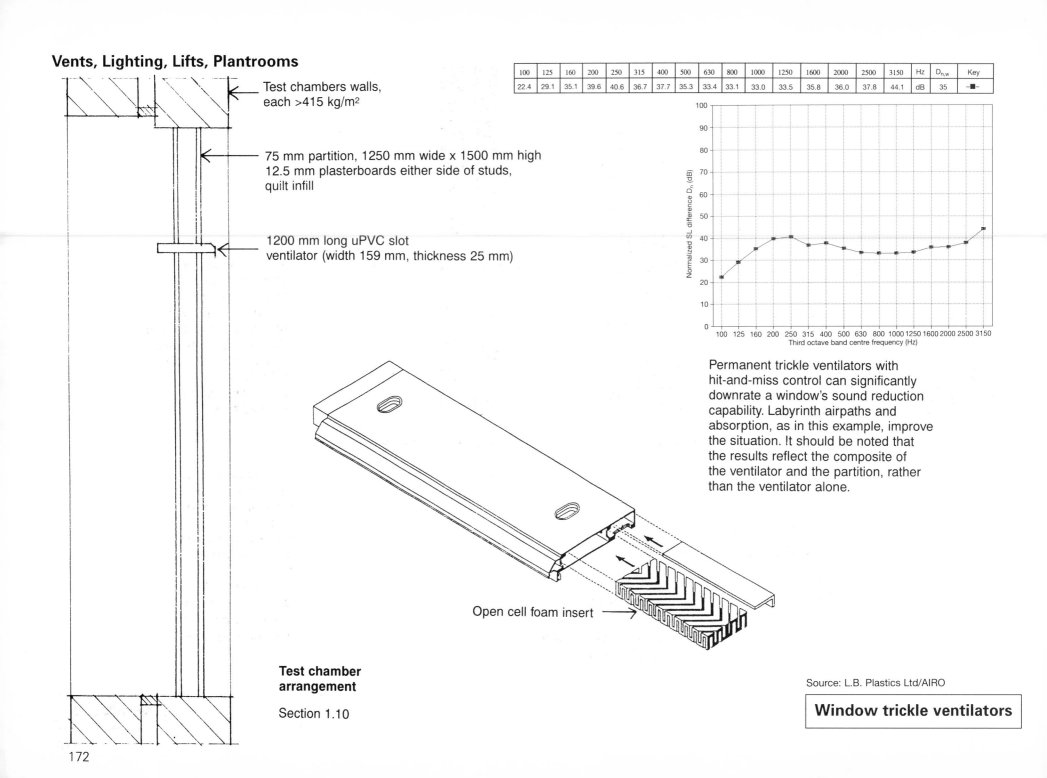

Test chambers walls,
each >415 kg/m²

75 mm partition, 1250 mm wide x 1500 mm high
12.5 mm plasterboards either side of studs,
quilt infill

1200 mm long uPVC slot
ventilator (width 159 mm, thickness 25 mm)

100	125	160	200	250	315	400	500	630	800	1000	1250	1600	2000	2500	3150	Hz	$D_{n,w}$	Key
22.4	29.1	35.1	39.6	40.6	36.7	37.7	35.3	33.4	33.1	33.0	33.5	35.8	36.0	37.8	44.1	dB	35	■

Permanent trickle ventilators with
hit-and-miss control can significantly
downrate a window's sound reduction
capability. Labyrinth airpaths and
absorption, as in this example, improve
the situation. It should be noted that
the results reflect the composite of
the ventilator and the partition, rather
than the ventilator alone.

Open cell foam insert →

Source: L.B. Plastics Ltd/AIRO

**Test chamber
arrangement**

Section 1.10

Window trickle ventilators

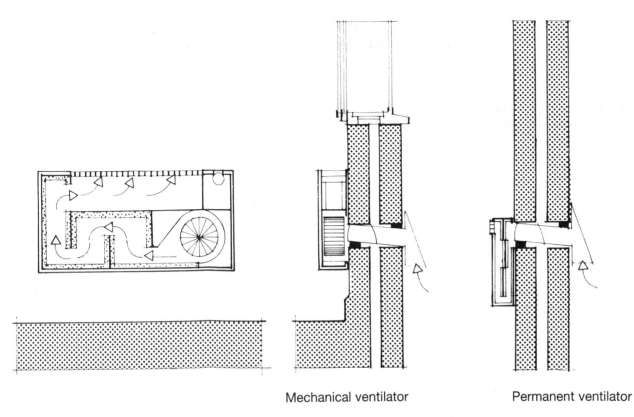

Mechanical ventilator

Permanent ventilator

Scale 1 : 20

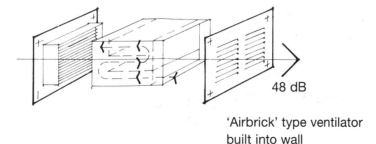

48 dB

'Airbrick' type ventilator
built into wall

Ventilators work by
labyrinth paths for
airways lined with
sound-absorbing material
absorbing external noise.
The fan in the powered
version must itself be
quiet. Grants allow
use in living rooms
and bedrooms.

Wall ventilators have
been used widely by
local authorities in
houses near noisy
motorways, railways or
airports to allow
attenuated
natural ventilation.
Grant aid is given for
new roads causing
$\geqslant 68$ dB L_{A10} (18 hr.)

Ventilators

173

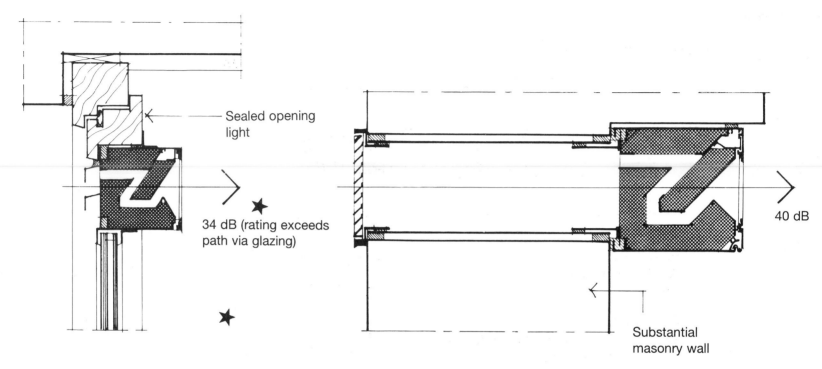

Sealed opening
light

34 dB (rating exceeds
path via glazing)

40 dB

Substantial
masonry wall

Model ZR 150

Sections
sectional sizes
100 × 100, 150 × 150

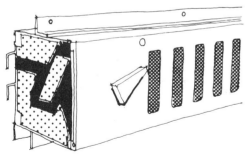

Model Z100

Linear sound-absorbers: ventilators with
anodized aluminium bodies. Ventilation
potential up to 200 m^3 of air/hour/metre
length. Use in offices, housing.

Linear trickle ventilators

Powered or passive ventilation

Source: Gretsch-
Unitas GmbH

Ventilators

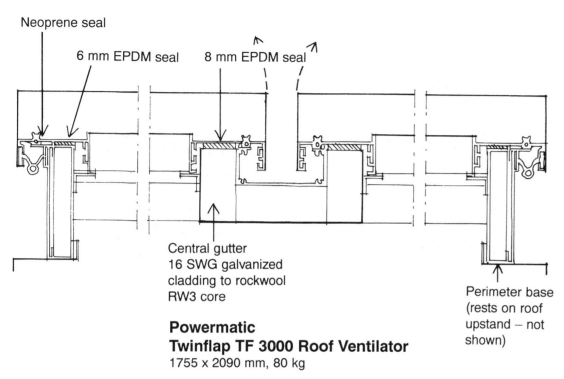

Neoprene seal

6 mm EPDM seal   8 mm EPDM seal

Central gutter
16 SWG galvanized
cladding to rockwool
RW3 core

Perimeter base
(rests on roof
upstand – not
shown)

Powermatic
Twinflap TF 3000 Roof Ventilator
1755 x 2090 mm, 80 kg

Standard industrial ventilators on fusible
links can downrate the sound insulation
of an auditorium roof and admit perceptible
levels of rain or hail noise. Uprated
versions like this can minimize the problem.

100	125	160	200	250	315	400	500	630	800	1000	1250	1600	2000	2500	3150	Hz	R_w
22.9	21.5	28.5	32.0	32.2	31.7	32.9	30.9	34.1	38.5	39.3	38.1	38.9	41.1	42.3	43.6	dB	38

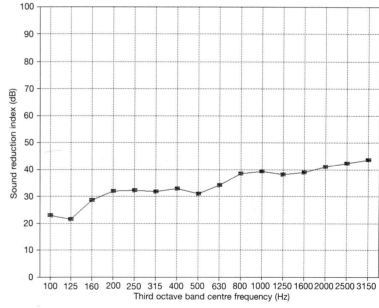

Source: Lidiard & Skelton Ltd/
University of Salford

Roof ventilators

Tungsten

Tungsten lamps give off negligible noise except when about to fail: the filaments then 'rattle'. Tungsten lighting is therefore used for anechoic chambers and other noise-sensitive rooms. Dimmer controls on lighting may cause some noise at low illumination setting.

Fluorescent

There is a great variation of noise from the main source, the control gear, even for fittings of the same type from the same manufacturer. The laminated iron core produces noise due to magnetization of the laminations, varying according to the type of circuit and wattage rating. The method of mounting fittings affects noise output: hanging fittings are preferable to solid fixing. In sensitive areas, remote control gear may have to be considered. Individual fittings may not be noisy. For instance a fitting recently tested had a worst case SWL of 23.3 dB at 630 Hz.

However, 32 such fittings in a room as a typical arrangement were calculated to produce a sound level approximating NR = 25 at 630 Hz

Source: University of Salford

Powerful lighting may cause significant noise at some particular frequency. The distribution at LHS is a total of 55 400 W luminaires (type HPI MBI special sports lights) mounted under high-level catwalks. In a multi-purpose sports hall of 11300 m^3 and RT = 2 seconds at mid-frequency. Ambient sound level for sports lighting on, house lights and ventilation off corresponds to NR = 30.

Source: Sandy Brown Associates

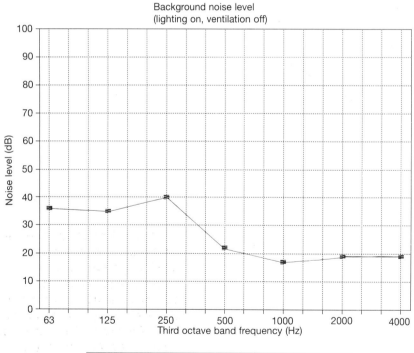

Background noise level (lighting on, ventilation off)

63	125	250	500	1000	2000	4000	Hz
36	35	40	22	17	19	19	dB

Lighting

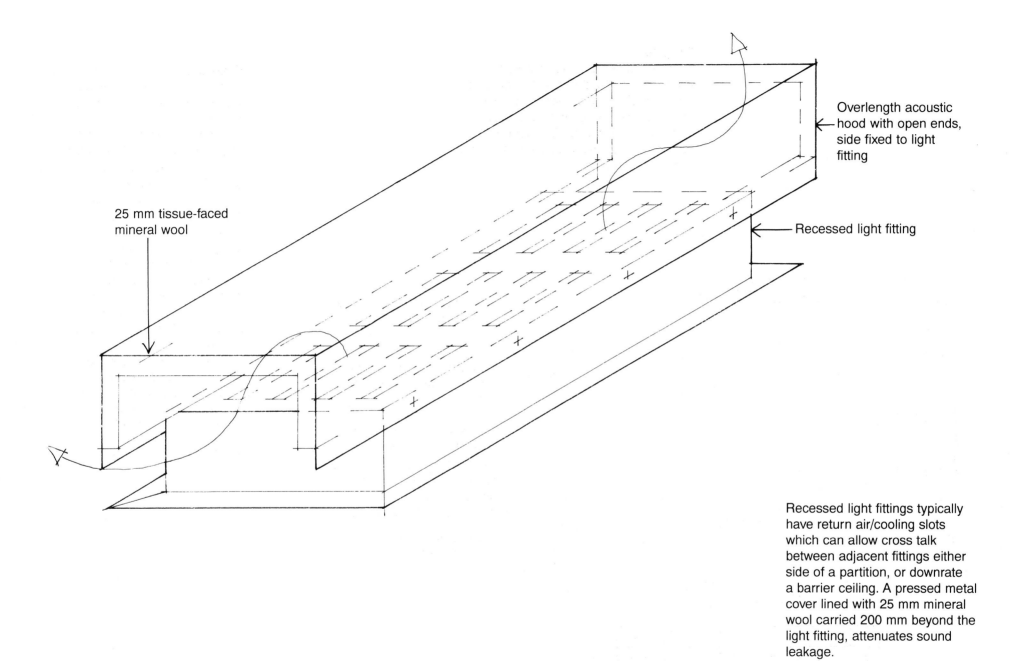

25 mm tissue-faced mineral wool

Overlength acoustic hood with open ends, side fixed to light fitting

Recessed light fitting

Recessed light fittings typically have return air/cooling slots which can allow cross talk between adjacent fittings either side of a partition, or downrate a barrier ceiling. A pressed metal cover lined with 25 mm mineral wool carried 200 mm beyond the light fitting, attenuates sound leakage.

Lighting

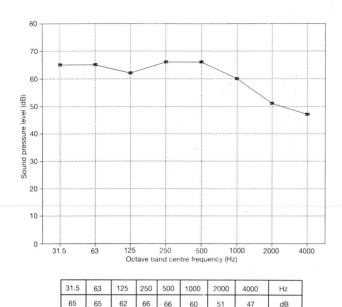

31.5	63	125	250	500	1000	2000	4000	Hz
65	65	62	66	66	60	51	47	dB

Single hydraulic lift motor/ pump unit

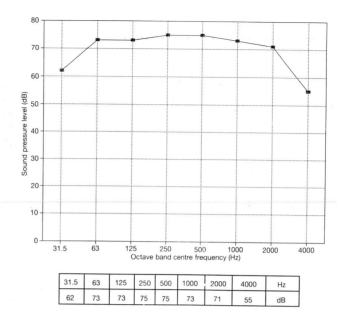

31.5	63	125	250	500	1000	2000	4000	Hz
62	73	73	75	75	73	71	55	dB

Double hydraulic lift motor /pump units

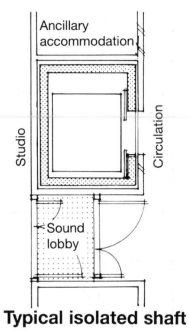

Typical isolated shaft

Advice notes

1. Hydraulic lift motors are more noisy than electric motors: minimize by specifying pump and motor to be submersible type and to have casings lined with sound deadening material.
2. Select lift doors for quiet operation.
3. Check high-speed/high-rise lifts for wind noise upshaft.
4. All machinery to be on anti-vibration mountings.
5. Avoid builder's work holes between lift shafts and other areas.
6. Choose electronic proximity switches, etc. as a way of avoiding 'clicking' working parts in control gear
7. Ensure good maintenance of lifts.
8. In refurbishment schemes, check noise from existing lift installations (older types, especially open shaft, were far noisier).
9. Don't forget noise from 'lift arrived' bells.
10. Avoid lift motor rooms next to sensitive rooms.

Plan arrangement

Lift noise is of particular concern in hotels or hospitals where the noise levels from machinery may not be high, but the discontinuity of operation draws attention to the noise. Typical sound levels within lift car are 65 dBA for hydraulic, 60 dBA for electric operation.

Lifts

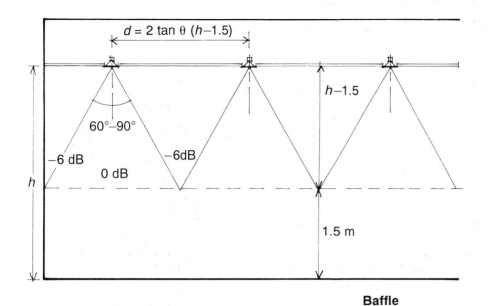

$d = 2 \tan \theta \, (h - 1.5)$

$60° - 90°$

-6 dB

-6 dB

0 dB

$h - 1.5$

1.5 m

h

Baffle

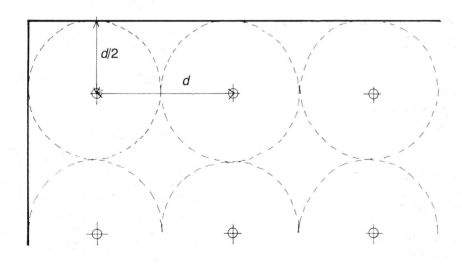

$d/2$

d

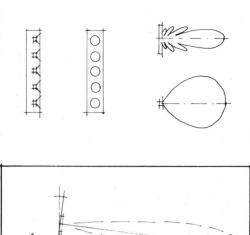

Column

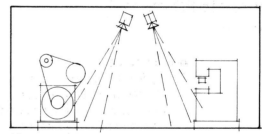

Horn

The design of sound systems for good audibilty is a field in itself. The component of main interest in architectural design is the loudspeaker. The baffle, or cabinet, loudspeaker is a non-directional, low output type for office, restaurant, shopping malls, the column loudspeaker is directional in the vertical plane, used in churches, sports halls. The horn loudspeaker is directional in both planes. Used in workshops, along corridoors, outside public address for any arrangement, to direct sound where needed, i.e. to the listener plane.
Have enough loudspeakers of adequate output, and enough absorption to control reverberant sound levels.

Loudspeakers

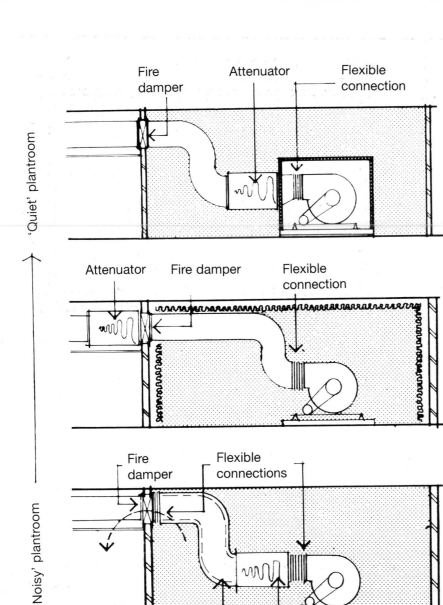

'Quiet' plantroom

'Noisy' plantroom

1. Noise enclosed at source

Acoustic enclosures to noisy items of plant within plantroom

A.V. mounts to isolated base.

Good to enclose noise at source but this may not be possible if there are many noise sources, or plant items requiring complete access and ventilation to all sides.

2. Plantroom lined with sound absorbent quilt spaced off walls.

Enclosure of individual items of plant may not be practical. Lining of plantroom may reduce reverberant sound.

3. Substantial room enclosure ensures isolation. Good insulation value to walls, roof, floor: separate structure if possible. Airborne sound level inside plantroom high, particularly with amplification factor of hard finishes which increase noise level within by up to 9 dB

Particular care re. noise breakout via ductwork necessary. For very noisy plant and sensitive rooms around all measures may be necessary: enclosure of plant, linings to plantroom, substantial fabric.

Plantrooms

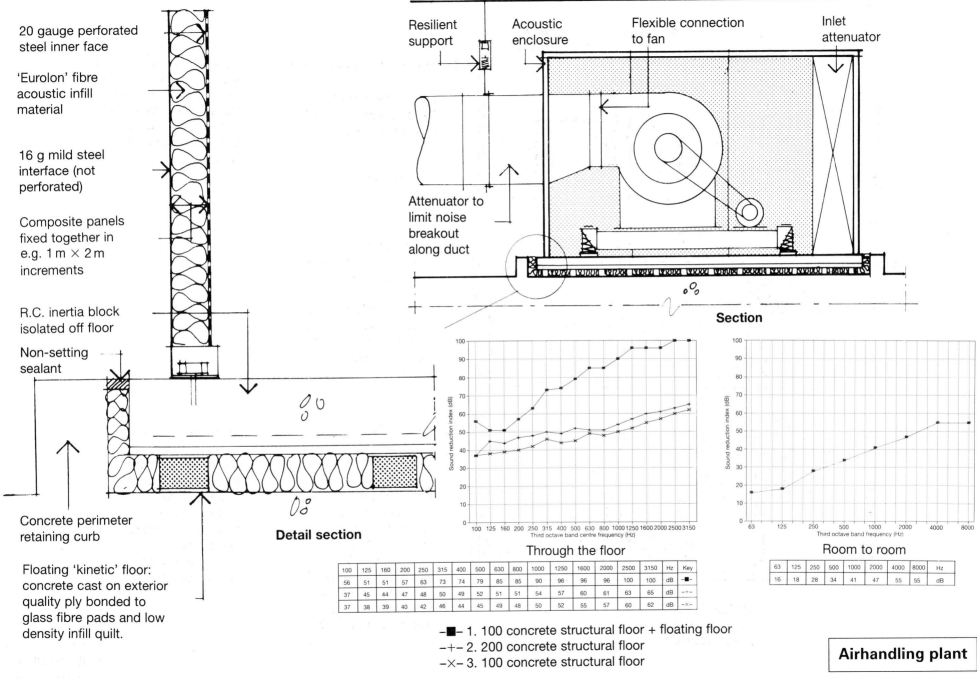

20 gauge perforated steel inner face

'Eurolon' fibre acoustic infill material

16 g mild steel interface (not perforated)

Composite panels fixed together in e.g. 1 m × 2 m increments

R.C. inertia block isolated off floor

Non-setting sealant

Concrete perimeter retaining curb

Floating 'kinetic' floor: concrete cast on exterior quality ply bonded to glass fibre pads and low density infill quilt.

Detail section

Resilient support

Acoustic enclosure

Flexible connection to fan

Inlet attenuator

Attenuator to limit noise breakout along duct

Section

Through the floor

Sound reduction index (dB) / Third octave band centre frequency (Hz)

100	125	160	200	250	315	400	500	630	800	1000	1250	1600	2000	2500	3150	Hz	Key
56	51	51	57	63	73	74	79	85	85	90	96	96	96	100	100	dB	-■-
37	45	44	47	48	50	49	52	51	51	54	57	60	61	63	65	dB	-+-
37	38	39	40	42	46	44	45	49	48	50	52	55	57	60	62	dB	-×-

-■- 1. 100 concrete structural floor + floating floor
-+- 2. 200 concrete structural floor
-×- 3. 100 concrete structural floor

Room to room

Sound reduction index (dB) / Third octave band frequency (Hz)

63	125	250	500	1000	2000	4000	8000	Hz
16	18	28	34	41	47	55	55	dB

Airhandling plant

181

Louvres, screens

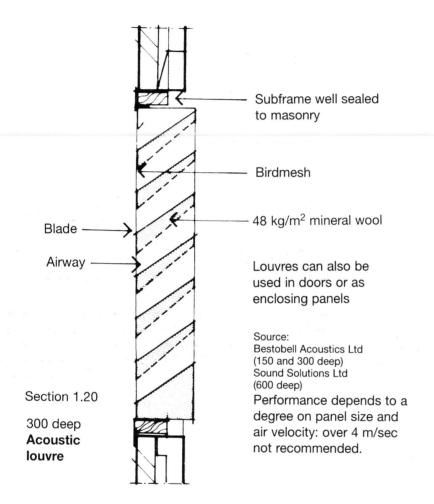

Subframe well sealed to masonry

Birdmesh

48 kg/m^2 mineral wool

Blade

Airway

Louvres can also be used in doors or as enclosing panels

Source:
Bestobell Acoustics Ltd
(150 and 300 deep)
Sound Solutions Ltd
(600 deep)
Performance depends to a degree on panel size and air velocity: over 4 m/sec not recommended.

Section 1.20

300 deep Acoustic louvre

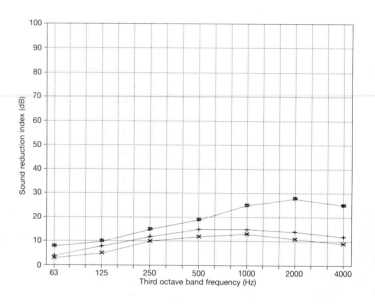

Frequency (Hz)	63	125	250	500	1000	2000	4000	Louvre depth (mm)	Key
Sound reduction index (dB)	8	10	15	19	25	28	25	600	—■—
	4	8	12	15	15	14	12	300	—+—
	3	5	10	12	13	11	9	150	—×—

Louvres

Screens

Insertion loss is defined as the sound level difference before and after inserting a sound absorber or barrier between noise source and reference point.

'Gullfiber' modular acoustic screen 2 m × 1 m × 40 mm
Finish: painted steel.
Perforations both sides (one side perforated optional)
Absorption coefficients
125 – 4 k Hz
0.15 0.40 0.80 0.90 0.90 0.85

Source: Lund Institute of Technology

(Insertion loss test by room method to ISO 354)

Distance from source (m)	80	100	125	160	200	250	315	400	500	630	800	1000	1250	1600	2000	3150	3500	4000	Hz	Key
1.5	8	7	6	10	15	14	16	15	13	14	21	25	24	25	24	25	27	26	dB	–■–
3	5	6	8	9	11	11	12	11	11	17	20	21	17	20	20	21	21	21	dB	–+–

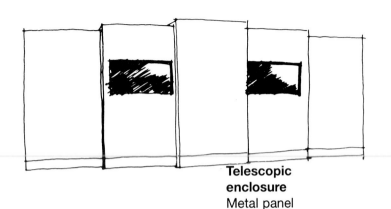

Telescopic enclosure
Metal panel
Own ventilation extract

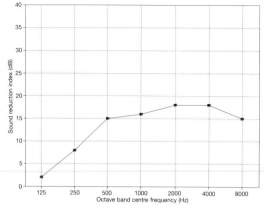

Typical performance of
metal panel
enclosure

Source: The Noise Control Centre Ltd

125	250	500	1000	2000	4000	8000	Hz
2	8	15	16	15	15	15	dB

Air intake via
attenuator

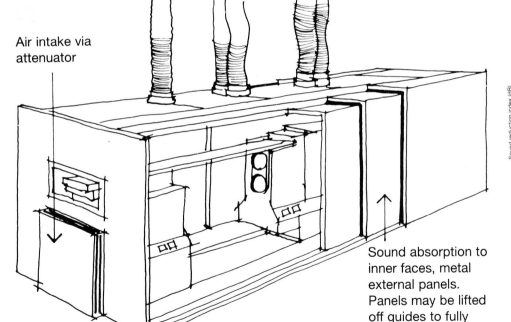

Sound absorption to
inner faces, metal
external panels.
Panels may be lifted
off guides to fully
expose machinery

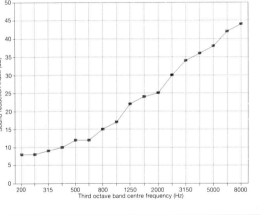

Typical performance of enclosure
by proprietary limp low-stiffness
acoustic curtains

Source: Bestobell Acoustics

200	250	315	400	500	630	800	1000	1250	1600	2000	2500	3150	4000	5000	6300	8000	Hz
8	8	9	10	12	12	15	17	22	24	25	30	34	36	38	42	44	dB

Such systems should be considered to screen
presses, machine tools, pumps, compressors, etc.
mounted within working areas. Neither system is
effective to screen low-frequency noise, but gives
useful improvement at speech frequencies.

Machinery enclosures

184

5 DEFINITIONS

Weighted standardized impact sound level $L'_{nT,w}$

This is a single-figure descriptor obtained from one-third octave band values of the standardized impact sound levels $L_n{'}_{T,w}$.

It is obtained in exactly the same way as the weighted normalized impact sound level, L_{nw}.

See BS 5821, Part 2: 1986 and BS 2750, Parts 6 & 7: 1980.

Standardized impact sound level L'_{nT}

This is the impact sound level measured between two rooms under field conditions and standardized to a reverberation time of 0.5 s, i.e.

$$L'_{nT} = L' - 10 \log \frac{T}{0.5}$$

where L' is the measured impact level.

See BS 5821, Part 2: 1986 and BS 2750, Parts 6 & 7: 1980.

Weighted normalized impact sound level L_{nW}, L'_{nW}

This is a single-figure descriptor obtained from one-third octave band values of the normalized impact sound levels L_n (Laboratory) or L'_n (field). The normalized levels are compared with a set of weighting curves and the curve is found for which the total adverse difference between the normalized level and the curves is less than but as close to 32 dB as possible. Adverse differences occur when the normalized levels fall above the rating curve.

The weighted normalized impact sound pressure level is the sound pressure level at 500 Hz on the standard curve which meets the above criterion. For an L_{nW} or L'_{nW} of 60 the curve is defined by

Frequency Hz	Level dB	Frequency Hz	Level dB
100	62	630	59
125	62	800	58
160	62	1000	57
200	62	1250	54
250	62	1600	51
315	62	2000	48
400	61	2500	45
500	60	3150	42

Other curves are obtained by moving the one-third octave up or down in 1 dB steps.

See BS 5821, Part 2: 1985 and BS 2750, Parts 6 & 7: 1980.

Impact noise level, L

This is the sound pressure level measured in a one-third octave band when a standard tapping machine is operating on the floor above the room.

Impact sound

Impact sound refers to the sound produced when a short-duration impulse, such as a footfall, acts directly on a structure.

The frequency content of the sound will depend upon the duration of the impact, a short, sharp event giving a broadband frequency content while a longer-duration event caused, for example, by having a resilient layer over the structure, will contain mainly low-frequency sound and will be subjectively less disturbing.

Normalized impact noise level

The impact noise level as measured in the laboratory will depend upon the acoustic characteristics of the receiving room, so to normalize results the measured noise levels are corrected to a constant 10 m² of absorption; hence

$$L_n = L - 10 \log (A/A_0)$$

where A is the actual sound absorption in the receiving room in the one-third octave band under consideration, and $A_0 = 10$ m².

L'_n is used if flanking cannot be eliminated.

See BS 5821, Part 2: 1984 and BS 2750, Parts 6 & 7: 1980.

Weighted standardized level difference $D_{nT,w}$

To obtain a single-figure rating value from field measured values of the standardized level difference, D_{nT}, the one-third octave values are weighted using the same method used to obtain the weighted sound reduction index, R_W.

Absorption

Absorption is the term applied to the process by which energy is removed from a sound field. Most materials will, to a greater or lesser extent, absorb sound, i.e. convert acoustic energy into heat. However, to be an efficient absorber a material should generally have an open surface structure which allows sound to enter, and internally it should provide many interconnected pathways through which the sound may pass to dissipate its energy by means of viscous losses. Good fibrous absorbents are glassfibre and mineral wool.

In acoustics, A has a more specific meaning. It is the product of the area, S, of an absorbing material and its absorption coefficient, α. So:

$A = S \times \alpha$ m² or Sabines.

If there are several absorbing surfaces whose areas are S_1, S_2, S_3, etc., then the total absorption is

$A_T = S_1\alpha_1 + S_2\alpha_2 + S_3\alpha_3 + \dots$.

Air absorption

The absorption of sound by air is significant for propagation over long distances and in large enclosures. High frequencies are absorbed the most and the absorption is dependent both on temperature and humidity.

Standardized sound level difference D_{nT}

The standardized sound level difference is used to assess airborne sound insulation between rooms in buildings. As the sound level difference across a partition will depend upon the absorption in the receiving room it is recommended (BS 5821: 1984) that the measured level difference is corrected, to a standard receiving room reverberation time of 0.5 s. Hence:

D_{nT} = measured level difference – 10 log (T/0.5) dB;
T = reverberation time of the receiving room (seconds).

Diffuse sound level

When the sound energy in an enclosure is uniform throughout the space, the sound field is said to be diffuse. This is normally the case for enclosures with conventional aspect ratios and small absorption which is uniformly distributed throughout the enclosure.

Norris–Eyring equation

This equation is a modified form of the Sabine equation and is suitable for use when the average room absorption coefficient is greater than 0.1:

$$T = \frac{0.161V}{-2.3S \log_{10}(1 - \overline{\alpha})} \quad \text{seconds}$$

Reverberance

When a sound source in an enclosure is turned off, the sound does not immediately stop but persists for a short time due to the reflection of energy from the walls of the enclosure. Similarly, it takes a finite time for sound level to reach its equilibrium value after the source is turned on. This behaviour is known as reverberance and is a major factor in determining the general level or quality of sound in any enclosed space.

Reverberation time

The time which is taken for the reverberant sound energy in an enclosure to decay to one millionth of its equilibrium value, i.e. by 60 dB, after the source is turned off, is known as the reverberation time. The reverberation time is frequency dependent and it is customary to measure its value in octave or one-third octave bands.

Sabine equation

The Sabine equation gives the reverberation time in terms of room volume and total room absorption as:

$$T = \frac{0.161V}{A} \quad \text{seconds}$$

where V is in cubic metres and A in square metres.

The equation is valid for diffuse sound fields only and gives the best results when the average absorption coefficient is less than 0.1. However, it is often used when this condition is not met. For large enclosures air absorption is included so that:

$$T = \frac{0.161V}{A + 4mV} \quad \text{seconds}$$

where m is a sound attenuation coefficient.

Values for $4m$ are as given in the table below.

Air absorption (values of $4mV$, in m² units for a volume of 100 m³ at 20 °C):

Frequency (Hz)	Relative humidity (%)						
	20	30	40	50	60	70	80
125	0.06	0.05	0.04	0.04	0.03	0.03	0.02
250	0.14	0.13	0.12	0.11	0.10	0.09	0.08
500	0.25	0.25	0.26	0.26	0.26	0.25	0.25
1000	0.57	0.47	0.46	0.46	0.48	0.50	0.51
2000	1.78	1.21	1.00	0.90	0.88	0.88	0.88
4000	6.21	4.09	3.10	2.60	2.27	2.08	1.95
8000	19.00	14.29	11.00	8.95	7.61	6.69	6.04

Sound absorption coefficient

The sound absorption coefficient is the quantity used to describe how well a particular material absorbs sound energy. It is denoted by α and is defined as:

$$\alpha = \frac{\text{sound energy not reflected from material}}{\text{sound energy incident upon material}}.$$

For a perfect absorber α would equal 1, while for a perfect reflector α would equal zero.

The absorption coefficient varies with frequency and also with the angle at which sound strikes the material. Because of the angular dependence it is usual to measure α in diffuse sound fields so that the sound effectively strikes the material at all angles of incidence. α measured under these conditions is known as the random incidence absorption coefficient and is denoted by $\overline{\alpha}$. It is usually measured in one-third or octave bands.

Frequency

If vibrations are given to a medium in a regular manner then a regular progression of pressure maxima and minima will be observed at any point in the medium. When two adjacent maxima or minima, or for that matter any two adjacent paths of equal pressure, pass the points, we say that one complete cycle has passed. The number of such cycles which pass per second is referred to as the frequency of the wave.

The unit of frequency is the hertz (Hz). If 500 cycles occur in one second the wave has a frequency of 500 Hz.

Pascal (Pa)

Pascal is the unit of pressure, and sound pressures are measured in pascals (Pa).

The smallest sound pressure that the average human can detect is around 2×10^{-5} Pa.

Humans begin to perceive sound as painful when the sound pressure is around 20 Pa.

Atmospheric pressure has a value of 10^5 Pa.

$$
\begin{aligned}
1 \text{ pascal} &= 106 \text{ micropascal } (\mu Pa) \\
&= 1 \text{ newton/metre}^2 \ (N/m^2) \\
&= 10 \text{ microbar } (\mu bar).
\end{aligned}
$$

Sound level difference between two spaces

The sound level difference between two spaces separated by a partition depends upon the value of the sound reduction index, the area of the partition and the acoustic properties of the two spaces:

1. room-to-room
$$L_{p2} = L_{p1} - R + 10 \log_{10} (S/A) \text{ dB};$$

2. inside-to-outside
$$L_{p2} = L_{p1} - R + 10 \log_{10} S - 20 \log_{10} r - 17 + DI \quad \text{dB};$$

3. outside-to-inside
$$L_{p2} - L_{p1} - R \ T \ 10 \log_{10} (S/A) - K + 6 \text{ dB}.$$

L_{p1} is the sound pressure level on the source side (dB);

L_{p2} is the sound pressure level on the receiver side (dB);

S is the area of the partition (m²);

R is the sound reduction index of the partition (dB);

A is the absorption in the receiving room (m²);

DI is the directivity index of the facade;

r is the distance of the receiver from the partition;

k is a constant, the value of which depends on where, external to the partition, the sound pressure level was measured:

k = 6 dB if measured very close to the partition;

k = 2.5 dB if measured about 1 m away;

k = 0 dB if the measured position is far from facade.

Directivity factor (Q)

The directivity factor is the ratio of the intensity of sound in a given direction from a source to the intensity in the same direction of the source radiated uniformly.

Directivity index (DI)

The directivity index is defined as

$$DI + 10 \log_{10} Q \text{ dB}$$

where Q is the directivity factor of the source in a given direction.

	Directivity index (dB)
Omni-directional source radiates spherically	0
Omni-directional source on flat plane: radiation confined to a hemisphere	+3
Omni-directional source at junction of two flat planes; radiation confined to ¼ sphere	+6
Omni-directional source at junction of three flat planes; radiation confined to ⅛ sphere	+9

Octave band

Two frequencies are said to be an octave apart if the frequency of one is twice, or more precisely $10^{0.3}$, the frequency of the other.

Contiguous octave bands have centre frequencies which are also related by a factor of two ($10^{0.3}$). The centre frequencies and bandwidth of standard octave bands are shown in Table 6.1.

Octave band sound pressure level

The sound pressure level measured when only frequencies within an octave are passed is known as the octave band sound pressure level. Analysis of sound into octave bands transmitted through partitions is frequently used to assess the sound insulation.

One-third octave band

Two frequencies are said to be one-third of an octave apart if the frequency of one is 1.26, or more precisely $10^{0.15}$, times the other. There are three one-third octaves in each octave band. The standard centre frequencies and bandwidths of one-third octaves are shown in Table 6.1.

Weighted sound level difference D_W

The weighted level difference is obtained from level differences, measured in one-third octave bands in exactly the same way as the weighted sound reduction index R_W is obtained.

Sound insulation

Airborne sound insulation refers to the process of separating, by a physical barrier, a space to be protected from a space containing a noise source. With noise insulation the sound is effectively prevented from travelling in a specific direction by an impervious barrier. The greater the surface mass of the barrier, the greater the insulation will generally be. Unlike sound absorption, sound insulation does not remove energy from the sound field, it merely redirects it.

Sound reduction index SRI

The sound reduction index is the measurement generally used to express the insulation properties of a partition in decibels. It is defined as:

$$SRI = 10 \log_{10} \left(\frac{1}{\text{transmission coefficient}} \right) \quad dB.$$

The sound reduction index is frequency dependent and is usually measured in octave or one-third octave bands.

If the transmission coefficient $\tau = 0.01$, i.e. 1% of the incident sound energy is transmitted by the partition, then the sound reduction index is 20 dB; with $\tau = 0.001$, the SRI is 30 dB, etc. Hence for 50 dB insulation, which for example may represent a reasonable reduction between attached dwellings, the incident energy per square metre must be reduced by a factor of 0.00001.

Weighted sound reduction index R_W

This is a weighted single-figure descriptor of the sound reduction performance of a partition measured under laboratory conditions. The sound reduction index in each of the one-third octave bands from 100 Hz to 3150 Hz is compared with a standard set of curves. The value of R_W for a given partition is obtained from the standard curve which, when compared with the measured SRI values, produces an adverse deviation as close to -32 dB as possible. Only the SRI values which fall below a particular standard curve are considered in the sum.

Positive deviations from the standard curve are not taken into account. The standard values for the curve corresponding to an R_W of 52 are:

Frequency Hz	Reference value (dB)
100	33
125	36
150	39
200	42
250	45
315	48
400	51
500	52
630	53
800	54
1000	55
1250	56
1600	56
2000	56
2500	56
3150	56

The R_W value is the value in decibels of the reference curve at 500 Hz.

To obtain other reference curves the one-third octave band values are changed in 1 dB steps up or down.

6 TABLES

Table 6.1 Octave and one-third octave centre frequencies and band limit frequencies

Band number	Preferred centre frequency (Hz)	Octave Band limits	Octave Centre	Third-octave Centre	Third-octave Band limits
		22.39			22.39
14	25			25.12	
					28.18
15	31.5		31.62	31.62	
					35.48
16	40			39.81	
		44.67			44.67
17	50			50.12	
					56.23
18	63		63.10	63.10	
					70.79
19	80			79.43	
		89.13			89.13
20	100			100.00	
					112.20
21	125		125.89	125.89	
					141.25
22	160			158.49	
		177.83			177.83
23	200			199.53	
					223.87
24	250		251.19	251.19	
					281.84
25	315			316.23	
		354.81			354.81
26	400			398.11	
					446.68
27	500		501.19	501.19	
					562.34
28	630			630.96	
		707.95			707.95
29	800			794.33	
					891.25
30	1000		1000.00	1000.00	
					1122.02
31	1250			1258.93	
		1412.54			1412.54
32	1600			1584.89	
					1778.28
33	2000		1995.26	1995.26	
					2238.72
34	2500			2511.89	
		2818.38			2818.38
35	3150			3162.28	
					3548.13
36	4000		3981.07	3981.07	
					4466.84
37	5000			5011.87	
		5623.41			5623.41
38	6300			6309.57	
					7079.46
39	8000		7943.28	7943.28	
					8912.51
40	10000			10000.00	
		11220.18			11220.18

Table 6.2 Sound reduction indices

	kg/m²	OBCF (Hz)						Mean
		125	250	500	1000	2000	4000	
Single glazing (mm)								
4-mm glass in aluminium frame, 100-mm opening		10	10	11	12	12	13	11
4 mm	10	20	22	28	34	34	29	28
6 mm	15	18	25	31	36	30	38	29
6.4 mm laminated		22	24	30	36	33	38	30
12 mm	30	26	30	35	34	39	47	35
19 mm	49	25	31	30	32	45	47	35
Double glazing: glass/air space/glass (mm)								
Sealed units								
3/12/3		21	20	22	29	35	25	25
4/12/4		22	17	24	37	41	38	30
6/12/6		20	19	29	38	36	46	30
4/12/12		25	22	33	41	44	44	35
6/12/10		26	26	34	40	39	48	34
6/20/12		26	34	40	42	40	50	39
6.4 lam/12/10		27	29	37	41	42	53	38
Separate panes								
6/150/4		29	35	45	56	52	51	44
6/200/6		37	41	48	54	47	47	46
4/200/4		27	33	39	42	46	44	39
4/200/4, opposite sliders open 25 mm		15	23	34	32	28	32	27
4/200/4, opposite sliders open 100 mm		10	16	27	25	27	27	22
Masonry/blockwork								
102-mm single-leaf fairfaced		36	37	40	46	54	56	45
Single-leaf plastered both sides	240	34	37	41	51	58	60	47
Cavity brickwork with ties	480	34	34	40	56	73	76	52
Double leaf brickwork plastered both sides	480	41	45	48	56	58	60	51
100-mm lightweight blockwork fairfaced	125	32	32	33	41	49	57	41
100-mm blockwork plastered both sides		32	34	37	45	52	57	43
100-mm blockwork with plasterboard on dabs both sides		28	34	45	53	55	52	45
200-mm fairfaced light weight blockwork	250	35	38	43	49	54	58	46
200-mm blockwork plastered both sides		37	39	46	53	57	61	49
200-mm blockwork plasterboard on dabs both sides		33	39	50	55	56	60	49
Three-leaf brickwork plastered both sides	720	44	43	49	57	66	70	55
Two leaves of 100-mm dense concrete blocks, 50-mm cavity, 13-mm plaster both sides, cavity ties		35	41	49	58	67	75	52

	kg/m²	OBCF (Hz) 125	250	500	1000	2000	4000	Mean[a]
Stud partitions								
9-mm plasterboard on 50 × 100 mm studs at 400 mm centres		15	31	35	37	45	46	35
13-mm plasterboard on 50 × 100 mm studs at 400 mm centres		25	32	34	47	39	50	38
13-mm plasterboard on 50 × 100 mm studs at 400 mm centres, 25 mm mineral wool between studs		25	37	42	49	46	59	43
6-mm ply on 50 × 50 mm studs at 600 mm centres		10	14	22	28	42	42	26
Double 13-mm plasterboard on 146-mm steel studs at 600 mm centres		32	41	47	49	53	58	47
Sheet materials/boards								
9-mm ply on frame	5	7	13	19	25	19	22	18
25-mm T & G timber boards	14	21	17	22	24	30	36	25
5-mm ply/1.5-mm lead/5-mm ply composite sheets	25	26	30	34	38	42	44	36
Two layers of 13-mm plasterboard	22	24	29	31	32	30	35	30
1.2-mm steel sheet, 18 g	10	13	20	24	29	33	39	26
6-mm steel plate	50	27	35	41	39	39	46	38
Profiled metal sheeting		18	20	21	21	25	25	22
0.8-mm steel trapezoidal section, 50-mm deep cladding panels		14	17	18	20	29	31	22
Duct cladding: plaster/mineral wool	30	11	13	12	12	12	21	12[b]
Duct cladding: lead foil/mineral wool	12	7	8	7	7	7	7	7[b]
50-mm woodwool slabs, screeded to source side	28	26	28	30	32	33	36	30
100-mm woodwool slabs, screeded to source side	50	28	28	32	34	33	38	31
Doors								
43-mm flush, hollow-core door, normal hanging	9	12	13	14	16	18	24	16
43-mm solid core door, normal hanging	28	17	21	26	29	31	34	26
50-mm steel door with good seals		21	27	32	34	36	39	32
Acoustic metal doorset, double seals		36	39	44	49	54	57	47
Floors								
235-mm T & G floorboards, floor joists, 13-mm plasterboard and skin	31	18	25	37	39	45	45	35
235-mm T & G floorboards, floor joists with 50-mm sand between, 13-mm plasterboard and skin		35	40	45	50	60	64	49
100-mm reinforced concrete slab	250	37	36	45	52	59	62	49
200-mm reinforced concrete slab	460	42	41	50	57	60	65	53
300-mm reinforced concrete slab	690	40	45	52	59	63	67	54
200-mm o/a: 125-mm concrete slab and screed on 13-mm nominal glass fibre	420	38	43	48	54	61	63	51

[a] Average 125–4000 Hz octaves. SRI (100–3150 Hz) 0–2 dB lower.
[b] + value on duct performance.

Table 6.3 Absorption coefficients

	OBCF (Hz)					
	125	250	500	1000	2000	4000
'Hard' finishes						
Water or ice	0.01	0.01	0.01	0.01	0.02	0.02
Smooth concrete, unpainted	0.01	0.01	0.02	0.02	0.02	0.05
Smooth concrete, sealed or painted	0.01	0.01	0.01	0.02	0.02	0.02
Concrete blocks, fairfaced	0.05	0.05	0.05	0.08	0.14	0.20
Rough concrete	0.02	0.03	0.03	0.03	0.04	0.07
Brickwork, flush-pointed	0.02	0.03	0.03	0.04	0.05	0.07
Brickwork, 10-mm-deep pointing	0.08	0.09	0.12	0.16	0.22	0.24
Plastered walls	0.02	0.02	0.03	0.04	0.05	0.05
Painted plaster	0.02	0.02	0.02	0.02	0.02	0.02
Ceramic tiles	0.01	0.01	0.01	0.02	0.02	0.02
Marble, terrazzo	0.01	0.01	0.01	0.01	0.02	0.02
Glazing (4 mm)	0.30	0.20	0.10	0.07	0.05	0.02
Double glazing	0.15	0.05	0.03	0.03	0.02	0.02
Glazing (6 mm)	0.10	0.06	0.04	0.03	0.02	0.02
Ceilings						
13-mm mineral tile, direct to floor slab	0.10	0.25	0.70	0.85	0.70	0.60
13-mm mineral tile, suspended 500 mm below ceiling	0.75	0.70	0.65	0.85	0.85	0.80
Metal planks, slots 14% free area, mineral wool overlay and void	0.50	0.70	0.80	1.0	1.0	1.0
Metal tiles 5% perforated, 20-mm quilt overlay and void	0.13	0.27	0.55	0.79	0.90	1.0
Woodwool slabs	0.40	0.40	0.70	0.70	0.70	0.80
Panels						
Solid timber door	0.14	0.10	0.06	0.08	0.10	0.10
9-mm plasterboard on battens, 18-mm air space with glass fibre	0.30	0.20	0.15	0.05	0.05	0.05
5-mm ply on battens, 50-mm air space with glass fibre	0.40	0.35	0.20	0.15	0.05	0.05
Suspended plasterboard ceiling	0.20	0.15	0.10	0.05	0.05	0.05
Steel decking	0.13	0.09	0.08	0.09	0.11	0.11
Ventilation grille (per m²)	0.60	0.60	0.60	0.60	0.60	0.60
13-mm plasterboard on frame, 100-mm air space with glass fibre	0.30	0.12	0.08	0.06	0.06	0.05
13-mm plasterboard on frame, 100-mm air space	0.08	0.11	0.05	0.03	0.02	0.03
2 × 13-mm plasterboard on frame, 50-mm air space with mineral wool	0.15	0.10	0.06	0.04	0.04	0.05
22-mm chipboard on frame, 50-mm air space with mineral wool	0.12	0.04	0.06	0.05	0.05	0.05
16-mm T & G on frame, 50-mm air space with mineral wool	0.25	0.15	0.10	0.09	0.08	0.07
22-mm timber boards 100-mm-wide, 10-mm gaps 500-mm air space with mineral wool	0.05	0.25	0.60	0.15	0.05	0.10
Treatments						
Curtains in folds against wall	0.05	0.15	0.35	0.40	0.50	0.50
25-mm glass fibre, 16 kg/m³	0.12	0.28	0.55	0.71	0.74	0.83
50-mm glass fibre, 16 kg/m³	0.17	0.45	0.80	0.89	0.97	0.94
75-mm glass fibre, 16 kg/m³	0.30	0.69	0.94	1.0	1.0	1.0
100-mm glass fibre, 16 kg/m³	0.43	0.86	1.0	1.0	1.0	1.0
25-mm glass fibre, 24 kg/m³	0.11	0.32	0.56	0.77	0.89	0.91
50-mm glass fibre, 24 kg/m³	0.27	0.54	0.94	1.0	0.96	0.96

	OBCF (Hz)					
	125	250	500	1000	2000	4000
75-mm glass fibre, 24 kg/m^3	0.28	0.79	1.0	1.0	1.0	1.0
100-mm glass fibre, 24 kg/m^3	0.46	1.0	1.0	1.0	1.0	1.0
50-mm glass fibre, 33 kg/m^3	0.20	0.55	1.0	1.0	1.0	1.0
75-mm glass fibre, 33 kg/m^3	0.37	0.85	1.0	1.0	1.0	1.0
100-mm glass fibre, 33 kg/m^3	0.53	0.92	1.0	1.0	1.0	1.0
50-mm glass fibre, 48 kg/m^3	0.30	0.80	1.0	1.0	1.0	1.0
75-mm glass fibre, 48 kg/m^3	0.43	0.97	1.0	1.0	1.0	1.0
100-mm glass fibre, 48 kg/m^3	0.65	1.0	1.0	1.0	1.0	1.0
25-mm acoustic plaster to solid backing	0.03	0.15	0.50	0.80	0.85	0.80
9-mm acoustic plaster to solid backing	0.02	0.08	0.30	0.60	0.80	0.90
9-mm acoustic plaster on plasterboard, 75-mm air space	0.30	0.30	0.60	0.80	0.75	0.75
50-mm mineral wool, 33 kg/m^3	0.15	0.60	0.90	0.90	0.90	0.85
75-mm mineral wool, 33 kg/m^3	0.30	0.85	0.95	0.85	0.90	0.85
100-mm mineral wool, 33 kg/m^3	0.35	0.95	1.0	0.92	0.90	0.85
50-mm mineral wool, 60 kg/m^3	0.11	0.60	0.96	0.94	0.92	0.82
75-mm mineral wool, 60 kg/m^3	0.34	0.95	1.0	0.82	0.87	0.86
25-mm mineral wool, 25-mm air space	0.10	0.40	0.70	1.0	1.0	1.0
50-mm mineral wool, 50-mm air space	0.50	0.70	0.90	0.90	0.90	0.80
50-mm mineral wool (96 kg/m^3) behind 25% open area perforated steel	0.20	0.35	0.65	0.85	0.90	0.80
Floor finishes						
Cord carpet	0.05	0.05	0.10	0.20	0.45	0.65
Thin (6-mm) carpet on underlay	0.03	0.09	0.20	0.54	0.70	0.72
Thick (9-mm) carpet on underlay	0.08	0.08	0.30	0.60	0.75	0.80
Wooden floor boards on joists	0.15	0.11	0.10	0.07	0.06	0.07
Parquet floor on timber joists and deck	0.20	0.15	0.10	0.10	0.05	0.10
Parquet laid on concrete	0.04	0.04	0.07	0.06	0.06	0.07
Vinyl or linoleum on concrete	0.02	0.02	0.03	0.04	0.04	0.05
Vinyl and resilient backing on concrete	0.02	0.02	0.04	0.05	0.05	0.10
Miscellaneous						
Audience on timber seats (1/m^2)	0.16	0.24	0.56	0.69	0.81	0.78
Audience on timber seats (2/m^2)	0.24	0.40	0.78	0.98	0.96	0.87
Audience per person, seated	0.33	0.40	0.44	0.45	0.45	0.45
Audience per person, standing	0.15	0.38	0.42	0.43	0.45	0.45
Seats, leather covers (per m^2)	0.40	0.50	0.58	0.61	0.58	0.50
Upholstered seats (per m^2)	0.44	0.60	0.77	0.89	0.82	0.70
Floor and upholstered seats (per m^2)	0.49	0.66	0.80	0.88	0.82	0.70
Areas with audience, orchestra, or seats, including narrow aisles	0.60	0.74	0.88	0.96	0.93	0.85
Orchestra with instruments on podium, 1.5 m^2/person	0.27	0.53	0.67	0.93	0.87	0.80
Shading factor (apply to finishes under seats, x coefficient)	0.80	0.70	0.60	0.50	0.40	0.20
Air 30% RH (per m^3 at 20°C)	–	–	–	0.005	0.01	0.04
Air 50% RH (per m^3 at 20°C)	–	–	–	0.005	0.009	0.03
Air 70% RH (per m^3 at 20°C)	–	–	–	0.005	0.009	0.02
Office furniture (per desk)	0.50	0.40	0.45	0.45	0.60	0.70

Values exceeding 1.0 have been rounded down to 1.0.

INDEX